Storm of the Century

Storm of the Century
the Labor Day hurricane of 1935

Willie Drye

WASHINGTON, D.C.

Published by the National Geographic Society

Library of Congress Cataloging-in-Publication Date

Drye, Willie.
Storm of the Century: the Labor Day Hurricane of 1935/ by Willie Drye.
    p.cm.
Includes bibliographical references and index.
ISBN 0-7922-8010-5
Florida Keys (Fla.)—History—20th Century. 2. Hurricanes—Florida—Florida Keys—History—20th Century. I. Title

F317.M7 D79 2002
975.9'41062—dc21   2002021945

Contents

To my wife, Jane Morrow,
whose love, support, and faith in me
made this book possible.

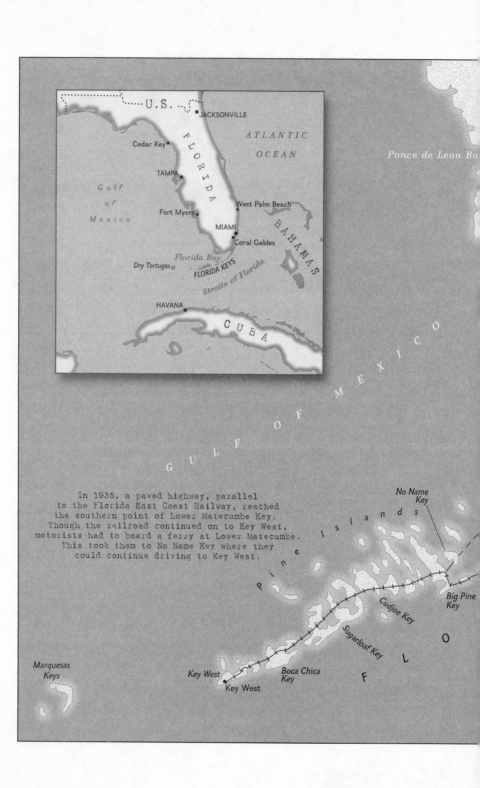

In 1935, a paved highway, parallel
to the Florida East Coast Railway, reached
the southern point of Lower Matecumbe Key.
Though the railroad continued on to Key West,
motorists had to board a ferry at Lower Matecumbe.
This took them to No Name Key where they
could continue driving to Key West.

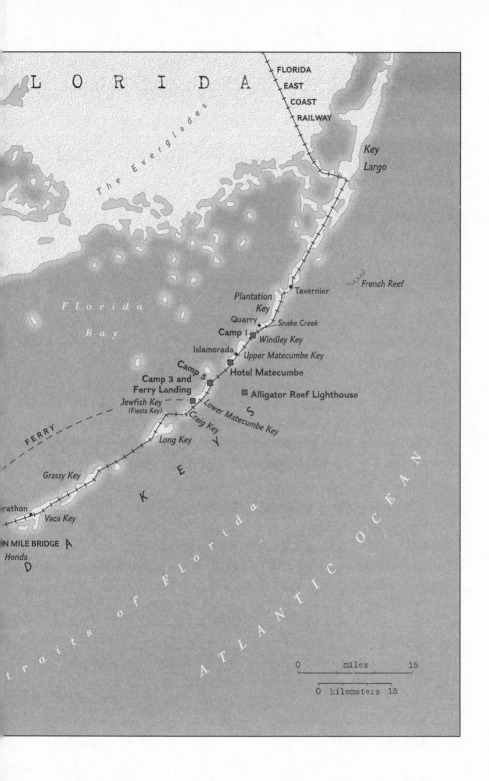

F L O R I D A

FLORIDA
EAST
COAST
RAILWAY

The Everglades

Key
Largo

French Reef

Tavernier

*Plantation
Key*

Florida
Bay

Quarry — *Snake Creek*

Camp I
Windley Key

Islamorada
Upper Matecumbe Key

Camp 5
Hotel Matecumbe

**Camp 3 and
Ferry Landing**

■ Alligator Reef Lighthouse

Jewfish Key
(Fiesta Key) — *Lower Matecumbe Key*

FERRY

Craig Key

S

Long Key

Y

K

E

Grassy Key

rathon

Vaca Key

N MILE BRIDGE A

Honda

D

S t r a i t s   o f   F l o r i d a

A T L A N T I C   O C E A N

0 ___ miles ___ 15

0 kilometers 15

Sunday, September 1, 1935

In the waning days of the summer of 1935, a patch of bad weather—thunderstorms, wind, and rain—blew off the west coast of Africa and rumbled across the Atlantic Ocean. As the weather system approached the Bahamas in late August it picked up a counterclockwise circulation imparted by the rotation of the Earth, drew energy from salt water that had baked for months beneath the blazing summer sun, and evolved into a tropical storm.

It was the time of year when such storms often form in that part of the world, although the 1935 season had been relatively quiet. The summer's first hurricane hadn't formed until August 18 a few hundred miles east of Puerto Rico. It had stayed well offshore from the United States as it churned northward, weakened as it reached the cool North Atlantic, and plowed into Newfoundland with 60-mile-an-hour winds.

There was something different about the second storm of the season, however. This one would become a small hurricane of tremendous power that would cause havoc far out of proportion to its diminutive size. It would strike the Florida Keys with a force beyond any human standard of measurement. Hurricanes weren't named in 1935, but the storm that formed off the Bahamas in late August would become the most powerful hurricane ever to strike the United States. This anonymous killer would spread grief throughout the country. Its aftermath would reverberate for months through the highest government offices in Washington, D.C., and then it would quickly fade from the nation's collective memory.

But when the storm crossed Andros Island in the Bahamas during the evening of Saturday, August 31, 1935, it did little more than rustle trees and snap some branches. Steering clear of shipping lanes and eluding the primitive, porous hurricane detection system of that era, the storm slipped quietly into the Straits of Florida, within easy striking distance of Florida or Cuba. There it found perfect conditions for strengthening, and its energy exploded overnight.

It was exactly the kind of hurricane one might expect to form in the middle of the Great Depression, when so many forces—economic, political, even natural—seemed to be aligning solely for the purpose of punishing those least capable of protecting themselves. In 1935 the United States was in the grip of a bewildering paradox of poverty in the midst of plenty. In the cities, hungry men got into fist-fights over garbage discarded by restaurants, and people lined up for blocks to receive a cup of soup or a sandwich. Meanwhile, farmers slaughtered livestock, poured out milk, and burned grain because no one could buy what they produced. Then the banks foreclosed on the farms, forcing the bankrupt farmers off their land. Farmers who managed to hold on to their property didn't fare much better. A prolonged drought put hundreds of thousands of people on the brink of starvation and made dust of the topsoil in the Midwest. The prairie winds whipped the dust into thick, choking clouds that towered over the land and turned midday to dusk.

About two million men roamed the country on freight trains seeking work that wasn't there.

The misery wasn't confined to the United States. As poet W. H. Auden noted, "waves of anger and fear" encircled the globe during the 1930s. In Germany, a mediocre landscape artist who'd found a brilliant new career in politics steadily strengthened his grip on the German people, built horrible new weapons of war, and started hatching one of history's vilest schemes for world conquest. In Japan, ambitious military warlords seized power and plotted a brutal campaign to dominate Asia and the Pacific Ocean. In Italy, the posturing buffoon who controlled the government dreamed of creating a new Roman Empire as he prepared to unleash mechanized warfare on a poor African nation that had been a cradle of civilization but now could barely feed its people.

The malignancies bedeviling the world seemed to feed this storm. How else could it have acquired such awful power? And when this witches' brew of wind and water had achieved an unearthly strength, it found hundreds of down-and-out men who'd been ground beneath the heel of the Depression and were completely unprotected from its onslaught, and it steered straight for them.

It was another of the harsh ironies of the time that the men were put in the path of this vicious storm because their government was trying to help them. They were American military veterans, and they were very much on Ed Sheeran's mind at daybreak on Sunday, September 1, 1935. The men—most of whom had served in what was then called the Great War—were sleeping in shacks all around Sheeran as the sun crept above the horizon of the Atlantic Ocean and began its spectacular ascent into the heavens above the Florida Keys.

Sheeran had already been at work for several hours. It didn't matter to him that it was Labor Day weekend or that he'd intended to spend the holiday with his wife in their comfortable home in the Miami suburb of Coral Gables. A bad storm was prowling the seas somewhere east of the Keys, and from Sheeran's point of view only a fool would sit still and do nothing when he knew trouble might be heading his way.

The U.S. Weather Bureau had been issuing advisories on the storm for two days. The agency hadn't said yet that the disturbance posed a direct threat to the Keys, but that meant nothing to Sheeran. He trusted his own observations and judgment more than those of men sitting in offices many miles away. And in 1935, meteorologists didn't have much more to work with than Sheeran did.

There were no weather satellites to pinpoint a tropical weather system and chart its development and movement, no hurricane-hunting airplanes to penetrate the heart of the storm to obtain

3

invaluable information about whether it was weakening or intensifying. Meteorologists relied on reports from ships at sea for much of their information about violent storms, and when a hurricane was roaming the ocean, captains were trying to put as much distance as they could between their ships and the bad weather.

Sheeran was 65 years old, but advancing age had done little to diminish his energy. The Wisconsin native had spent most of his adult life working in South Florida and the Keys. In September 1935 he was supervising the construction of one of the highway bridges that would finally link the Lower Keys with the Upper Keys and the mainland. The project was part of a New Deal effort to help Depression-wracked Key West, whose 12,000 residents were trying to survive on an average income of seven dollars per month. Some of the veterans worked for Sheeran, although the federal officials in charge of the vets camps had created so many regulations about their work hours it was difficult to get much use out of them.

Sheeran had learned to keep his wits about him, establish his priorities, and focus on his work in difficult situations. He had served as a combat engineer in France in 1918 and was wounded when he refused to stop working on a bridge simply because the Germans were shooting at him. His stubborn dedication to his job had earned him a Purple Heart, a promotion from captain to major, and a citation for bravery from General Pershing himself.

He had weathered many hurricanes and developed a skill for detecting them that was almost a sixth sense. A distant hurricane telegraphs its approach in a subtle but unmistakable code that is written in the clouds, the sea, and the air. Sheeran had learned to recognize these subtleties, and on September 1, 1935, he was dead certain of two things: This was a bad storm and it was headed his way.

Months earlier, Sheeran had prepared for the possibility of a hurricane when he ordered his crew to dig a 1,000-foot canal at the southern tip of Lower Matecumbe Key. He was responsible for a lot of expensive floating construction equipment that, if left in exposed waters, would easily be destroyed by a hurricane. As the sun came up Sunday morning, Sheeran and his men were moving the equipment into the canal, where the sheltered water and surrounding mangroves would provide some protection from the winds and rough seas he was certain would be upon them in another day or two.

But he was powerless to do anything about the 400 or so men dozing in the flimsy shacks of the three work camps that had been established in the Upper Keys a few months earlier. The vast majority of the veterans had no idea of the power of a hurricane or how vulnerable the slender, low-lying Keys were to these storms.

As Sheeran worked, horrible memories of a tragedy that occurred 29 years earlier in an identical setting kept flashing through his mind. In 1906 he was working on the construction crew building the famous Key West Extension of the Florida East Coast Railway from Miami to Key West. Hundreds of men hired for the massive project were housed in work camps and houseboats in the Keys. Most of them had never been in the tropics and knew nothing of the danger of the storms that sometimes come roaring off the ocean in late summer and early fall.

In mid-October the Keys natives (known as Conchs—the tough shellfish that were a staple of their diet) told railroad construction supervisors that a powerful storm was headed their way. The Conchs pleaded with the bosses to evacuate the workers, but their warnings were ignored. The hurricane struck the Keys with winds of more than 130 miles per hour on the morning of October 18, 1906.

At least 130 workers were killed. Many died when the hurricane yanked a houseboat from its moorings at Long Key and hauled it out to sea. The storm pulled the houseboat far beyond any hope of rescue and then methodically smashed the vessel and spilled the doomed occupants into the churning ocean.

Corpses washed up on beaches for days afterwards.

Now Sheeran feared another slaughter was in the making. He knew the veterans' poorly built wooden shacks would be useless in the face of a hurricane's fury. The only way to protect the men was to load them aboard a train and get them off the islands. But Sheeran was employed by the Florida State Highway Department and didn't have the authority to order a special train for the vets. Evacuation was up to the federal officials in charge of the work camps, and he wondered if they were taking the threat seriously.

One of the officials, Sam Cutler, had been gathering information about the storm since the previous afternoon. At age 59 the assistant administrator had never been in a hurricane, but he was cautious by nature, and his training as a safety engineer had reinforced this tendency. Cutler was in temporary command of the work camps during the holiday weekend because his boss, 45-year-old Ray Sheldon, had decided to take a brief honeymoon in Key West with his wife of one week. Cutler wanted to evacuate the veterans immediately, but that decision would have to be made by Fred Ghent, the administrator in charge of the veterans work program in Florida.

Fred Ghent's office was almost 500 miles up the coast in Jacksonville. He had a lot on his mind that weekend. When he was hired in April 1935 as administrator for the work program, Ghent seemed perfect for the job. He was compassionate and wanted to help the veterans get their lives back on track. But officials in Washington had decided to terminate the program, and in early August Ghent was told he'd soon be out of a job. The news was a bitter surprise, and he planned to get his mind off things for a while by spending Sunday, September 1, on a Jacksonville golf course.

At the same time Sheeran was moving his equipment into sheltered waters, Fred Ghent sleepily answered his ringing telephone. It was Ray Sheldon calling from Key West. Sheldon said he'd just talked to the U.S. Weather Bureau's office there, and the meteorologist had suggested he might want to take the next ferry back to the work camps in the Upper Keys. The storm that had crossed the Bahamas the night before might make the waters too rough for the ferry in a day or two. Ghent hated to interrupt Sheldon's brief honeymoon, especially since he didn't think this storm would amount to much. But someone had to be there to take charge. Ghent reluctantly ordered his assistant to return to the camps. Soon Sheldon and his bride were on their way out of Key West to catch the 8 a.m. ferry at No Name Key.

In the camps, many veterans continued sleeping until the oppressive heat of the late summer day slowly baked them into the bleary and painful wakefulness that accompanies a nasty hangover. They rolled out of their bunks and lined up at barrels of ice water to slake their intense thirst. As they waited their turns they greeted others who joined them in line, calling many of the newcomers by nicknames: "Chain Gang," "Big Boy," "Mad Dog," and "Slim."

The men sipped cups of water and discussed the events of the previous evening with wry humor. They chatted about the storm they heard had formed somewhere out there over the Atlantic. All summer, they had been hearing warnings that a hurricane was coming, and they wanted to see one. They had faced real danger in France 18 years ago, they reminded each other, and they sure as hell weren't afraid of a little wind and rain. Besides, it would cool things off and blow away the damned mosquitoes for a few days.

The men living in the Keys work camps in the summer of 1935 represented a cross section of America's Depression casualties. Many were well-trained professionals who were earning good livings and raising families before the economic crash threw them out of work. Others had been bouncing from job to job for a decade or more since their discharge from the military, unable to stay with one job and put down roots. Some of the men in the Keys were making a genuine effort to turn their lives around. A few even brought their families down to the islands, rented cottages, planted gardens, and seemed settled for the first time in years.

But drinking and despondency were serious problems in the work camps. Many vets felt they had landed at the end of the world in the isolated, sparsely populated Florida Keys and had nothing more to lose. One veteran who worked on the bridge construction crew told friends he intended to make his tomb of one of the concrete support arches. When the crew started pouring concrete for arch number 61—his payroll number—he planned to leap into the wet cement and be buried alive. For the vets, drinking was an escape from the ruins of their lives. They were, in a very real sense, the dregs of the "Lost Generation"—men who had been profoundly changed by their experiences in World War I.

Most of the men in the Keys work camps had been members of the American Expeditionary Force (AEF). When they boarded troopships for Europe in April 1917, they were the United States' contribution to the massive conflict that had been greedily swallowing lives by the millions for three years. The world simply hadn't been prepared for the astonishing death toll of the Great War. Dramatic improvements in weapons in the late 19th and early 20th centuries made the slaughter inevitable. Author Donovan Webster noted that warfare hadn't changed much in almost 1,000 years until Alfred Nobel's invention of dynamite in 1866 "boosted the bloody art of war from bullets and bayonets to long-range high explosives."

Despite the staggering loss of life after three years of fighting, the Allies—Great Britain, France, and Italy—and the Central Powers—Germany, Austria-Hungary, and Turkey—were still locked in a stalemate when the Americans arrived.

The American Expeditionary Force commander, Gen. John Pershing, kept his green troops in training camps for the better part of a year getting them ready for the fight. The Americans saw their first real combat in June 1918 at Château-Thierry and Belleau Wood in northern France and immediately distinguished themselves as fierce and daring fighters. When U.S. Marines under Col. Wendell Neville arrived near the scene of a German advance, a French officer told him Allied troops had been ordered to retreat. "Retreat hell," Neville growled. "We just got here." The colonel's Marines dug in and stopped the Germans with devastatingly accurate rifle fire.

But the Americans also faced the Germans' murderously effective weaponry, and they paid a terrible price. At Belleau Wood, where American soldiers fought in bitter trench warfare, "masses of earth, chunks of rock, splinters of trees leaped into the air as the shells exploded," recalled Lt. Col. Frederick Wise. "Machine-gun and rifle bullets thudded into the earth unendingly."

When the fighting ended in November 1918, American casualties stood at more than 364,000 dead, wounded, and missing. American losses didn't compare with the staggering death toll suffered by the Europeans, but it was a bloody toll for scarcely a year of actual fighting. Still, the Americans' brief participation tipped the balance in the Allies' favor, forcing the Central Powers to surrender.

The Western world rejoiced at the capitulation of the Central Powers. But the horrible experience of combat left permanent psychological scars on many members of the AEF, who discovered they couldn't easily settle back into civilian life. Many years later, this condition would be called post-traumatic stress disorder. In 1919 it was known as shell shock.

Like their counterparts in Europe whose lives had been shattered, many servicemen had seen their beliefs destroyed by the brutality of modern warfare. The wholesale, indiscriminate slaughter and destruction of the war crushed any conviction that humanity was progressing toward a peaceful, benevolent civilization. Many who survived the conflict were certain their lives were meaningless.

But life continued after the war. The distractions of the 1920s helped some people forget the horrors of the conflict. Americans largely ignored Prohibition while making millionaires of the gangsters who sold them watered-down drinks at outrageously inflated prices in illegal speakeasies. When they weren't drinking gin and dancing, they amused themselves with fads such as crossword puzzles and flagpole sitting—and everyone seemed to be getting rich in the stock market. For a while, it was easy to believe Republican Presidents Warren Harding, Calvin Coolidge, and Herbert Hoover when they said the United States had entered a new era of perpetual prosperity that would permanently eliminate poverty.

The decade that followed the war was a time of empty euphoria however, when many Americans pursued pleasure and wealth because there seemed to be nothing else to do and no reason to look for anything more. And no one seemed to notice or care that the machinery of commerce was becoming dangerously unbalanced.

The stock market crash in 1929 and the ensuing Depression came just as veterans were entering what were supposed to be their most productive years. Now, instead of building careers and raising families, hundreds of vets were sweating, swatting mosquitoes, drinking bootleg whiskey, and building a bridge in the remote Keys for a dollar a day plus food and housing—if the term "housing" could be applied to a 10-by-20-foot cabin with a canvas roof where four men slept.

But they were on a payroll, and in that respect they were a lot better off than the millions who'd long ago lost hope of finding jobs. Federal officials in Washington regularly received letters from unemployed veterans who'd heard about the work program and would gladly have endured the discomfort and isolation of the Keys in exchange for a regular paycheck. By September 1935 the Depression was approaching the end of its sixth year. President Franklin D. Roosevelt's many New Deal programs had rescued millions from the brink of starvation. But America's economy was still in disrepair. Almost 20 percent of the nation's workforce was still unemployed, and many of those who had jobs were working in unhealthful or dangerous conditions for bare subsistence wages.

Still, Americans mired in the middle of the Great Depression managed to find some distractions from the grimness of the times. In the summer of 1935, many people were enjoying the illusion of wealth and power by buying expensive real estate—with play money—and trying to bankrupt their opponents in a wildly popular new board game called Monopoly. Sports entered a new era when lights were erected at Cincinnati's Crosley Field, and on May 24, 1935, the hometown Reds beat the visiting Philadelphia Phillies 2-1 in the first major-league baseball game played at night. And a struggling bandleader named Benny Goodman electrified an audience in Los Angeles when he and his bored musicians suddenly cut loose with blaring brasses, wild improvisations, and throbbing drums while playing for a dance in August 1935. The moment marked the birth of a new genre of popular music that came to be called swing.

Humorist Will Rogers kept Americans chuckling during the hard times with his bipartisan barbs at politicians of all stripes. "There is something about a Republican that you can only stand him just so long," he once observed, "and on the other hand, there is something about a Democrat that you can't stand him quite that long."

As the Labor Day weekend of 1935 approached, however, Americans were mourning the loss of Rogers's homespun, incisive wit. He was killed in a plane crash in Alaska on August 15. Millions of Americans learned details of Rogers's death in the weekly newsreels that preceded feature films in theaters across the nation. Hollywood was cranking out a steady stream of movies intended to take America's collective mind off the problems of the day. A frothy new comedy called *Top Hat* featuring Fred Astaire and Ginger Rogers had been released just in time for the Labor Day weekend of 1935.

As audiences were lining up to watch Astaire and Rogers dance cheek to cheek on Saturday evening, August 31, the S.S. *Dixie* left its berth in New Orleans and set sail for New York. The liner carried 233 passengers who hadn't been as troubled by the Depression as many other Americans. Aboard the liner were several doctors, a Yale University professor with a fondness for playing poker and the piano, a movie actress, a Catholic priest, honeymooners, and a young woman who was bored almost beyond endurance. As the ship sailed across the placid waters of the Gulf of Mexico, Charlotte Brown could find nothing better to do than write a letter to her mother in Philadelphia. "It's the quietest crowd I ever saw," Brown complained, "and there's no excitement."

Capt. Einar Sundstrom commanded the *Dixie*, and he hoped the voyage stayed boring. He knew rough weather had been reported

11

around the Bahamas, but he'd sidestepped many storms during his 34 years at sea and figured he could outwit this one. As the sun came up Sunday morning, September 1, the *Dixie* was steaming southeast in the Gulf toward the tip of the Keys. Soon Sundstrom would take the ship around Key West and swing her northeast into the Straits of Florida and the Gulf Stream. The *Dixie* was due in New York on Thursday, September 5, and Sundstrom looked forward to spending a few days with his wife and two daughters in his trim, two-story brick house in the Long Island village of Little Neck.

While Ed Sheeran eyed the horizon suspiciously and directed his work crew on Lower Matecumbe Key, the architect of the programs that had given jobs to the needy veterans in the Keys finally escaped the withering heat of Washington. As the rising sun bathed the Hudson River Valley in its soft, elegant light, President Roosevelt's special train pulled into the station at Highland, New York. FDR was helped into a waiting car for the short drive across the Hudson River to Springwood, his estate in Hyde Park.

It had been a long and busy summer for the President. The first session of the 74th Congress had lasted 235 days, the longest since 1922. The marathon assembly was part of Democratic strategists' careful preparation for the upcoming political season. An election year was only a few months away, and politicians were feeling the primal urge to begin that odd courtship ritual with voters known as campaigning. With that in mind, leaders of the overwhelmingly Democratic Congress kept lawmakers in the capital through the summer hoping to resolve all controversial legislation so Republicans would have less ammunition to use against Democratic candidates.

They'd nearly succeeded in clearing the decks of potentially troublesome issues. They hit a snag in the last hours when Senator Huey Long, the renegade Democrat who'd turned his home state of Louisiana into a personal fiefdom, began a filibuster against the last piece of New Deal legislation. Long didn't think the bill provided enough funding for loans to cotton and wheat farmers and vowed to prevent the Senate from voting on it. His windy blustering blocked action on the bill that also would have provided funding for one of FDR's New Deal center-pieces—Social Security. When the gavel fell to end the first session, Long dashed out a side door of the Senate chamber and boarded a train for New York. There he told a reporter that Congress was "a bunch of cowards" for knuckling under to FDR and boasted he'd be elected President in 1936 on a third-party ticket if the Republicans again nominated Hoover and Roosevelt was the choice of the Democrats.

Roosevelt planned to spend several weeks at Hyde Park, but he wouldn't be idle. He also had his eye on the 1936 election. The President hadn't said whether he would seek a second term, but he was going to work on a series of speeches about the accomplishments of the New Deal that would lay the groundwork for that announcement. He intended to deliver the speeches in late September during a cross-country trip that would have the appearance and trappings of a fall campaign tour.

FDR and his strategists knew they'd be facing opposition from both sides of the political spectrum. Some Americans—such as Long—were convinced that Roosevelt's policies hadn't done enough to pull the nation out of the Depression and wanted a more radical shift to the left. Many businessmen were weary of New Deal regulations on industry and wanted a conservative Republican President at the helm of American government. The Republican leadership also was desperate to avoid a repeat of the 1934 elections, when Democrats nearly chased them out of Washington by winning about 70 percent of the seats in the U.S. Senate and House of Representatives.

Roosevelt knew the political waters would soon be heating up. But as he joined his wife, Eleanor, and his mother, Sara, for breakfast at Springwood on Sunday morning, September 1, 1935, he had no idea that a potentially serious political problem was brewing for him 1,200 miles to the south in the warm waters of the Straits of Florida. And FDR's legendary charm and political shrewdness would be powerless against the forces fueling this problem.

13

chapter one

A Remote Paradise

When Bernard Russell was a boy walking to school, he'd sometimes take off his shoes, tie the laces together, and toss them across his shoulder. Then he'd walk barefoot down the sandy beach to the Matecumbe School in the seaside village of Islamorada in the Florida Keys.

Russell's occasional choice of routes was part schoolboy whimsy and part convenience. In the 1930s much of the Keys was still covered with dense underbrush. Walking along the beach was easier, and he could also study the Atlantic Ocean, which laps at the shores of Upper Matecumbe Key. The turquoise waters often resemble a giant saltwater lake, thanks to the coral reefs that parallel the Keys and act as a breakwater, keeping the breakers four miles or so offshore.

The Alligator Reef Lighthouse stands guard over the reefs. The 136-foot-tall lighthouse rises above the remains of the U.S.S. *Alligator,* which wrecked on the reef in November 1822. The lighthouse's unique nighttime signal—five consecutive flashes of a white light and one flash of a red light at intervals of five seconds—had warned mariners of the reef since 1873.

At high tide, the Atlantic was only about 100 feet from the front door of the two-room schoolhouse that Russell attended. In June 1935 Russell was 16 years old and part of the largest graduating class that Matecumbe School had ever produced. Nine students received diplomas for completing the nine grades the school offered. In the remote, sparsely populated Keys, parents who wanted their children to finish their secondary education had to send them to live with friends or relatives in Key West or Homestead to attend high school.

That summer, Russell had become friends with schoolmate Laurette Pinder, who was 17 and lived at the other end of the island. There was something a little special about this friendship, and both teenagers realized it.

The 48-star American flag that snapped in the sea breeze in front of the Matecumbe School identified Islamorada as part of the United States. But in many ways Islamorada was much further removed from the mainland—and mainstream America—than the 40 or so miles of coral and salt water that separated the village from the tip of the Florida peninsula. Automobiles, telephones, and a few other early-20th-century technological advances had found their way to Islamorada by the summer of 1935. But the people on the islands between Key West and the peninsula still lived much as their grandparents in the previous century had.

Key West, 75 miles to the south over land and water, had a population of about 12,000, but fewer than 1,000 residents inhabited the islands between Key West and the mainland. Two small electric plants—one at Tavernier north of Islamorada and the other at Marathon to the south—provided electricity for the few residents in those villages, but the other communities outside Key West were without power. At nightfall, Islamorada residents lit their kerosene lanterns.

Islamorada and the other tiny communities on the string of coral islands that make up the Keys did have a link of solid steel connecting them to the mainland and the modern world—the Key West Extension of the Florida East Coast Railway (FEC). In 1935 the daily arrival of the southbound passenger train from Miami to Key West—the southernmost island in the 130-mile chain—was a major event in Islamorada. When the snorting, smoking, steam-powered locomotive chuffed to a stop around 9:30 a.m. at the Islamorada station, village residents gathered to greet passengers, pick up packages, board the train, or just watch the commotion.

On most mornings a few residents were likely to be coming and going at the post office, where Bernard's father, John Russell, was postmaster. The building housing the Post Office was literally a stone's throw from the train station. After checking their mail they might step around to the small store that John Russell and his brother Clifton owned in the rear of the same building. They could buy a soft drink for a nickel and sip it as they stood on the post office porch, shaded from the tropical sun by an overhang supported by three columns. It had been built in 1928 of native coral salvaged from the tailings left behind after the island's first road had been graded. Bernard Russell, 10 years old at the time, had driven a Model T dump truck slowly along the road while others picked up chunks of coral and tossed them onto the back of the truck. When the daily train arrived, the post office idlers often stepped off the porch and strolled up unpaved DeLeon Street to join the other onlookers at the depot.

A passenger who gazed out the coach window during the brief stop at Islamorada might have wondered why anyone would want to live there. Even with the railroad and the highway linking the Upper Keys to the mainland, the remoteness of the islands was unsettling to many outsiders. The sun-drenched outcroppings that divide the Atlantic Ocean and the Gulf of Mexico are so unlike any other place on Earth that first-time visitors a century ago often found the Keys eerie and foreboding. In 1908 writer Ralph Paine described the islands as "worthless, chaotic fragments of coral reef, limestone and mangrove swamp...aptly called the sweepings and debris which the Creator hurled out to sea after He finished shaping the Florida peninsula."

For the most part, the rest of the world ignored the Keys. "There were never enough people on those Keys to really make big news, or anything like that, and a lot of it has never had any attention paid to it," said William Johns, a reporter for the *Miami Daily News* who was based in Homestead in 1935.

The nearest doctors and dentists—and other securities and advantages of civilization—were many miles away. Other than the train, the only way to get to Key West was to drive onto a ferry at Lower Matecumbe Key, seven miles south of Islamorada, for a four-hour boat ride to No Name Key. From there, it was a 45-mile drive to Key West. Or you could go by sailboat. If luck and the wind were with you, you could sail to Key West in a few days. If the wind was against you or the weather suddenly turned bad, the trip could take much longer.

The railroad right-of-way had been hacked through a dense tropical jungle, and much of Upper Matecumbe and the other Keys were still covered by a thick tangle of ferns, buttonwood, mangrove, poisonwood, and palm trees. Over the years Islamorada residents had worn a series of foot trails through the underbrush, but in 1935 there still were places on the island where you couldn't see the sun.

The train passenger might have noticed the outdoor privies in Islamorada. In 1935 the number of outhouses far exceeded the number of telephones on Upper Matecumbe Key. Indoor toilets wouldn't have been of much use anyway because a plentiful supply of fresh water was required to flush them. Fresh water doesn't occur naturally on the Keys, and rainwater for drinking was collected in large cisterns. Every drop was far too precious to be used for indoor plumbing.

The islanders kept a close watch on their cisterns. Pools of fresh water inevitably became a hatchery for mosquitoes. Avoiding the stinging insects was all but impossible. They were everywhere, especially during the summer rainy season. Many residents kept a small pot of pyrethrum burning near their doors. The fumes—a natural insecticide—discouraged mosquitoes from coming into their houses. Anyone venturing outside—especially after dark during the summer—would be surrounded within seconds by a cloud of the buzzing bloodsuckers. The islanders slept with mosquito netting around their beds, and when they went outside they often wore hats with fine mesh netting that covered their faces. They also wore clothing that nearly covered their bodies despite the heat. Men typically wore denim overalls over a long-sleeved shirt. Women often wore long-sleeved dresses and an old-fashioned sunbonnet.

Living in the middle of the Atlantic meant constantly watching the weather—especially from August to November, when hurricanes were often forming somewhere beyond the horizon. The U.S. Weather Bureau tried to monitor hurricanes and issue reasonably accurate advisories and warnings, but keeping track of a hurricane in 1935 was a tricky job. Meteorologists relied heavily on information about weather conditions from ships at sea and from trained weather observers stationed along the coast who sent information several times a day about wind speed, barometric pressure readings, and other details to the U.S. Weather Bureau. Forecasters did the best they could with the tools and information they had, but sometimes they were just wrong about where a hurricane was and where it was heading.

Island residents knew the only storm warning they could really count on was their barometers and their own knowledge of the natural indicators that told them when a hurricane was heading their way.

"My dad lived by the barometer," Bernard Russell said. "He read that every day, like he did his Bible."

Despite the isolation and inherent dangers, however, life on the isolated Keys offered some benefits not known elsewhere. Crime was almost nonexistent, and many residents of the close-knit Keys communities didn't bother locking their doors when they left their homes. And while millions of Americans in other parts of the country struggled to put food on their tables during the 1930s, the Keys were surrounded by a sort of saltwater pantry that helped mitigate the cruelest effect of the Depression—hunger.

Lobster—which the locals called crawfish—was abundant on the Atlantic side of the islands, and queen conchs were plentiful farther south. Pompano, tuna, grouper, and snapper could be reeled in farther offshore. The deeper waters teemed with big game fish, such as sailfish, swordfish, tarpon, and amberjack, and many islanders augmented their seafood diets with small produce gardens.

Fewer than 1,000 people lived on the Keys outside of Key West, and most of those residents lived in the Upper Keys, the segment of islands stretching southward from Key Largo to Long Key. Tomato gardens and key lime groves dotted the interior of the Upper Keys. Some residents used the railroad to ship their produce to markets on the mainland. Others made a living by plucking sponges from the surrounding waters and selling them in Key West.

The Middle Keys—the islands between Conch Key and Pigeon Key—and the Lower Keys, which encompassed the southernmost islands outside of Key West, were virtually uninhabited in 1935.

Islamorada's only church—Matecumbe Methodist—stood next to the oceanfront school. In the summer of 1935, Rev. S. E. Carlson was a relative newcomer to Islamorada, and he and his wife were still getting to know their new congregation. The couple lived in a one-story wood-frame house near the church.

Many of the pioneers who settled the Keys in the mid-19th century rested in a small cemetery next to the Methodist church. The most prominent grave was that of Etta Pinder, a 14-year-old girl who'd drowned in 1914. Her grief-stricken parents stationed a marble angel at the head of their daughter's grave to watch over her eternal slumber.

Life moved mostly to the rhythms and whims of the sea. Islamorada residents lived on or near the beach, but their modest houses bore no resemblance to the oceanfront mansions that line much of Florida's coast today. In 1935 air-conditioning was decades away from being commonplace. In Islamorada, homes, the school, and the church were built on the beach to take advantage of the cool breezes blowing in from the ocean.

Sometimes in the summer, those cooling winds come in the form of a sudden storm. The oppressive heat cooks up a squall that sweeps across the islands from the Atlantic or Florida Bay. Rising winds sway the palms and rustle their fronds, and across the water the horizon no longer separates the ocean and the sky. The rain begins with a few big drops that slam heavily into the ground and raise little puffs of dust. Soon it is coming down in dense silvery sheets, visibility drops to almost zero, and the turquoise waters are pocked by a million tiny splashes.

Occasionally the grim-looking clouds spit out a brilliant, jagged lightning bolt that briefly illuminates everything with an eerie bluish tinge. Sudden sharp cracks of thunder shake the Earth. The temperature plummets and the wind gusts suddenly to maybe 30 or 40 miles per hour. It can all seem quite impressive—and perhaps a bit frightening—to a newcomer who has never seen one of these garden-variety summer storms. But it usually doesn't last more than 30 minutes. The squall lumbers away as quickly as it came and the wind dies back down and pretty soon it's so still and stiflingly hot, that fierce little storm seems like a fleeting dream.

The houses on the beach were sturdy enough to easily withstand these brief, intense blows, but Keys residents had no illusions about whether their homes would endure the fury of a hurricane. Many had built even sturdier shelters near the center of the island where they rode out the hurricanes that occasionally visited the islands.

The shelter that John Russell built for his family was typical of the structures that had been erected by his neighbors. The buildings were constructed with thick timbers that often were held together by long, heavy-duty railroad bolts. Russell had even anchored his to the coral island with long steel bolts. The postmaster wasn't one to belittle the power of a hurricane, but he thought his hurricane house would stand up to most anything the sea could throw at it.

Russell and his neighbors were less certain, however, about how they would protect themselves from problems they feared the railroad would eventually cause when an especially bad hurricane came their way.

When the Key West Extension—more popularly known as the Overseas Railroad—was completed in 1912, it joined the slender strand of islands like a string of pearls and, for the first time, threw them open to the outside world. But the seafaring Conchs complained loudly when workers started building the roadbed for the railroad. Instead of constructing bridges across the shorter spans between the islands, Henry Flagler's engineers decided to support the tracks by building causeways. Unlike bridges, the solid causeways blocked the tidal flows. In some places the causeways were elevated as much as 13 feet above normal low tide. The natives shook their heads in dismay. To them, the railroad looked like nothing more than a giant dike, and they feared that one day a hurricane would pile up water against it until it was well above their heads. "It'll drown us like rats," they muttered.

In spite of its drawbacks, the railroad brought many benefits to the islands, and the 110-mile train trip down the Keys was a thrilling ride. The rails crossed about two dozen islands, and a series of causeways and bridges spanned almost 18 miles of water. Crossing the magnificent bridges—especially the Seven-Mile Bridge near Marathon and the spectacular steel suspension span at Bahia Honda—offered an unparalleled view of the Atlantic Ocean and Florida Bay. The bridges were just wide enough for the train tracks, so passengers looking out the coach windows saw only water beneath them and got the sensation that they were floating over the ocean.

They could see squadrons of pelicans gliding inches above the waves, following the contours of the swells. They could watch seagulls wheeling and floating in the sea breeze, and if they were lucky they might see a dolphin or a manta ray leap from the brine beneath them. Passengers on the daily northbound evening train from Key West to Miami got a special treat—they could watch the vividly colorful tropical sunset that marks the end of the day in the Keys.

The railroad was a testament to the iron will and unlimited wealth of Henry Morrison Flagler, who, with his Standard Oil Co. partner, John D. Rockefeller, amassed one of the great fortunes of the 19th century. Flagler made several visits to Florida between 1878 and 1883 and was so charmed by the graceful antiquity of St. Augustine that he decided to build a hotel there. He also literally invented Florida tourism when he bought a small group of railroads to create the Florida East Coast Railway. As he extended the line down the coast from Jacksonville he built more hotels along the way.

By 1896 Flagler's railroad had reached Fort Dallas, a small, sleepy settlement on Biscayne Bay that would soon be called Miami. There wasn't much there except mosquitoes, alligators, swamps, and a few orange groves. But Key West, 160 miles to the south, was Florida's largest and wealthiest city, and Flagler couldn't rest until he figured out a way to use his railroad to take advantage of the island city's excellent deepwater harbor. He knew that a rail terminal at Key West would be hundreds of miles closer to the planned Panama Canal than seaports on the U.S. mainland, and he figured he could make additional millions hauling the world's freight to and from the tip of the Keys. He foresaw still more profits from a "train-boat" that would transport passenger and freight cars between Key West and Havana, Cuba, only 90 miles apart across the Straits of Florida.

In 1904 Flagler took on a task that seemed impossible—building a railroad across the low-lying Florida Keys to Key West. He considered running the railroad through the Everglades to the tip of the Florida peninsula, then building a bridge to carry his trains across Florida Bay to one of the Keys. But he rejected that plan in favor of an island-hopping route across the string of low-lying islands. Work began in 1905, and Flagler pushed the project to completion despite hurricanes, labor problems, and enormous cost in both money and human lives.

The final tab for the railroad was more than $27 million, or about $212,000 per mile. But the cost in human lives was even more staggering. About 300 construction workers died during the six years it took to build the Overseas Railroad. Many were killed in October 1906 when a powerful hurricane blasted across Cuba and struck the Keys.

The Conchs knew a storm was rising. Rufus Johnson was one of the longtime Keys residents who tried to warn construction supervisors that the hurricane was bearing down on them. "I went [at] 11 o'clock at night and asked the men to get out, when they were building the railroad there," Johnson recalled many years later. "And the bosses said, 'You don't know anything.'"As it turned out,

Johnson knew far more than the bosses realized, but they ignored his warning and refused to evacuate the workers, many of whom were living aboard a large houseboat docked at Long Key. The FEC had also built a two-story, wood-frame administration building there.

As the hurricane drew nearer to the Keys, William Saunders—who worked on the construction crew—noticed that none of the Conchs employed by the FEC showed up for work. "I am sure that the men whose forefathers had lived on the Keys had developed some sixth sense regarding the approach of a hurricane," Saunders said.

Saunders had lived in South Florida 15 years and experienced four hurricanes. "I thought that I had learned all there was to know about such storms," he said. "But [this] was by far the worst, and I found out a lot more about them."

Early in the morning of October 18, 1906, the winds began howling at Long Key. Around 7:30 a.m. the storm pulled the houseboat from its moorings. With perhaps 150 workers—including Saunders—aboard, the houseboat was dragged helplessly into open water, where huge waves pounded it mercilessly. Some of the men were so terrified they drank teacups of laudanum, an opium derivative used for pain relief, and lay down to die.

They didn't have long to wait. Around 9 a.m. the hurricane smashed the houseboat's upper deck. A few minutes later the wind and pounding waves shattered the remnants of the boat, spilling the workers into the furious sea.

Saunders and six others managed to grab a large piece of wreckage and ride it like a raft. "It is hard to describe the way the waves rose up some three stories, then broke over us and the raft, with tons and tons of water," Saunders said. He hung on grimly, motivated by more than a simple dread of death. He was afraid his family couldn't collect his life insurance policy if he should be lost at sea.

Saunders and 48 other survivors were eventually plucked from the ocean.

The hurricane's eye passed over Pigeon Key, about 20 miles south of Long Key where the FEC had another camp for railroad construction workers. Earle Hartridge, a construction engineer at Pigeon Key, thought he was going to die.

"We thought we would never survive it," Hartridge said. He and some friends took shelter in a warehouse on the tiny island. As the storm raged outside, the men hastily scrambled atop a large pile of cement and dug a crater there. The hurricane destroyed the warehouse, but Hartridge and his companions were safe in their makeshift shelter.

Farther up the coast, the hurricane also sank the *Saint Lucie*, a steamboat with dozens of construction workers aboard. Survivors clung to lifeboats or wreckage and tried to keep their heads above the roiling ocean. "The sea, which had abated some, picked up again," said W .J. Grant, second officer of the *Saint Lucie*. "Great God, I have never seen it so high. The rain was blinding and beat our faces like shot. I could see nothing more until a sea pitched us out of the lifeboat and into the mangroves on the shore."

The hurricane killed about 130 FEC workers. The furious storm and death toll made a strong impression on Ed Sheeran, a 36-year-old Wisconsin native who was working on the railroad construction crew. Sheeran blamed the tragedy on the supervisors' poor judgment and ignorance about the power and danger of hurricanes. When he was given a supervisory position after the 1906 storm, he became highly skilled at detecting hurricanes. In the isolated Keys, he knew his life and those of his workers depended on it.

"We had no communication whatsoever," Sheeran said. "No telephone, no radios, no wireless—nothing but boats from Key West, and it took 10 days to get them. We absolutely relied on our barometers. We studied them and studied the wind. We talked to the natives."

Sheeran learned how to calculate a hurricane's approximate position and direction of travel using only his barometer and subtle weather indicators. "If I can get the speed of the wind on each side of me, I can tell pretty well where the storm is," he said. "It follows low areas. People that have never been in those storms don't know them." Two more hurricanes pounded the Keys before the railroad was completed in 1912, but under Sheeran's guidance only 13 men were lost because of these storms.

The first FEC train rolled into Key West in January 1912, and the railroad quickly became a boon to the islands. Besides allowing them to ship their produce to markets, the railroad in a sense finally linked the Conchs to civilization. Now Key West and Homestead were only a few hours away, and some of the hardships of living on the isolated islands were eased. An Islamorada resident could now be in Key West by noon for an appointment with a doctor or dentist and be back home at 7:45 p.m. on the northbound evening train.

The major cities of the East Coast were also linked to the Keys. A passenger could board a train in Washington, D.C., and be in Key West about 40 hours later. The railroad started bringing a new kind of visitor to the Keys—one who came purely for pleasure and brought plenty of money to pay for it.

The remote tropical environment and splendid fishing appealed to well-heeled sportsmen who could afford to escape the cold winters of the Northeast and Midwest. In Islamorada, a "millionaires row" was created, anchored by the Matecumbe Club, an exclusive fishing resort formed by a group of very wealthy businessmen affiliated with the New York Cotton Exchange. In 1917 club members built a handsome, two-story lodge, white with green shutters, on a palm-shaded stretch of beach on Upper Matecumbe. A two-story porch, supported by four columns of California redwood, overlooked the Atlantic. Inside, members relaxed on wicker furniture in a comfortable lodge after spending a day on the water. Trophy catches hung on the walls of the lounge

The rich part-time residents provided a small economic boon for the Conchs. During the winter they hired the natives as fishing guides. During the summer they paid them to look after their large, empty homes.

Ed Butters had also come to the Keys for the first time on a fishing trip in 1926, and he "loved every minute of it," according to his wife, Fern. Butters moved his wife and parents to Florida in 1926 when he got a job on the construction crew building the new Dade County Courthouse in Miami. Ed and Fern opened a small inn on Key Largo in late 1926. Thomas Edison, who had moved to Fort Myers, became a regular guest. During one of his visits he apologized to Fern because he'd stained a beautiful hand-embroidered tablecloth. The stain wouldn't come out, but the tablecloth became one of Fern's most prized possessions.

Ed bought an old U.S. Navy lifeboat, put a motor in it, and developed a reputation as one of the best fishing guides in the Keys.

In 1932 the Butterses sold their inn on Key Largo and used the money for a down payment on the Russell Arms Hotel on Upper Matecumbe Key. They renamed it the Hotel Matecumbe.

Former millionaires who'd gone bust during the Depression came to the Keys either to forget about their losses or to try to amass new fortunes. George Merrick, who created the visionary development of Coral Gables during the outrageous Florida land boom of the early 1920s, came to the Keys after he went broke on the eve of the Depression. He opened the Caribee Colony a few miles south of Islamorada near the southern tip of Upper Matecumbe Key. The little resort featured small cottages and a restaurant that became famous for its coconut pies.

Miami businessman Roland W. Craig had built his own little village on a small island between Lower Matecumbe Key and Long Key that had been created by the FEC to support a railroad bridge. Craig ran a yacht supply business, a small grocery store, and post office on his island, which was accessible only by boat or by the railroad. Craig also talked the FEC into letting him name the island Craig Key, and the little settlement became known as Craig.

But the most famous resort was the Long Key Fishing Camp, 17 miles down the railroad tracks from Islamorada. The visitors who stepped off the train at the small Long Key station entered a world of splendid, pampered isolation.

People had been coming to Long Key for the fishing for thousands of years. The Calusa Indians were the first, drawn to this place of crystal clear waters and abundant marine life. Spanish explorers also fished there in the 17th and 18th centuries.

Soon after the Key West Extension was completed, the railroad converted the large administration building at Long Key into a handsome, comfortable lodge with accommodations for 75, and 14 surrounding bungalows were renovated to house guests as well. The camp was open from late December to early April, when the weather in the Keys is at its most pleasant and the mosquitoes virtually disappear. During the season, the yachts of some of the world's wealthiest people were anchored at the camp's marina.

A caretaker looked after the expensive amenities during the off-season. In 1935 the caretaker was James E. Duane, Jr., who was also a trained observer for the U.S. Weather Bureau. Duane filed daily reports of wind speeds, barometric pressure readings, and other information to meteorologists in the bureau's Key West office.

A few members of the exclusive fishing club built their own houses at Long Key. One of the most luxurious belonged to the Countess of Suffolk, England, who spent $25,000 (an enormous sum in an era when a six-room house with a two-car garage in Detroit was selling for about $2,800) to build a bungalow she used for only a few weeks each winter. The countess furnished her pricey tropical getaway with expensive art objects collected during her travels.

The porches of the lodge and first row of bungalows overlooked a wide white-sand beach, and the buildings were shaded by a grove of coconut palm trees. Wooden walkways were woven among the palms, connecting the bungalows and linking them with the lodge.

Guests could stand on the beach, look southward, and see the famous Long Key Viaduct, which carried the railroad from Long Key across more than two miles of water to Conch Key. The seemingly endless procession of arches marching toward the horizon was so handsome that the FEC used a stylized drawing of a train crossing the viaduct as a logo for the Overseas Railroad.

Those who came to the fishing camp expected to pay handsomely for their fun, and during the early 1930s the Depression seemed to be of little or no consequence to its affluent visitors. At the same time coal miners were earning $14 per week, and $25 would have paid the weekly salary of a bus driver or a schoolteacher, guests at the Long Key Fishing Camp were happily spending $6 to $8 per night for a room in the lodge, and those who stayed in the bungalows were paying a daily rate of $8 or $9 each. The camp also had a fleet of a dozen 34-foot cabin cruisers that guests could rent for $25 a day.

Visitors to Long Key included those with names synonymous with American capitalism—Vanderbilt, Guggenheim, and Gillette—as well as politicians and European royalty. President Herbert Hoover fished at Long Key, and so did President Franklin Roosevelt. Author Zane Grey was a regular at Long Key, and the wife of newspaper publisher William Randolph Hearst dropped in a time or two, as did baseball great Lou Gehrig.

The fishing was superb, and the camp management kept detailed records of the catches and awarded prizes to the visitors. But the fishing alone wouldn't have drawn the cream of world society to a remote island in the middle of nowhere. Long Key Fishing Camp was a picture-perfect tropical setting.

Zane Grey, who wrote about fishing and the outdoors as well as his many Western novels, combined fishing and writing when he went to Long Key. During a 1912 visit he divided his time between working on *The Light of Western Stars* and fishing for tarpon. Enchanted by Long Key, the author praised the "eternal moan out on the reefs," and wrote "always by the glowing, hot colorful day or by the soft dark night with its shadows and whisperings on the beach, that significant presence—the sense of something vaster than the heaving sea."

A staff of 60 employees waited on the guests and went to great lengths to preserve the camp's carefree, disconnected isolation from the problems troubling the rest of the world. Radios and newspapers were prohibited, and guests could bask in the sun and escape the dreary early-1930s landscape of breadlines, hungry families, and dispirited men. But as the yachts began arriving at Long Key for the 1934–35 season, casualties from the Depression were appearing in the Keys like debris washing ashore from a distant shipwreck.

Only a few miles up the railroad tracks from the exclusive fishing club, weary men were stepping off the FEC train and blinking in wonder at their strange tropical surroundings. The accommodations awaiting them were a good bit less sumptuous than those at Long Key. The men were housed in tents that had been set up on hastily erected wooden platforms. Most of the men were well into their middle age and all were veterans of the U.S. military. Most had served during what was then known as the Great War or the World War, although some had fought during the Spanish-American War and a handful had been peacetime soldiers.

The standoffish Conchs eyed the newcomers uneasily, perhaps sensing that their presence heralded profound changes in their islands.

The events that led to the veterans' arrival in the Keys began during the summer of 1932 in Washington, when President Herbert Hoover stubbornly denied the harsh reality of the Depression and seemed determined to ignore its effects on the nation's wage earners. When the bottom fell out of the stock market in 1929 and the U.S. economy entered a free fall, Hoover insisted that the hard times were only temporary, despite an unemployment roll that increased from 1.5 million in October 1929 to at least 3.2 million by March 1930. When thousands of jobless men started selling apples on the streets of New York and oranges in New Orleans, the President said the men had left their regular jobs because they could make more money peddling fruit. During the winter of 1931, Hoover insisted that no one was starving or freezing, despite growing evidence to the contrary.

The harshest effects of the Depression weren't as visible on the sparsely populated Upper Keys, but in Key West the situation was every bit as desperate as it was on the mainland. The industries that had once made Key West prosperous and populous were long gone. The city's residents got by with fishing, a little income from tourists, and occasionally bootlegging booze from nearby Cuba. And Key West had its own tropical version of the street corner fruit vendors in the larger mainland cities. Instead of selling apples and oranges, Key West's jobless residents sold coconuts and limes.

Hoover refused to abandon his staunchly Republican belief that the nation's economy eventually would right itself without government intervention and insisted that the nation adhere to its traditional economic policies. But the ranks of the unemployed steadily increased. As the 1932 election approached, *Fortune* magazine published the results of a survey that concluded that 34 million Americans—more than one-fourth of the nation's population—had no income. And *Fortune* didn't even include 11 million farm families in its survey.

While Hoover insisted that the nation's economy was fundamentally sound, others feared the deprivations caused by the Depression could have serious consequences and eventually undermine the stability of the government.

One of the staunchest advocates for change was the governor of New York, Franklin D. Roosevelt, a Democrat who persuaded his state legislature to create the Temporary Emergency Relief Administration. The program, which was directed by Harry Hopkins, provided work relief that helped jobless New Yorkers get through the winter of 1931–32.

Roosevelt's programs attracted the attention of national Democratic leaders looking for a candidate to oppose the luckless Hoover in the 1932 presidential election. With the skillful support of Louis Howe and other advisers, Roosevelt launched his campaign for the White House on April 7, 1932, when he addressed the nation during the *Lucky Strike Radio Hour*. He called for a new approach to economic recovery—a plan that built "from the bottom up and not from the top down" and focused on "the forgotten man at the bottom of the economic pyramid."

The pledge to help the forgotten man resonated with American voters and became a major theme of Roosevelt's campaign. When he won the Democrats' nomination in July, he promised to remember the "men and women forgotten in the political philosophy of government" if he became President.

Thousands of destitute veterans were among the jobless ramblers roaming the country in search of work. The ex-servicemen became more visible during the summer of 1932 when they converged on Washington seeking help. They hoped to persuade Congress and Hoover to approve early payment to them of a bonus that had been authorized in 1924, when times were good and the United States was still feeling a swell of patriotic pride for the troops who helped defeat Germany in 1918. The bonus plan called for each vet to receive about $1,000 as a reward for their wartime service. Payment was due in 1945.

But in 1932 the veterans were desperate. They came to Washington on whatever transportation they could find to demand immediate help. Some vets on the West Coast started their trip by blocking railroad tracks and climbing aboard an eastbound freight train when it was forced to stop. Others formed caravans of battered trucks and automobiles and took up collections to pay for gasoline as they passed through towns en route to the nation's capital.

Many brought their hungry families with them and set up a giant city of tents, lean-tos, and shacks in the southeastern corner of Washington. Others moved into a row of abandoned, partially demolished buildings on Pennsylvania Avenue that were being removed to make way for new government buildings.

The vets, who became known as the Bonus Marchers, wanted Congress to give them a $500 bonus immediately instead of waiting another 13 years for the full amount. But President Hoover staunchly opposed an early payment.

Tension mounted in the capital during the spring and early summer as the ranks of the vets and their families steadily increased. Washington was uneasy about the presence of the veterans, and many in positions of power were tired of the sight of the shabby former soldiers and wanted them gone. Brig. Gen. George Mosely proposed that the Bonus Marchers be arrested and sent to concentration camps on "one of the sparsely inhabited islands in the Hawaiian group not suitable for growing sugar." As far as the general was concerned, the vets could languish indefinitely in the distant tropics and those in authority back in Washington "would not worry about the delays in due process of law in the settlement of their individual cases."

Public opinion was critical of the Bonus Marchers. A June 1932 *Washington Post* editorial complained that the veterans "can not revert to a soldier status and secure special favors in the midst of millions unemployed." The *Louisville Courier-Journal* was even sharper, accusing the men of deliberately "drawing themselves further and further apart from the rest of the population as a specially privileged class ready at all times to bring political pressure to bear on a Government which showers them with dollars."

By June about 20,000 veterans and their families had gathered in the capital. Their cause was championed by Representative Wright Patman, a Democrat from Texas who introduced a bill in the House of Representatives that would authorize immediate payment of the bonus. Representative Hamilton Fish, a Republican from New York, led the opposition and classified it as a test of national character. The debt wasn't due, Fish said, and Congress could not allow itself to be "coerced by any groups" into approving the bill for early payment of the bonus.

It seemed that Congress was listening to the veterans' pleas. On June 15, 1932, the House of Representatives approved Patman's bill. But two days later the Senate defeated the bill, dashing the vets' hopes for receiving their money. Many Bonus Marchers left town, but a hardcore group of about 8,000 remained, many of them vowing to stay until 1945, if necessary.

Elsewhere, the sympathies of many Americans were swinging in favor of the ex-servicemen. In Las Vegas, Vice President Charles Curtis was confronted in late July 1932 by hecklers wanting to know why the Hoover Administration didn't at least give food to the veterans still bivouacked in Washington. Curtis snarled back that he'd helped many more people than the "dirty cowards" who confronted him.

Hoover wasn't completely unsympathetic. The President allowed medical supplies and some surplus Army equipment to be given to the vets, but like many others in positions of power he was getting tired of the Bonus Marchers. He had the gates to the White House chained shut and erected barricades on the streets nearest the mansion. By July 28 the President's patience was gone. He ordered that U.S. Army troops be used to evacuate the veterans from their camps on the government property on Pennsylvania Avenue.

Hoover's instructions stated that the troops should "use all humanity consistent with the due execution of the order." But Gen. Douglas MacArthur, who was in charge of the operation, decided there was "incipient revolution in the air." His troops moved in with tanks, tear gas, and bayonets, burning the vets' makeshift camps and driving them out of the District of Columbia.

Newspaper photos of the rout horrified Americans, who stared in disbelief at pictures of U.S. troops battling bedraggled ex-servicemen while their families sought shelter on the porches of Washington homes.

Hoover's hopes of winning reelection were minimal before July 1932. MacArthur's brutal treatment of the Bonus Marchers all but guaranteed the President would be defeated. In Hyde Park, New York, Roosevelt sat on the porch of his home with Felix Frankfurter listening to news broadcasts about the veterans' rough eviction from Washington. "Well, Felix," FDR said, "this will elect me."

Roosevelt won a landslide victory in November, and voters made it clear they wanted to give the new President a free hand in dealing with the Depression by sending overwhelming Democratic majorities to the Senate and House of Representatives.

While the President-elect pondered how he was going to tackle the difficult task ahead of him, he was reminded often of the "forgotten man" he'd promised to remember. One reminder appeared in the March 1933 edition of *Atlantic Monthly* magazine in an essay by Wilson Follett. In "The Forgotten Man to His President," Follett wrote that when Roosevelt had spoken of the forgotten man, he was referring to "us, the plain folk...whose votes put the rungs in your ladder." By electing Roosevelt, voters had said, "We live in America, too. It is high time someone thought of us for a change; and, mark you, we mean sooner or later to be remembered."

On March 4, 1933, Franklin Roosevelt stood beneath a gray sky on the steps of the U.S. Capitol to be sworn in as the nation's 32nd President. When the moment came for FDR to take the oath of office, he laid his left hand on his family's 17th-century Dutch Bible. It was opened to a verse that was very important to the incoming chief executive—the 13th verse of the 13th chapter of First Corinthians. Roosevelt's choice of verses gave a clear indication of how he intended to confront the dire emergency awaiting him. The King James English translation reads: "And now abideth faith, hope, charity, these three; but the greatest of these is charity."

Exactly how he was going to apply these virtues, however, had not been worked out. When FDR took the reins of government, the New Deal was still "a happy phrase he had coined during the campaign, and its value was psychological," said Frances Perkins, who became Roosevelt's secretary of labor. "It made people feel better, and in that terrible period of depression they needed to feel better."

At the core of the nebulous New Deal, Perkins said, was "the forgotten man, the little man, the man nobody knew much about." Under Roosevelt, he "was going to be dealt better cards to play with."

It was nearly too late. As Roosevelt took the oath of office, banks across the country were failing, unemployment had hit a stunning 25 percent, and thousands of jobless, homeless Americans were living in shabby encampments known as Hoovervilles.

One of the driving philosophies behind FDR's New Deal was to try something, anything, to get the nation back on track. If one solution didn't work, it was withdrawn and another was quickly substituted. His approach was reflected in the flurry of bills his administration sent to Congress between March and June 1933—the first 100 days of his new administration. The Democrat-controlled Congress passed them all, creating dozens of new federal agencies and programs aimed at resuscitating the nation's comatose economy.

Among the new agencies was the Federal Emergency Relief Administration, or FERA. The legislation that established FERA—based on the statewide Temporary Emergency Relief Administration FDR had created in New York—also appropriated $500 million to be used directly for relief for the nation's jobless. Half of the money would be given directly to the states. The rest would be doled out as matching funds, with the states receiving one dollar in federal money for every three dollars they spent on relief.

Soon after FDR took office, veterans began drifting back into Washington to renew their demand for the bonus payment. The new President—who had been shocked by the brutal eviction of the Bonus Marchers only a few months earlier—seemed genuinely interested in helping the men. He rode out to the veterans' encampment, waving his hat in greeting and chatting with them. He provided tents, mess halls, showers, and other comforts and sent his wife, Eleanor, to talk to them. And he insisted that the vets be provided an endless supply of coffee. "Just let free coffee flow all the time," he said. "There is nothing like it to make people feel better and feel welcome."

Roosevelt's desire to help the veterans may have been sincere, but the man who waved his fedora and extended a friendly helping hand to the vets was also one of the shrewdest politicians ever to hold America's highest elected office. The veterans reassembling in Washington were a political liability for his fledgling administration. As he labored to somehow pull the nation out of the quagmire of the

Depression, he could ill afford for Americans to again see hungry, desperate families besieging the capital to plead for help. Like his predecessor, Roosevelt opposed early payment of the veterans' bonus. But if he was going to oppose the bonus, he had to find another way to get them out of Washington and put them to work. That would be difficult, however, since most of the veterans were too old for the newly formed Civilian Conservation Corps (CCC) that had been created to build public works projects across the United States.

As the veterans began drifting back into Washington, lyricist Al Dubin sat down to write songs for an upcoming movie musical to be produced by Warner Brothers. Dubin was deeply moved by the plight of the men who had been treated as heroes in 1918 only to be booted out of the nation's capital 14 years later when they were in desperate need of help. With this in mind, he wrote "Remember My Forgotten Man," which he described as "a plea for the United States' vast army of unemployed, so many of whom were ex-servicemen reduced to standing in breadlines."

"Remember My Forgotten Man" became the rousing finale for *Gold Diggers of 1933*, which was released in May of that year. The song begins with Joan Blondell speaking the lyrics:

> *Remember my forgotten man?*
> *You put a rifle in his hand.*
> *You sent him far away*
> *You shouted "Hip hooray,"*
> *But look at him today.*

Etta Moten sang the lyrics as she looked down from her apartment at a street scene unfolding beneath her. A police officer, about to arrest a tramp snoozing beside the apartment step, discovers that the shabbily dressed man is wearing a war medal inside the lapel of his jacket. The cop releases the tramp.

Dubin's lyrics put a face on the "forgotten man" and became a catchy reminder that Americans who'd put their lives on the line for freedom were now suffering horribly because of the Depression. And the Roosevelt Administration tried to help them.

By the summer of 1935 the administration had found what seemed like a good solution. Hundreds of veterans who had come to Washington because they didn't know where else to turn were boarding southbound trains with tickets to a place most of them had never heard of. They'd been told there would be work—a highway construction project—when they got to their destination. But when they stepped off the train on a tiny, remote, sparsely populated island in the Atlantic Ocean, they wondered whether someone was indeed remembering them or trying very hard to forget them.

chapter two

Forgotten Men

On the evening of July 7, 1935, a violent thunderstorm rolled off the Atlantic Ocean and lashed the Upper Keys with driving rain and strong winds. The squall made an impression on John Ambrose, a war veteran from Baton Rouge, Louisiana, who rode out the rough weather in a construction camp on the beach at Lower Matecumbe Key.

Ambrose was one of the hundreds of out-of-work veterans who had been sent to the Florida Keys from Washington. Vets had been arriving by train in the Keys since November 1934. Their project, one of hundreds of New Deal construction projects under way throughout the country, was to build a highway bridge that would run parallel to the Florida East Coast Railway, establishing another link from Key West to the mainland. By the summer of 1935, the three oceanfront work camps had become rustic villages with populations larger than any of the island settlements outside of Key West.

The men also had their own weekly newspaper, the *Key Veteran News*. Ambrose, a highly skilled and talented draftsman, was the staff cartoonist for the newspaper and also wrote a weekly news column. The power of the summer storm fascinated Ambrose, and he described it in the July 13 edition.

"Shacks creaked and canvas billowed and cracked," he wrote. "Throughout the night the wind rose and fell and caused deep concern to many unfamiliar with tropical storms."

The squall "threatened to develop into a mild form of hurricane," he continued, adding that the thunderstorm "was a real blessing in disguise for the mosquitoes were completely blown away."

The storm's ferocity caused an uneasy stirring among the men living in the cabins on the beach. Not long after the blow, Ambrose noted that some of his Camp 5 neighbors seemed to be expecting "a gosh-awful tornado or hurricane." The men had "buttressed, lashed, moored and supported...all four sides and the roof" of their little one-room home.

He couldn't resist teasing the men about the improvements they'd made to their quarters. "Everything has been anchored but the family cat," Ambrose wrote. "Wouldn't it be awful if a hurricane arrived and playfully tossed it up on the railroad track in spite of the network of fortifications surrounding it?"

Only an outsider would describe a hurricane as "playful." The Conchs feared and respected the powerful storms that the Atlantic hurled at them every year or so, and anyone with notions that hurricanes were fun had some harsh lessons to learn. But then the strangers who had been arriving by the hundreds in the isolated islands were an odd bunch. Most of them had served in the war, and many of them had put their lives on the line in the fierce fighting in France that eventually defeated Germany. Some bore scars from bullet and shrapnel wounds, and others had permanent health problems because they had been exposed to toxic gas.

Still others had been wounded in a less obvious but perhaps more debilitating way. The intense, prolonged strain of combat had permanently altered their perception of the world around them and their place in it. Even before the Depression turned everything upside down, these unhappy men realized they didn't belong in the workaday world of wives and children, careers and promotions, pensions and planned retirements. Their emotional stability had been undermined by nagging self-doubt, mistrust of others, and constant fears that something terrible could happen at any moment.

Some of them endured their alienation in a sullen, confused, and passive silence. Others were enraged that they had, in effect, been evicted from society and denied the one thing upon which Americans in particular base so much of their personal identity and self-respect—a steady job.

In some ways, being sent to the isolated, sparsely populated Keys made their problems worse. Now they had a steady job, but for many of them that was no longer enough to banish the personal demons that hounded them. There wasn't much to do in their spare time to take their minds off their frustrations except fish, write letters home, or get drunk. Quite a few chose the last form of amusement.

But drinking didn't help them forget their fears and disappointments. Booze ignited the simmering coals of their anger, burning away the restraints that held it in check when they were sober. They became mean drunks, searching for a target for their blazing, inarticulate fury. Lots of times the only thing within reach was each other, and so drunken brawls became common in the work camps.

The first fight erupted as soon as the vets drew their first pay in early November 1934. Glenn Robertson, a lawyer from Johnson City, Tennessee, whose practice had evaporated with the Depression, described the drinking spree in a November 10, 1934, letter to a friend.

"Last night was pay day, the first one, and we surely had a terrible time, worse than I ever saw in a CCC camp, or any other place—some of the men are just animals," Robertson wrote.

The drunken brawling would become a payday ritual for many of the veterans. The sober, hardworking Conchs looked on in frightened astonishment and tried to remember their Methodist teachings of tolerance and compassion, but sometimes it wasn't easy.

Farther down the islands, Key West residents were trying to understand how they had become so impoverished. Jobs and money had once been abundant there.

As the 19th century drew to a close, Key West was Florida's largest city and among the wealthiest in the United States The city's 20,000 residents had prospered thanks to a collection of thriving industries.

The marine salvaging industry started the city on the road to prosperity in the mid-19th century. The salvagers—known locally as wreckers—started raking in handsome profits before the Civil War by rescuing crews and cargoes from ships that ran aground on the reefs a few miles offshore. Among the many Cuban influences on the city was a cigar-making industry employing more than 11,000 workers, and 90 percent of the sponges sold in the United States at the turn of the century came from the waters around Key West. The military's presence kept still more employed. Key West also was a port of call for the Mallory Steamship Lines, and that provided several hundred more jobs. But one by one, Key West's bustling industries started going belly-up as the new century turned the corner.

Improvements in marine navigation technology meant that shippers could sail safely past the reefs that had once been such an expensive bedevilment to them, and so the wreckers were out of work. The cigar makers were lured to Tampa when that city offered them tax reductions. The spongers moved to Tarpon Springs just down the coast from Tampa, and the military started closing bases in Key West after World War I. The steamship company also closed its offices there.

By the late 1920s Key West was on the skids. Within two short decades, the city's tax base and more than 14,000 jobs had vanished. Even the Florida East Coast Railway, Monroe County's largest taxpayer, was forced into bankruptcy and operated under the supervision of court-appointed receivers. With the nation and the world sliding into a deep economic depression there were no prospects that new industry would come to Key West anytime soon.

Those residents who could afford to, left town. But about 13,000 who were either too poor or too stubborn to move stayed and tried to scratch out a living as best they could.

A promising young writer named Ernest Hemingway found the dilapidated town charming when he and his second wife, Pauline Pfeiffer Hemingway, stepped off a passenger ship from Cuba in 1928. Three years later the couple bought a rundown Spanish colonial mansion on Whitehead Street that had been a showpiece when a wealthy wrecker built it in 1851. Pauline started fixing the place up, and her husband's growing circle of celebrity friends began finding their way to Key West.

Hemingway's stature as an author grew as he worked on his books, collected sizable royalty checks, and entertained his friends—whom he dubbed the Mob—with fishing trips on the Gulf Stream and parties in his spacious home. In the spring of 1934 he spent $3,000—money he'd been paid by *Esquire* magazine—as a down payment for a fishing yacht that he named *Pilar*. He persuaded friends at the nearly deserted U.S. Navy base near his home to let him dock the boat there.

As Hemingway prospered, happily trolling the Gulf Stream aboard *Pilar*, many of Key West's impoverished natives wondered where their next meal would come from and municipal leaders fought a losing battle to keep the city solvent.

By the summer of 1934 the city faced a bond debt of $5 million that it couldn't pay, plus another $270,000 in interest that was due. Added to that was about $150,000 in past due operating expenses and more than $113,000 in unpaid salaries to city employees. Among the unpaid workers were the garbage collectors, who showed their frustration by letting the trash pile up.

Finally, city and county leaders threw in the towel. The local governments were flat broke.

On July 1, 1934, Key West and Monroe County leaders passed joint resolutions declaring that due to financial distress they were handing over the responsibilities of local government to David Sholtz, the governor of Florida. He immediately declared that the entire city of Key West was on welfare and thus subject to the jurisdiction of the Federal Emergency Relief Administration. The governor's declaration made Key West's problems the official responsibility of Julius Stone, director of the Florida Emergency Relief Administration (Florida ERA), the state agency charged with implementing the Federal Emergency Relief Administration's program in Florida.

Sholtz's declaration landed Key West's story in newspapers across the country, which was exactly what Julius Stone wanted.

"I knew it didn't mean a thing," Stone said of the declaration, "but I thought it sounded pretty dramatic."

He also knew the governor's move might have been illegal because it had been Stone's suggestion. "I got away with it because we were so far off that no one knew what we were doing," Stone said. "And also because I chose a time when [Harry] Hopkins was on a long vacation."

In 1929 Julius Stone, who held a doctorate in organic chemistry from Harvard, had been hired to work under Harry Hopkins, who was running New York's state welfare program under then Governor Franklin Roosevelt. Stone's agile mind quickly adapted itself to administration. When FDR was elected President, Hopkins became his right-hand man and the director of Roosevelt's Public Works Administration (PWA), the New Deal program created to put the nation's unemployed back to work by building federally funded projects. Hopkins then hired Stone as one of his assistants.

By August 1934 the PWA had hired about 675,000 workers and was spending $39 million per week on projects. Some were massive and far-reaching, such as the Tennessee Valley Authority, which would bring cheap electricity to much of the Southeast. On a smaller scale, dozens of courthouses, baseball parks, and other public buildings were built across the country.

Stone received a budget of $2 million in federal money to use in Key West. Within a couple of days after being handed the keys to the city, he announced that the shabby little town would be cleaned up and repackaged as a tourist destination. Stone predicted Key West would become "the Bermuda of Florida."

The idea of converting Key West into a tropical tourist town had merit. The lowest recorded temperature in the town's history was only 41 degrees, and its winter highs were usually in the 70s, making it a perfect getaway for winter-weary residents of large Northeastern cities. The turquoise waters offshore offered excellent fishing, and beneath the accumulated grime of impoverished neglect Key West's houses were a fascinating blend of architectural styles and influences. Cuban, Bahamian, and Creole cultures had also come together to create a vibrant tropical environment in Key West.

Converting the dingy little town into a tourist attraction would take a lot of hard work, however. Among Stone's first acts was putting the city's garbage trucks back on the streets, which were clogged with weeks of accumulated garbage. Ten trucks operated 18 hours a day for several months to haul away the trash.

Stone also hired public relations specialist M. E. Gilfond, who cranked out news releases about the economic miracle occurring in Key West.

Stone made sure the nation was watching the transformation of Key West. He put the credibility and prestige of the New Deal on the line in August 1934 when he wrote an article for the *New York Times* in which he boasted that the FERA's effort in Key West would become a model for solving the problems plaguing the rest of the nation.

He planned to capitalize on the unique beauty beneath the city's shabby, dilapidated exterior. "Ours is a job of preservation rather than demolition," Stone told a Miami radio audience on August 24, 1934. The city's old houses would be restored and its "romantic lanes and byways" would be preserved, he promised. "We want visitors to breathe and feel the romance and lure of the sea, and the tradition of the pirate and wrecking enterprises of old."

The clever, resourceful, and quick-witted Stone clearly enjoyed being placed in a position of absolute authority. "With a scratch of my pen I started this work in Key West, and with a scratch of my pen I can stop it," he boasted to a reporter for the *Key West Citizen*.

While Stone relished his new authority in Key West, FDR and his advisers in Washington, D.C., were still puzzling over what to do about the desperately needy veterans who again were converging on the nation's capital seeking help. When Stone announced the plans to convert Key West to a tourism economy, a solution for the problem of what to do with the veterans suddenly materialized.

Stone and other Florida ERA officials wanted to make it quicker and easier for tourists to drive from Miami to Key West. Building a highway to replace the slow ferry at Lower Matecumbe Key would cut hours off the trip but also meant building bridges to connect the islands. An island-hopping highway running the length of the Keys had long been a dream in South Florida, but the state high-way department had flatly refused to provide funding for such a project.

Stone, with a few scratches of his powerful pen and the backing of Uncle Sam's treasury, announced in October 1934 that the Florida ERA would use federal money to build the bridges and connect and improve the roads that already existed on some islands, and thus create a 150-mile Miami-to-Key West highway. And instead of using CCC labor, jobless veterans—including the remnants of the Bonus Marchers who were returning to Washington—would be sent to the Florida Keys, organized into camps and put to work on the projects.

It would be an ambitious undertaking, perhaps not quite as spectacular as the Overseas Railroad but still a monumental project. The same long stretches of open water—such as the seven-mile span between Knight Key and Little Duck Key—would have to be bridged. There wouldn't be another highway like it in the world.

Roosevelt Administration officials didn't reveal who had suggested sending the veterans to the Keys, but Louis Howe, widely regarded as the brains behind FDR's 1932 run for the White House, was often given credit for the idea.

The plan also had the fingerprints of Harry Hopkins on it. Sending the vets to the Keys to build the road followed the boiler-plate philosophy of the New Deal recovery effort: that paying jobless people to work on public projects would restore their self-respect and self-confidence and benefit the larger society. "Give a man a dole and you save his body and destroy his spirit," Hopkins said. "Give him a job and pay him an assured wage, and you save both the body and the spirit."

But the plan also had some uncomfortable similarities to the one General Moseley had suggested in 1932 for getting the Bonus Marchers out of Washington—send them to a sparsely populated warm-weather island far from the nation's capital and forget about them.

As far as President Roosevelt and his advisers were concerned, sending the veterans was a best-of-both-worlds solution—it provided help for them and a political benefit for the Roosevelt Administration. The vets would have employment for which they would be paid $30 a month plus housing and food, and they would be in one of the most isolated regions of the United States, more than 1,100 miles from Washington and thus out of the columns of the nation's newspapers.

More veterans work camps would be established in other parts of Florida and in rural South Carolina for other federally funded projects.

Officials said nothing publicly about the political benefits of removing the veterans from Washington. Stone said later that they were only being prudent when they decided to send the vets as far from large cities as they could.

"We thought we were giving these fellows a chance to get away from the big cities with temptation to spend money," Stone said. "Here there was sunshine, fresh air, and quiet."

Not to mention boredom, isolation, and clouds of mosquitoes.

The first men sent to the Keys would be housed in two work camps supervised by. Col. G. S. Robinson for FERA

One camp would be built on the beach overlooking the Atlantic on Windley Key and the other on the beach at the foot of Lower Matecumbe Key next to the ferry dock. The camp at Windley Key was designated Camp 1. The men housed there would work in a quarry on neighboring Plantation Key that would provide fossilized coral stone for the construction projects. The other camp would be designated Camp 3, and the veterans there would work with civilians employed by the state highway department to build the three-and-a-half-mile highway bridge between Lower Matecumbe Key and Jewfish Key.

B. M. Duncan, a state highway department engineer who lived in Key West, was in charge of the bridge and highway construction project. His assistant was Lawrence Bow, a Keys native. Although the veterans would be paid with federal funds, Duncan and Bow, who were state employees, would supervise their work.

In early November 1934 about 50 vets stepped off the FEC train at Windley Key, two miles up the tracks from Islamorada. Their first task was to clear away brush and start work on Camp 1.

The men who followed were from all across the United States and all walks of life. They included Jimmy Conway, a former professional boxer from Brooklyn, New York, who had once been a legitimate contender for the heavyweight championship. In his prime, Conway had gone the full 15 rounds in a bout with heavyweight champ Jack Britton. Conway lost the fight on points but impressed everyone with his durability and potential. He'd won more than $20,000—a small fortune in those days—before falling on hard times.

Arthur Mewshaw had been an attorney in Charlotte, North Carolina. John T. McNulty was a former actor who had performed on Broadway and landed parts in several movies before being wounded in the war. He resumed his career after returning from France and had been a stage manager until he lost that job.

Bill Hendren had been a high school principal before landing in the Keys. Other veterans had worked at large newspapers such as the *New York Times, New York Herald,* and *New York World* before the Depression.

But although the work camps offered the men at least a theoretical chance to get their lives back on track, the program was beset with problems from the moment the first veterans arrived on Windley Key. The friction began with the primitive living conditions. The vets were housed in tents and had no place to take a bath or relieve themselves.

B. M. Duncan and Lawrence Bow also weren't happy about being required to use the veterans on their highway construction project.

The vets—angry, alienated, out of shape, and annoyed by mosquitoes and sleeping in tents—were less than enthusiastic about doing hard labor in the muggy Keys.

Duncan and Bow were accustomed to the hot, humid weather, and to working with and supervising men who wanted the job and knew how to do it. If a man didn't want to work, they didn't have much use for him; there were too many men begging for jobs to waste time with a bunch of surly veterans. Nor did they have time to make the vets comfortable in the work camps. Duncan and Bow weren't social workers. They were construction foremen with a work schedule to meet. It didn't make sense to them that they should have to mollycoddle a bunch of grown men.

Resentment festered on both sides, and would soon lead to a showdown.

A few weeks after the camps opened, a small group of angry veterans went to Miami to meet with E. J. Close, operations director for the Florida ERA. The vets told him that conditions were intolerable and asked him to come see for himself.

Close went to the Keys with several other local officials, including the city engineer of Homestead. In a brief report he wrote after his inspection, Close noted that camp sanitation was "terrible" and there was no discipline. He suggested that new supervisors experienced in dealing with veterans be brought in immediately to correct the problems before they got worse.

Close's report started the wheels of bureaucracy turning, albeit very slowly. On December 3 William H. D. Hinchman, the Federal Emergency Relief Administration's assistant regional engineer for the Southeast, met with Colonel Robinson to discuss the problems in the Keys. Robinson quickly made it clear that he had a low opinion of the veterans. About 40 percent of them were "psychos," and the entire group completely ignored the rule prohibiting whiskey in the camps, he said.

Robinson acknowledged that there was very little discipline in the camps, but said that was only a serious problem on paydays. "On that day, there is nothing we can do with them, and since I have taken the stand that Washington wants these men to stay here I have put up with things that I would not stand under ordinary conditions."

Robinson's claim that the vets' drinking was a problem for only a couple days each month didn't square with what Hinchman had heard, however. FEC trains went through the camps each day, and passengers were continually seeing drunken veterans, creating a serious public image problem that had to be eliminated, he said. Hinchman and Robinson decided to build canteens for the veterans, hoping this would at least keep their drinking out of public view.

Despite having a clear picture of the problems in the camps, federal administrators moved very slowly to correct them. On Christmas Eve, Albert Keith, a veteran from Atlanta at Camp 1, wrote a letter to the office of the U.S. Attorney General saying that conditions were unbearable.

"We have no recreation, there are no regulations and no order among the men of the camp," Keith wrote. "I have never been affiliated or connected with such a disrupted and disorganized mob. It reminds me of an insane asylum."

When Keith didn't get a response to his letter, he and three other veterans sent a telegram to Louis Howe, one of President Roosevelt's closest advisers, telling him that conditions were "desperate" and that 200 men in Camp 1 were going to leave if conditions weren't improved immediately.

With the railroad hauling dozens of veterans away from Washington every week and depositing them in the remote Keys, FDR was ready to publicize his position on early payment of the bonus. On New Year's Eve, 1934, he announced that he opposed paying the bonus before it was due in 1945. The veterans most in need of help were already getting federal assistance, and the government was giving "very definite and distinct preference" to hiring veterans for its relief work, the President said. Besides, he added, it would cost too much to pay the bonus ahead of schedule.

In the meantime, the Florida ERA's effort to bring tourists to Key West was already paying dividends even though work on the new bridge and highway had hardly started. Stone and his assistants organized local residents into work details. Brightly colored signs with the slogan "Help to All Who Help Themselves" started appearing in the windows of homes and businesses as Key West residents pitched in enthusiastically to clean up their town and repair the many shabby buildings that had been eyesores for so long.

Gilfond and his staff, which included talented graphic artists, launched a nationwide advertising campaign to lure tourists to Key West. When the visitors arrived they were given a booklet published by the Florida ERA that included a map of the city's attractions.

The effort was a rousing success. About 40,000 tourists visited Key West during the 1934–35 season, and the city's income from tourism increased by about 43 percent. Even Dizzy Dean, the star pitcher for the St. Louis Cardinals, briefly visited the city during a cruise after his team's victory in the 1934 World Series. Dean, nattily attired in a tropical-weight suit and two-tone shoes, stepped off the cruise ship long enough to be photographed at the Key West docks.

Not everyone in Key West was happy about all of the new visitors, however.

No one had bothered to confer with Ernest Hemingway before putting his house on the maps that were handed out to the visitors. The author's home was listed as attraction number 18, and a fair number of those 40,000 tourists tramped onto his property and peered into the windows of his home or gawked at him from the sidewalk as he tried to relax on his porch with a drink and a cigar. One especially bold visitor opened the front door of Hemingway's home and marched into his living room as though he were walking into a museum.

Hemingway made light of the intrusions in a column in the April 1935 issue of *Esquire* magazine, describing himself as "a modest and retiring chap" with no desire to compete with the other tourist attractions listed on the map. But behind the humor, the author was livid, and the fact that he was an anti–New Deal Republican who despised Julius Stone only added to his rage.

When Florida ERA leaders decided in early 1935 to replace dozens of outhouses in Key West with a modern sewer system, Hemingway saw an opportunity to regain some privacy. The streets were ripped up to lay the new pipelines, and the paving bricks that had been removed were stacked at the same Navy yard where Hemingway docked his yacht. The author bought 19,000 of them for $38 and put his handyman, Toby Bruce, to work building a six-foot-tall wall around his property. He urged Bruce to get the project completed before the onset of the worst part of the hurricane season in August.

While Hemingway cursed the tourists and tried to wall them out, hundreds of vets were arriving on the islands to the north of Key West. By early February 1935 about 600 men were living in the Upper Keys and working on the road construction project.

But camp administrators still hadn't improved the substandard living conditions that had so angered Albert Keith and other veterans months earlier. The men were arriving faster than carpenters could build even minimal housing for them.

"They had to rush to get up tents of any description that they could get hold of—circus tents, squad tents—and try to cut lumber and get it as soon as they could to start building shacks for them," said Hubert Nichols, an engineer from Homestead who was working on the bridge construction project.

The hastily built housing made some veterans uneasy.

"I would like to say that they were supposed to block up the shanties but the way they were blocked it was suicide for hurricane weather," said Abraham Fox, a veteran from Los Angeles who was assigned to Camp 1. "They had sawed off trees into blocks a foot and a half or two feet long and set them on top of the ground and then the house set on these. For bracing they nailed boards down the sides of the shanties onto the blocks. That was awful...I laid there many a night knowing that it would be like a matchbox if a storm hit."

Keys natives weren't impressed with the work camps either. Rufus Johnson, who'd lived on the islands for more than 50 years, said the camps wouldn't withstand even strong breezes. "I saw them blown to pieces with a common north wind," he said.

Winds also frequently blew down a tent used for storage at the work camps, Johnson said. "I saw a big tent for storing things there one night, and the next morning it would be all to pieces," he said.

Johnson warned one administrator about putting the camps so close to the ocean. "I told him we had high tides in October, higher than any time of the year," he said. "I said in October the tides will put that mess hall under water. He said 'You think so?' and I said 'I know so.' He said how would it be to put a lot of boards and things around it, and I said, 'Mister, water has got more power than anything in the world.'"

But state and federal officials dithered about how to resolve the housing problems. A proposal to convert boxcars into temporary housing was dropped when officials decided that would cost too much.

In late February Joseph Hyde Pratt, a FERA regional engineer in Raleigh, North Carolina, made several inspection visits to the veterans camps. He was accompanied by others, including Fred Ghent, the director of safety for the Florida ERA. Pratt was very upset with living conditions in the camps and especially displeased by the way Duncan and Bow were running them.

The camps should have been put into "first-class condition" before the veterans started work on the bridge, Pratt said. But the camps were still filthy, and were only getting worse with more men pouring in every day.

The inspectors also learned that two veterans had died from spinal meningitis—a disease caused by bacteria that can thrive and spread in crowded living conditions.

Duncan received a letter on February 26, 1935, detailing the dirty and dangerous conditions the inspectors had found in the camps and ordering him to immediately make the camps as sanitary as possible and keep them that way.

By late February the men in Camp 3 had formed a five-member grievance committee to take a list of demands to administrators. The vets wanted improved sanitation in the camps. They also were upset because they thought they had not been paid as much as promised for their work, and because B. M. Duncan and Lawrence Bow were hiring skilled workers from outside the camps instead of using veterans who had the same skills and could do the same work.

Duncan responded to their demands by ordering the five members of the grievance committee to be thrown in jail. He didn't bother to get a warrant for their arrest or even have them charged with a crime. The veterans were outraged. On February 25 the men in Camp 3 went on strike to protest the arrest of their comrades.

Two days later, Pratt, Fred Ghent, and Sam Cutler, another engineer, who was Ghent's assistant, were back in the Keys to meet with Duncan and Bow. But Duncan had gone to Miami to meet Governor David Sholtz and ride the FEC train with him to Key West.

Despite the terrible conditions in the camps, Bow said he didn't think they should give in to the veterans' demands because it would only encourage them to ask for more concessions.

Ghent and Cutler left around 5:30 p.m. When they reached Miami they stopped to buy an afternoon newspaper. They were astonished to learn that National Guard troops had been sent to Islamorada. Ghent realized that Duncan had gone behind the backs of state and federal administrators and persuaded Monroe County Sheriff Karl Thompson to ask the governor to send troops to the Keys.

The strike and the presence of the National Guard attracted the press to Camp 3, and on Saturday, March 2, FERA engineer Marvin Porter went to the Keys to meet with the veterans, and then returned to Miami with Duncan for a conference with Pratt and Stone.

Porter told Duncan that his authority over the veterans would be reduced. Porter also concluded that the arrest of the five-member veterans grievance committee that had prompted the strike had been illegal. He ordered that the camps' sanitation must be improved immediately, and that Florida State Highway Department officials—most notably Duncan and Bow—not have any part in supervising the work camps. Every camp administrator should either be a veteran or an employee of the Florida Emergency Relief Administration, he said.

Stone, Pratt, and Porter also decided to make a major change in administering both the veterans camps and the construction project. They would divide the authority, putting the state highway department engineers in charge of the actual bridge and highway work and using Florida ERA administrators to supervise the veterans camps.

It was a decision that seemed completely practical and necessary at the time, but the division of authority would have terrible consequences in a few months.

Two days later, the veterans returned to work, but the strike had made Sheriff Thompson and Keys residents nervous, and the National Guard remained. Federal officials realized they were dealing with a group of men who were so troubled and volatile that they would have to be handled very carefully. Camp administrators in the Keys should not make the bridge construction their main concern, Pratt said.

"A large percentage of these veterans are problem cases and they do not seem to be able to assume responsibility, but want to be taken care of," Pratt later wrote in a report. "Most of them when handled right are willing to work and will work diligently and well. The work of the veterans, however, should not be the main consideration, but secondary to their welfare."

Fred Ghent's assistant, Sam Cutler, remained in the Keys to supervise the veterans working on the bridge being built at Camp 3. The Harvard-educated Cutler seemed, to the FERA engineers, to be the kind of administrator they needed to supervise the unruly veterans. Those who had worked with him respected his judgment and character and considered him to be an unusually capable administrator.

"I considered [Cutler] rather an exceptional person because he had all the markings of a gentleman and he was very conscientious," said Paul Vander Schouw, an administrator in Florida's transient division. "At the time he made [safety] inspections he was very conscientious in his reports. He was a man who could be rigid in his official duties and still be quite agreeable in personal relationships."

But some of the people in the work camps regarded Cutler differently. His Ivy League training and cautious nature, as well as his professional background, made him an object of derision. Robert W. Ayer, Jr., who was a file clerk in the camps' administrative offices, said Cutler was "a very nervous sort of fellow" who "imagines things."

"He was probably the most nervous one there," Ayer said.

As the dust began to settle from the strike and the dramatic reorganization of the camps' administrative structure, Julius Stone launched a new publicity campaign to polish up the image of the veterans work program. On March 15 Stone told the United Press that Florida had been chosen for an important "sociological experiment" to rebuild the lives of "derelict World War veterans."

Stone said that 25,000 veterans eventually would be sent to the Keys for "reconditioning."

"Restoring the men to their former selves is paramount," Stone said, adding that the Keys had been chosen for the camps because they were far removed from the temptations of the city. The men would work on construction projects in the Keys, but the work would not be their main purpose for being there, he said.

Florida officials and residents were horrified at the prospect of 25,000 jobless, homeless veterans being herded into their state, and a few days after Stone's statement an embarrassed Harry Hopkins hastily explained that the federal government had no intention of sending that many men to the Keys.

Stone's comments about a social experiment in the Keys sounded a bit too good to be true to the *Washington Post*. In late March, after

Congress again failed to pass a bill allowing early payment of the veterans bonus, the *Post* sent reporter Edward T. Folliard to the Keys to take a look at the work camps.

William Hinchman took charge of the camps on March 18. His task was daunting, but he was determined to correct "the worst conditions from every angle that I have encountered during my experience with the Federal Emergency Relief Administration."

Hinchman established new priorities. He immediately pulled most of the veterans off of the bridge construction project and put them to work improving the camps that had been neglected by Duncan and Bow. "These two men, on account of their former experiences [as construction engineers] were interested primarily in the construction of bridges connecting the Keys and the development of a highway extending from the Florida mainland to Key West," Hinchman said. "The welfare and rehabilitation of the men sent to this area were never taken into consideration."

Soon after Hinchman took over, the *Washington Post* published two stories by Edward Folliard that were harshly critical of the veterans work program in the Keys. Folliard described the veterans as "working guests of Uncle Sam" who had gone on a "booze rampage" during the February strike. The work camps in the Keys were a "transplanted bonus camp."

The purpose of the camps in the Keys was to rehabilitate the veterans and "make them forget about a bonus march on Washington," Folliard wrote.

Hinchman set a whirlwind of changes into motion. He had the vets clean up their camps and plant palm trees. He obtained athletic equipment for the camps and urged the men to form baseball and volleyball teams. He gave them new khaki work uniforms. He tried to appeal to their sense of self-respect. And he allowed them to start their own weekly newspaper—the *Key Veteran News*.

Although Hinchman worked hard to improve the camps, he had no intention of staying in the Keys and looked for a permanent director for all seven veterans work camps in Florida. In late March Pratt suggested several possible successors for the job. He gave an especially high recommendation for one of the men.

"You have another good man down there now—Mr. Cutler," Pratt told Hinchman. "If you can use him to advantage, permanently, in connection with the camps, I shall be glad to have you do so. I consider him a very capable man in many ways."

By the end of March Hinchman had finished his reforms and prepared to leave the Keys. But before going he delivered speeches to the vets at both camps, telling them "bygones are bygones" and imploring them to improve their behavior. "All the veterans stationed in the Keys are getting a black eye because of your actions," he said. "They don't rate it. There are plenty of special men in these encampments."

The *Key Veteran News* carried Hinchman's remarks in its first issue on March 30, 1935. The newspaper also included a front-page story saying that the National Guard was protecting the veterans from "parasites" such as bootleggers.

It was a nice gesture toward the troops. Dealing with the veterans' fondness for strong drink was becoming tiresome for the soldiers and a ceaseless frustration for guard commanders.

"The chief source of all the trouble amongst the veterans seems to be caused by liquor," Lt. Col. M. R. Woodward of the Florida National Guard wrote in a memo to his superiors in April 1935. "One of the main functions of the guard is to keep out all illegal shipments of liquor. The veterans resort to drinking shoe polish, hair tonic, and other fluids that contain alcohol, and this creates a very bad condition when men become intoxicated on these drinks."

Islamorada natives were getting an eyeful of the vets' determined drinking. Bernard Russell, who was 16 in 1935, recalled that one day when he was minding the cash register at his family's small store in the rear of the post office building, a long line of veterans formed outside. The camp canteen apparently had run out of beer, and the men had lined up to buy bottles of rubbing alcohol and Coca-Cola. The teenager didn't know that the veterans were mixing the rubbing alcohol with the soda and drinking the noxious concoction. But when Russell's father, postmaster John Russell, saw the men leaving the store with their purchases, he knew instantly what they were doing and stopped the sales.

The postmaster was troubled by the frequent drunkenness of the veterans. "I often thought that it was almost a crime to allow so much drinking in the camps," he said. "When they got paid they would drink until it was all gone. Then they would wait until their allowances came again to get more."

The National Guard troops tried to cut off the vets' supply of hard liquor by searching everyone who got off the trains at the camps and setting up a roadblock at Plantation Key to search automobiles for booze. But protests from indignant tourists and residents put an end to those practices. Camp administrators still hadn't figured out how to curtail the payday drinking binges. "Every payday was just a big spree," said Hubert Nichols, an engineer for the bridge project.

Drunken brawls erupted regularly. "You'd see maybe a dozen at a time throwing beer bottles at each other and hitting each other over the head," Nichols said. "It looked like they would kill each other, but they always came through all right....They sure were a rough bunch down there. They drank whatever they could get."

The vets may have avoided killing each other during the brawls, but the payday fighting added to the workload of the camps' medical staff, which had converted a hotel at Snake Creek into a small hospital for the veterans. "We always had boom days then, suturing their wounds," said Lassiter Alexander, a physician who worked in the hospital.

The canteens weren't keeping the drunks entirely out of view. In March 1935 one of Roosevelt's closest advisors, Louis Howe, received a letter detailing the "disgusting experience" V. M. Ollier of Chicago had during a recent visit to the Keys with his family.

"Most of the [men] were in the most revolting stages of in-toxication I've ever seen," he wrote. Some were exposing themselves. Another approached Ollier's car to ask for money to get back to Washington. The angry visitor told Howe that the men didn't seem to appreciate what the government was trying to do for them.

On April 1, 1935, Fred Ghent—who'd become familiar with the veterans camps as the Florida ERA's director of safety—was named as Hinchman's replacement in charge of all veterans work camps in Florida. Ghent, an Alabama native, had lived in Florida since 1925. The *Key Veteran News* predicted that Ghent, who'd served in the U.S. Navy during World War I, would earn the veterans' respect because he had "a sympathetic understanding of their condition"—especially the circumstances that drove many of them to drink excessively.

"He believes that no man...is a habitual imbiber of liquor through choice, but that pressure from environment, reverses, etc. may be so heavy that one finally reaches a stage of despondency to the degree of inferiority complex, then resorts to stimulants with the hope of alle-viation," the *News* said.

Ghent had some quirks as an administrator, however, including a habit of convincing himself that events would always unfold according to his plans. His assumptions went beyond simple opti-mism. He would sometimes deny reality when it conflicted with what he wanted to believe.

It was an administrative trait that might have been harmless and even useful in different circumstances. But for the veterans under Ghent's supervision, it would be a precursor to tragedy.

Ghent's superiors in Florida weren't as impressed with his abilities as the FERA officials in Washington who appointed him. Conrad Van Hyning, director of the Florida ERA and Ghent's imme-diate supervisor, didn't think Ghent was the right man for the job despite his support from federal officials.

"He was probably too sentimental on the whole proposition," Van Hyning said. "He was the nervous type and likely to jump at decisions."

Another camp was established soon after Ghent took the helm of the veterans work program. The new installation, designated Camp 5, was built on the beach at the upper end of Lower Matecumbe Key. The camp was built on a narrow strip of land that was one of the lowest spots in the Keys It was anything but an ideal place for the third camp, but it was the only land that was available.

"At Camp 5, we were on the beach, at sea level, and at high tide the tide used to come right into the kitchen," said Joseph Fecteau, a veteran from Massachusetts. "In fact, at high tide it would come in and put the fire out. We could not do any cooking there in the rainy season....We [were] on the lowest part of the Keys up there, you see, between the Gulf and the Atlantic."

Work had scarcely begun on Camp 5, however, when federal officials told Ghent to stop adding new buildings to the work camps.

Still, the Florida ERA went ahead with plans to establish a headquarters for the three work camps at the Hotel Matecumbe. The deal was a windfall for hotel owner Ed Butters because it meant all of his space would be occupied indefinitely. The hotel's second-floor rooms would become offices and living quarters for 35 administrators and office staff, and Fern Butters and her cook would prepare three meals a day for the officials.

Meanwhile, Fred Ghent was worrying about shielding the veterans from the uncontrollable ravages of nature. In an April 9 letter to Pratt, Ghent pointed out that the Florida ERA administrators needed to make some kind of plans to protect the veterans from hurricanes.

"We do know...that this area is subject to hurricanes, and in view of this knowledge, it is our duty to every man employed on the Keys, in connection with this program, to furnish a safe refuge during the storm," Ghent wrote.

The islands were indeed subject to hurricanes.

The hurricane of October 1906 that had killed so many of the workers building the FEC's Overseas Railroad was only one of many powerful storms that had raked the Keys in the previous three decades. Hurricanes in 1909 and 1910 heavily damaged the railroad, and in September 1919 the strongest hurricane on record up to that time blasted Key West as it passed into the Gulf of Mexico. The storm—which nearly leveled the city—was so fierce that Sister Mary Louis Gabriel, a nun at the Convent of Mary Immaculate, dedicated Our Lady of Lourdes Grotto, a small shrine on the grounds of Saint Mary Star of the Seas Catholic Church where Key West residents could go to pray for divine protection from hurricanes.

In 1929 a hurricane crossed the Upper Keys at Key Largo, and in 1933—still the busiest hurricane season on record—three powerful storms approached the Keys but didn't make landfall in the islands.

While Ghent worked on plans to protect the veterans from hurricanes, he also made an effort to get to know the men, visiting the camps often during his first weeks as state administrator. During a lengthy April 24 meeting with the vets, Ghent commented on the biblical story of creation, noting that God made the Earth in six days. From somewhere in the crowd, one of the men immediately shouted, "He didn't use veterans' labor!"

Ghent addressed more serious matters as well, making a sincere effort to form a bond with the vets and promising to do his best to help. "I don't believe there is a man in the ranks who would be here if he wasn't a victim of the Depression and his financial condition, which was caused by something beyond his control," Ghent said.

He told the veterans he'd been in their shoes before.

"I have been along the road that most of you men have," he said. "I have been out of a job, and I have looked for a job, and I know the resistance you meet and the false promises you get when you are out looking for a job. It is the most discouraging, disappointing experience that any man can have during his lifetime....Almost every man here has lived long enough to find that his experience has been such that he could name his friends on one hand and not use all his fingers."

Ghent promised to meet with every man in the work camps to discuss his problems, adding that he hoped the individual meetings would "restore in your minds a bit of confidence in humanity."

Ghent told the veterans he had confidence in them. "I believe that human nature will react to reason and that any man who has reached the age of 35 will listen to anything that is reasonable," he said. And he said his own fate was in their hands as well.

"Gentlemen, I represent you first," Ghent said. "I represent the Florida Emergency Relief Administration forces second, and if we can't coordinate down here and put this show over, the first man to be fired will be me."

On May 13, officials decided the vets had settled down enough to allow the National Guard troops to leave the Keys. Their conduct had indeed improved, but it was still far from angelic. The weekly *Key Veteran News* contained frequent allusions and direct references to excessive drinking, including staff-drawn cartoons showing intoxicated and hungover veterans. And despite their military backgrounds, the men had little regard for any sort of authority.

"Now, the men didn't pay much attention to rules," said Loring Scott, a veteran from Indiana assigned to Camp 1. "As a matter of fact there were not many rules. They did about as they pleased in general deportment. Of course, there were some rules they didn't question. If a man didn't work, he didn't get paid, and he was reasonable enough to understand that. It seemed to be the inclination of the captains to be very lenient as to the conduct of the camps. A sort of sensitive spirit among the men. They didn't obey rules."

As the summer progressed the vets didn't confine their carousing to their camps. On weekends, especially around their monthly paydays, the vets boarded the FEC trains for Key West and Miami. Camp officials learned that Key West police were far more tolerant of the vets' drunkenness than cops in Miami and Homestead.

"They seem to be glad to have these men come to Key West," said Colonel Robinson. "If they get drunk they put them in jail until they are sober, and if they get into trouble they get in touch with me. When we were first here, 12 men received suspended sentences of 20 days in Homestead, but since that time I have discouraged the men from going to Homestead and have encouraged them only to come to Key West."

In the saloons of Key West, Ernest Hemingway was happy to hoist a glass and swap war stories with fellow veterans. Their adventures in Key West, Miami, and Miami Beach were often reported with sardonic "boys will be boys" humor in the *Key Veteran News*. The newspaper stories often mentioned the "18th floor," an inside reference to the Dade County Jail, which was located on the 18th floor of the Dade County Courthouse in Miami.

Their disruptive behavior wasn't confined to saloons. Sometimes the men weren't willing to wait for a regularly scheduled passenger train when they wanted to travel. On those occasions, they would use the same tactics employed by the West Coast Bonus Marchers in 1932. They'd block the railroad tracks with logs and whatever else they could lay their hands on and wait for a freight train. When the train was forced to stop, the men climbed aboard and demanded that the train take them to their destination. If they wanted to go shorter distances and didn't feel like walking or waiting for a train, they joined hands to form a human barrier and block the highway. When a car stopped, they'd pile in and tell the driver where they wanted to go.

The vets' behavior tried the patience of the Keys natives. Some of the veterans, however, attended services at Matecumbe Methodist Church, and John Russell, the postmaster, occasionally invited some of them into his home for dinner.

Others tried to provide the veterans with something to do in their spare time besides get drunk. Homestead librarian Lily Bow—whose son Lawrence Bow had been so staunchly opposed to giving in to their demands for better living conditions—sent books and magazines to the camps and wrote stories and poems for the *Key Veteran News*. The librarian doubtless felt some empathy for the veterans living in the isolated islands. She and her two young sons had lived on Cudjoe Key, not far from Key West, for a couple of years.

Ghent also hired a full-time recreation director for the veterans. Joseph Huau got busy setting up volleyball courts, organizing boxing matches, and laying out baseball diamonds. He also offered a sympathetic ear and served as a troubleshooter for camp administrators. "I was called on to mix with them to see if things could not be settled to clear their minds of any hard feelings toward the government," Huau said.

One of Huau's first projects was to organize baseball teams in the work camps. The sport became an obsession among the ex-servicemen, who turned out in droves to watch games between camp teams. The vets' teams also squared off on the diamond against teams of young men of the Upper Keys.

A smattering of former professional baseball players among the vets formed the nucleus of a veterans all-star team that was admitted to the Dade County League, which was composed of amateur teams in neighboring Dade County. The vets started work on a baseball park overlooking the mangroves on the banks of Snake Creek near Camp 1.

By mid-May 1935 Ghent's reforms had made the work camps a bit more comfortable for the veterans. Most of the men had been moved out of tents and were living in small cabins, which the veterans referred to as shacks. The cabins were arranged in neat rows. In Camp 1, the men erected facetious signs naming the unpaved streets in their camp after major thoroughfares in Washington, D.C., such as Pennsylvania Avenue and Vermont Avenue. The vets made mascots of several stray dogs, which they named Miami, Patsy, and Bonus. When Patsy gave birth to a litter of pups in late April 1935, the Camp 1 correspondent for the *Key Veteran News* reported the event.

By the summer of 1935, more work camps for veterans had been set up in other parts of Florida. In keeping with the South's unofficial but strictly observed policy of keeping the races separated, black veterans were housed in Camp 2 on Mullet Key near St. Petersburg. Camp

4 was established near Clearwater, Camp 7 was at Welaka, and Camp 9 was at Leesburg. A temporary camp, designated Camp 6, was set up briefly on No Name Key but was quickly closed.

Ghent returned to his office in Jacksonville after spending several weeks in the Keys. But he continued searching for solutions to the vets' persistent personal problems. In May he created a special staff of advisers to help the men get some relief from creditors back in their hometowns, untangle bureaucratic snarls with the Veterans Administration in Washington, and help them search for jobs. He also pressed ahead with efforts to establish some sort of hurricane protection.

A proposal to build a large, reinforced hurricane shelter for the veterans was dismissed because federal officials considered it too expensive. Ghent looked for another way to protect the men from storms.

On May 16, 1935, Ghent wrote a letter to Scott Loflin, a Jacksonville lawyer who was one of the receivers handling the FEC's bankruptcy, discussing a plan to use a special train to evacuate the veterans from the islands. Ghent said he wanted a train with five coaches, and he wanted it to be available 12 to 24 hours before a hurricane was expected to strike the Keys.

He added, however, that he would not pay to have a train standing by.

Two days after Ghent sent his letter to Loflin, the *Key Veteran News* reported on its front page that the two men had discussed hurricane evacuation, and that Loflin had told Ghent that all of the vets could be removed from the Keys in four to six hours. "Evacuation in Hurricanes Assured by Railroad Co-receiver," the headline read.

Ghent also promised the veterans that they'd be taken off the islands if a hurricane threatened the camps.

"Mr. Ghent said, 'We have trains waiting for you in Miami, where we can get you out of the Keys 24 hours before any storm hits you,'" said Clyde McCain, a veteran at Camp 3 from Los Angeles.

Ghent's problem—protecting the men from nature's ravages—seemed solved.

But Loflin had a different perception of the evacuation arrangements. On June 6 he sent a letter to Ghent telling him that the FEC would need 12 hours to put together an evacuation train and get it to the camps after officials had requested it. Loflin added that the FEC would not start assembling the train until camp officials told them where the men would be taken and gave assurances that arrangements had been made with local officials at the destination for water and sanitation services.

Loflin said nothing in his letter about keeping an evacuation train in constant readiness to send to the Keys. But Ghent had convinced himself that the FEC would have a train waiting in Homestead. Announcements were posted on camp bulletin boards telling the veterans that a special train would evacuate them from the islands if a hurricane threatened them.

The phantom train supposedly parked on a siding in Homestead was the first example of Ghent believing what was most convenient for him. It wouldn't be the last.

As the summer progressed, so did work on the bridge from Lower Matecumbe Key to Jewfish Key. By early June cofferdams were in place for the construction of the first four bridge supports. Workers started pouring the concrete for some of the supports on June 7, and a month later the work was completed. A pile-driving crew started preparations for 25 more supports. Plans called for 187 supports to be built for the highway bridge.

A combination of civilian laborers and veterans was being used on the project. Ed Sheeran, the survivor of the deadly 1906 hurricane, supervised the bridge construction.

By 1935 Sheeran was 65 years old, and what was left of his dark brown hair was flecked with gray. An old man's paunch encircled his waist. But he was still intensely focused on his work, and he was fiercely loyal to his friends and the men who worked under him.

Sheeran and other construction supervisors did the best they could with the veterans who'd been assigned to work with them. But fitting the men into daily work routines wasn't easy, especially since regulations imposed by the Florida ERA made it difficult for construction supervisors to use the vets efficiently.

Civilian workers reported for duty at 8 a.m. and were ferried out to the work site on a small boat. But veterans assigned to the bridge job didn't report for work until around 8:30 a.m., and a second boat had to be used to carry them to the work area.

Sheeran assigned the vets to clear brush on shore, unload construction materials, pour concrete at the construction site, and work as general laborers. A few veterans operated construction machinery such as derricks, cranes, and pumps.

But Hubert Nichols, who worked under Sheeran, said it was "just impossible" to use the veterans because of restrictions. Camp administrators insisted that the vets be back on shore promptly at 11:30 a.m. to go to lunch at their mess hall. The vets didn't return from their lunch break until around 1:30 p.m., and their workday ended at 3:30 p.m., which meant that they were available for work only about five hours per day.

Despite Ghent's improvements, the veterans still had to contend with uncomfortable living conditions that got worse with the arrival of the steamy Keys summer. Hordes of mosquitoes descended on the islands, precipitating another crisis for camp administrators.

"About the middle of June, the mosquitoes were so bad that it was almost impossible to stay there," said Loring Scott, the veteran from Indiana. "You had to stay in the house, or shack, or tent, or hut from the time it began to get dark until bright daylight. You just could not stay out there on those Keys."

Many veterans even kept their cabins darkened at night so the light wouldn't attract mosquitoes, Scott said. "That didn't happen every night, but we didn't have any light—half of those shacks were not lighted during June and July, and some nights you could not go outside of the shacks without the mosquitoes swarming all over you."

A group of vets met with Sam Cutler and told him they wanted to be transferred to other camps to get away from the relentless pests. Cutler said he couldn't do that, and the vets said they would quit if they had to stay in the mosquito-infested Keys. Camp administrators decided to bring in new weapons to fight the insects. Vets assigned to the recently created Camp 5 were given the task of mosquito control. A crew from Camp 5 constantly patrolled the islands, spraying puddles of standing water with oil to prevent mosquitoes from breeding there.

Meanwhile, more vets arrived in the Keys.

Soon after the July storm that so impressed John Ambrose, Sam Cutler went to the U.S. Weather Bureau's office in Miami to have the agency verify the accuracy of three barometers that would be put at the work camps.

Barometers had been around for hundreds of years, but in 1935 they were still the best way to monitor the approach of bad weather. It's difficult to think of air as having weight, but it does, and the weight is expressed as atmospheric pressure. In the 17th century, Italian physicist Evangelista Torricelli discovered that changes in atmospheric pressure had an odd effect on mercury. Torricelli invented the first barometer by filling a long glass tube with mercury and then turning the tube upside down and placing its open end into a small cistern of mercury. When bad weather caused the atmospheric pressure to decrease—that is, when the air became lighter—there was less pressure exerted on the mercury in the cistern. The mercury in the cistern would rise, and this allowed the mercury in the tube to drop. By marking the glass tube to measure inches, Torricelli was able to accurately monitor changes in atmospheric pressure.

When the weather is calm at sea level, the column of mercury in a barometer will stay at 29.92 inches on the glass tube. Barometers quickly became standard equipment on sailing ships when mariners discovered that the approach of bad weather at sea caused the mercury in the glass tube to fall to a lower level.

The hurricanes that form over the ocean, marked by extreme low pressure, have evoked fear and respect since prehistoric times. Indians living near the Atlantic called the powerful storms of late summer "hurracan," which also was their word for "evil spirit." Hurricanes had sent hundreds of ships to the bottom of the Atlantic. The barometer gave Euopean sailors a chance, at least, to detect these terrible storms.

Sam Cutler wanted to know more about hurricanes. While at the weather bureau's Miami office, he dropped in on meteorologist Ernest Carson. Cutler, true to his training, wanted to understand the threat hurricanes posed to the vets on the Keys. He also told Carson he wanted to receive any hurricane warnings issued by the Miami office.

Carson's Miami office was responsible for issuing warnings for the area from the northern end of Key Largo to West Palm Beach. Warnings for Islamorada, where the veterans work camps were located, were issued by the weather bureau's office in Key West. But the meteorologist told Cutler that he'd be glad to give him copies of any warnings issued by the Miami office.

Carson also passed along a weatherman's rule of thumb—a hurricane does not have to strike the Keys to cause hazardous conditions on the islands. Anytime a hurricane approaches the Keys or passes through the Straits of Florida—the narrow body of water that separates the Keys from Cuba and the Bahamas—conditions are very dangerous on the islands, Carson warned.

The information undoubtedly made an impression on Cutler, who had spent much of his career devising ways to minimize risks in the workplace.

The reason for the danger is simple—the Straits of Florida are only about 90 miles wide, and a hurricane can be several hundred miles wide, with hurricane-force winds of at least 74 miles per hour extending 50 miles or more all around the eye of the storm. The winds on the right side of the hurricane's eye are even more dangerous because they have the added force of the hurricane's forward speed. Thus, if a hurricane has 100-mile-per-hour winds at its center and the storm is moving at 15 miles per hour, the winds on the right side of the eye will be 115 miles per hour. Sailors refer to this part of a hurricane as the dangerous semicircle. A ship at sea will go hundreds of miles out of its way to avoid this part of a storm.

The winds on the left side of the eye are less dangerous because the storm's forward motion reduces their force. This means that the storm with 100-mile-per-hour winds at its center traveling at 15 miles per hour will have winds of only 85 miles per hour on its left side. Sailors refer to this side of a storm as the navigable semicircle, and if a ship's captain has to sail near a hurricane, he will try to position his vessel so that it is on the left side of the eye's forward motion.

A hurricane moving westward through the Straits of Florida subjects the Keys to the situation that sailors go to great lengths to try to avoid. The islands are squarely within the hurricane's dangerous semicircle. Unlike a ship at sea, however, the Keys can't maneuver away from the storm.

A hurricane in the straits is "one of the worst situations that you can get on the Florida Keys," said Ivan Tannehill, assistant chief of the weather bureau's Forecasting Division, in 1935. The stronger winds on the hurricane's dangerous semicircle pile up water against the islands, he said.

Weather bureau officials had long ago realized that one of their biggest problems was crafting hurricane advisories that alerted people to danger without creating panic. It was a difficult line to walk—so difficult, in fact, that the weather bureau reminded meteorologists of the agency's policy of issuing warnings in bulletins sent out every summer before each hurricane season.

The bulletin reminded meteorologists that when they ordered the red-and-black hurricane warning flags to be hoisted at coastal stations, they were telling residents "there is immediate need of precautionary measures to save life and property within the area encompassed by the warning."

In other words, if you see the hurricane warning flags flying, you are in danger and it's up to you to protect yourself.

The policy clearly defined the limits of the bureau's responsibilities. Forecasters should alert coastal residents that a hurricane could be heading their way, but they couldn't take responsibility for seeing that residents heeded those warnings. Still, weather bureau officials assumed people living on the coast wouldn't need much prompting to take action to protect their lives and property.

"Having given the warnings to constituted authorities and advised them as to precautionary measures that may be proper, the local official has done his full duty," the weather bureau statement said. "Whether or not the persons so warned do actually take the necessary precautions is a matter of their own responsibility."

The Conchs weren't likely to ignore an advisory telling them a hurricane was heading in their general direction. But newcomers—especially those who had been through a hurricane or two and thought they knew all about the storms—were another matter entirely.

In the 1920s new residents poured into Miami and South Florida, and thousands of them were killed by two powerful hurricanes. In September 1926 the eye of the worst hurricane on record until that time passed over downtown Miami. When the calm eye arrived, dozens of newcomers thought the storm was over and poured into the streets to see the damage. Many of them were killed a few minutes later when the backside of the hurricane's eye wall—the band of thunderstorms that forms around a hurricane's center— swept across the city.

In September 1928 thousands of migrant workers—most of them black—had arrived in the small towns around Lake Okeechobee to harvest the season's crops. They were completely unprepared for a vicious hurricane that shoved the huge, shallow lake's waters out of its banks and sent an eight-foot wall of water rolling across the Everglades. More than 1,800 people were killed, most of them poor black migrants.

The weather bureau was harshly criticized after both tragedies for not providing adequate warning. But a hurricane detection system that relied heavily on ships at sea for information about the location of storms was certain to be flawed, and any weather bureau bulletin that included the hurricane's location was basically an educated guess.

While Sam Cutler was learning about hurricanes, a new administrator for the Florida ERA arrived in Islamorada on August 1. Ray W. Sheldon was a Massachusetts native who'd lived in Florida since 1923. Sheldon was a construction engineer whom Ghent had hired in 1933 as director of safety for the Florida ERA in Volusia County. Sheldon had made a favorable impression on other Florida ERA administrators. His new job would be supervising the three veterans work camps in the Keys.

Sheldon's wife had died unexpectedly in 1934. But his life seemed to be on the upswing in August 1935. Besides moving from Daytona Beach to the Keys to start a new job, he planned to get married again. His bride-to-be was Gayle Colvert, 27, who had been working as a purchasing agent in Lakeland.

Sheldon had taken on a very difficult job. He was responsible for supervising about 700 men, many of whom were sullen and had little use for authority. Managing them efficiently would require an unusual combination of skills, and Sheldon's training and experience was that of an engineer, not a social worker or psychologist.

While Sheldon had impressed his bosses, the men who worked under him were learning that he wasn't easy to work for. He was dictatorial, wouldn't listen to the advice of his subordinates, and had a compulsive need to remind those under him that he was in charge.

"I found that advice or constructive criticism was definitely out of order," said John Good, who was in charge of supplies for the camps. "It seemed that in every case when we men who knew what should be done made the proper suggestion to Mr. Sheldon, we were never allowed to even finish stating the suggestion, much less being asked for advice as to what order should be given and how those orders should be carried out."

Many of the men around Sheldon decided to just keep their mouths shut.

"I thought Mr. Sheldon was the type that wouldn't listen to anybody else, and would do what he wanted to do, and what I could say would have no effect," said Wilbur Jones, an auditor for the camps. "Therefore, I would probably be better off if I just kept my opinion to myself."

Ghent's insistence on believing that everything would go as he planned, and Sheldon's assertion of authority by refusing to listen to his subordinates, would prove to be tragic flaws. Ghent and Sheldon were responsible for the safety of hundreds of men, yet a clear and unmistakable threat to the safety of the men in their care would be denied by one and ignored by the other.

Ghent came down to Islamorada to meet with Sheldon in early August. His instructions to the new administrator for handling the veterans were simple—"make them happy." Ghent also discussed hurricane preparation with Sheldon. He told Sheldon that they would use a special train to evacuate the veterans in the event of a storm. And he told Sheldon about the recently purchased barometers for each of the work camps to help monitor the movements of any hurricanes.

Unfortunately, the instruments couldn't foretell the approach of a serious political storm brewing just over the horizon.

On August 6, 1935, Ghent and his boss, Conrad Van Hyning, and another Florida ERA administrator, R. G. Unkrich, boarded a train for Washington, D.C. The veterans work program in Florida had grown steadily since the spring, but Ghent, Van Hyning, and Unkrich were concerned because federal officials in Washington seemed to be ignoring them. Ghent was especially frustrated because he felt that he had not received any definite instructions from Washington since he'd taken the job four months earlier. The Florida administrators wanted federal officials to tell them where the vets work program was going and how it was going to achieve its goals.

While the Florida administrators tried to get some direction from their counterparts in Washington, *New York Times* reporter Charles

McLean arrived in Kingstree, South Carolina, to take a look at a work camp there housing veterans who were building a public golf course in the little town near Charleston.

McLean toured the camps August 8 and 9, and, like Edward Folliard of the *Washington Post*, he found little to his liking. In a biting report he called the veterans work program "one of the strangest New Deal undertakings." He described the men in the South Carolina camp as "shell-shocked, whiskey-shocked and depression-shocked," and reported that 20 of them had wrecked a floor of the county jail after they'd been arrested during a recent payday drinking binge. Their behavior kept the little town of Kingstree "continually disturbed."

F. E. Simpson, a veteran at the South Carolina camp, fired back with an open letter accusing the *New York Times* reporter of having a drinking problem of his own that was so serious it had impaired his ability to accurately report what he had seen at the camp. The letter, published in the *Key Veteran News*, said that McLean had gone on a "debauch on moonshine" during his visit. Simpson said McLean was so drunk on August 9 that a group of Kingstree businessmen who came to his hotel room for an interview refused to talk to him.

As the *Times* bashed the veterans work program, Conrad Van Hyning learned in Washington that support for the work camps was falling rapidly in the Roosevelt Administration. Federal officials had decided to make major changes in the construction work in the Keys.

"We felt that the bridge project had not turned out to be a practical project for their work on the Keys [and] the camp situation wasn't satisfactory," Van Hyning said later.

The day after the *New York Times* story was published, the Florida ERA administrators prepared to leave Washington. On the afternoon of August 12, a discouraged Fred Ghent checked out of his hotel and made reservations to catch the 11:45 p.m. train for Florida.

A few hours before he had to catch his train, Ghent met Van Hyning, who had more bad news. He told Ghent that he would not be retained by the Florida ERA after the camps were closed.

The astonished Ghent immediately canceled his train reservations, deciding instead to stay in Washington one more day to try to scrounge up some job prospects.

On August 16 WPA administrator Harry Hopkins announced that all of the work camps in Florida and South Carolina would be closed November 1. The veterans would be assigned to another form of relief work or transferred to the CCC, which would take over the bridge and road construction project in the Keys.

The *New York Times* gave itself a pat on the back as it reported Hopkins's announcement. A *Times* editorial claimed that federal officials decided to close the camps after the newspaper had published stories "revealing their existence and describing conditions in them."

As the news of the closing swept through the veterans camps in the Keys, the season's first hurricane stirred in the warm waters east of Puerto Rico. The storm gained strength as it moved northwestward toward the United States, but around August 20 the hurricane made a sharp turn to the north and headed away from the mainland.

While the hurricane blew itself out over the open waters of the Atlantic Ocean, *Time* magazine gave another kick to the dying veterans work program. The August 26 edition of the magazine included a story that referred to the camps as "playgrounds for derelicts." The story added that the 11 veterans work camps—7 in Florida and 4 in South Carolina—housed about 2,500 "derelicts." About half of the men in the camps were "psychopaths," *Time* said.

On August 26 Ray Sheldon married Gayle Colvert in a quiet civil ceremony in Miami. He didn't have time for an immediate honeymoon, but he brought his new bride to the camps with the intention of taking off for a few days as soon as he could.

In the Keys, the veterans tried to cope with the news that the camps would be closed. On Friday, August 30, many of them were morose despite the approach of a convergence of events that otherwise would have had them in high spirits. A payday had arrived, the long Labor Day weekend awaited, and their beloved baseball team would play its first road game in the Dade County League in Ojus on the Monday holiday.

At 11:15 Friday morning, camp officials started handing out pay envelopes to the veterans at Camp 1 under the watchful eye of Deputy Sheriff Louis Maloney. When the pay call ended at Camp 1, the paymasters moved down the islands to the other two camps, stopping first at Camp 5 and then at Camp 3.

A number of vets departed immediately. Some headed north for Miami and Miami Beach. Others left for Key West.

Many who remained in the camps started their usual payday ritual.

"When we finished at Camp #3, it was around 2:15 or 2:30," Maloney said. "When we got back to the camps paid off first, about 75 percent of the men were drunk. This condition continued as long as they had money—as long as they could beg, borrow, or steal."

Civilian workers in the camps started clearing out for the holiday as well. Albert Davis, the barber at Camp 1, paused on his way out to check the latest notices on the camp's bulletin board.

"The bulletin board at Camp 1 showed a notice on Friday guaranteeing to remove the men from the camp within six hours after receipt of the first storm warning," Davis said.

Scarcely noticed amid the gloom, departures, and drinking was a bulletin from the weather bureau released at 9:30 p.m. Friday— far too late for publication in Friday's papers. Another tropical storm was brewing in the warm Atlantic.

"Conditions remain unsettled and slightly squally east of the Bahamas and north of Turks Island with evidence of a weak circulation but no strong winds," the bulletin read. "Seems to be working north-northwest or northward."

By Saturday afternoon only about 400 vets were left in the work camps. Many who remained settled down to read the August 31 edition of the *Key Veteran News*.

The newspaper tried to buck up its readers' sagging spirits by reminding them that no official orders to close the camps had been received from Washington, and until those orders were issued the men should consider Hopkins's announcement a "rumor."

Camp 5 correspondent John Ambrose also continued his mocking commentary on the hurricane season and the frequent rumors that a storm was bearing down upon them.

"Every day we hear discussion and dissertation upon the subject of the big wind, that all destroying tropical hurricane which has been fast approaching for the past month," Ambrose wrote in his weekly news column. "Where is the consarned thing? Is it possible that a hurricane of the proportions reported has been lost, or simply expended its velocity upon the thin atmosphere without even considering a visit to Camp Five? Aren't we important enough for the consideration of even a decrepit, spavined has-been of a tropical zephyr? Better luck next month, boys. Seek and ye shall find!"

It was a hellish thing to wish for. Around 1 p.m. that same day another bulletin from the U.S. Weather Bureau rattled across the Teletypes in newsrooms and Coast Guard stations.

"Tropical disturbance of small diameter but considerable intensity central about 60 miles east of Long Island Bahamas apparently moving west-northwestward attended by strong shifting winds and probably gales near center," the bulletin said. "Caution advised southeastern Bahamas and ships in that vicinity."

Unfortunately for the veterans, this "tropical disturbance" would be anything but the playful zephyr that Ambrose had described in one of his earlier columns, and it was going to do a lot more than chase away the mosquitoes for a few days.

chapter three

A Wind Stirs in the Atlantic

When the surface temperature of the Atlantic Ocean reaches 80 degrees, the water becomes a launching pad for hurricanes.

The warm water helps create rising currents of warm air, which lowers the atmospheric pressure where the air is rising. The rising air and diminished pressure pull in more air around the developing weather system, and the air currents can pick up a circular motion caused by the rotation of the Earth.

As the air currents converge at the point where the atmospheric pressure is lowest, the rotation gains momentum. A center of circulation forms. The weather system turns faster, and the winds gradually increase their speed. As the convergence becomes stronger, the winds increase and the atmospheric pressure around the center drops a little more. This causes more air to be pulled toward the center. Then the winds increase a little more, and the pressure drops still more. Warm water can cause this process to accelerate, and the warmer the water, the faster the process speeds up. When this happens, it's as though Nature has cranked up a huge rotary engine that's made of water, heat, and water vapor.

As summer progresses in the Northern Hemisphere, the intense heat of equatorial Africa generates thunderstorms that roll off the continent's west coast and ride the easterly trade winds across the Atlantic Ocean. As these disorganized thunderstorms—known as tropical waves—browse across water that has been cooking beneath the summer sun, they can pick up the circular movement and draw tremendous energy from the warm salt water.

The waters around the Bahamas and the tip of the Florida peninsula are often at least 80 degrees by the time the long Labor Day weekend arrives. Any tropical wave or storm that browses over this tepid water can get a jolt of energy capable of triggering a Jekyll and Hyde transformation. The moist heat from the water can quickly convert a weather system whose worst feature is some nasty squalls into a powerful, dangerous storm.

At 11 a.m. on Saturday, August 31, 1935, the surface temperature of the ocean between Florida and the Bahamas was 86 degrees. The water had become high-octane hurricane fuel.

Despite its fearsomeness, a hurricane is a surprisingly delicate thing—especially in its formative stages—and exceptionally warm water alone isn't enough to create a deadly storm. During a typical summer and fall, about 60 tropical waves blow off Africa and begin their journey across the Atlantic. Most of these waves become nothing worse than bad thunderstorms with some gusty winds.

But sometimes something more happens. Each summer anywhere from 5 to 15 tropical waves encounter conditions that allow them to develop into more violent and dangerous storms. The process starts when the disturbed weather picks up spin from the Earth. Once set in motion, the disturbance can coil tighter and tighter as it draws energy from the warm water. Its winds grow fierce as the atmospheric pressure at its center drops and more air rushes into the vacuum.

If conditions allow, the storm continues to develop. It officially becomes a hurricane when its strongest winds reach 74 miles per hour. If the momentum continues, the hurricane becomes stronger and stronger. A tightly coiled band of thunderstorms forms around the center of the hurricane. This band, known as the eye wall, contains the hurricane's fiercest winds. But inside the eye wall, all is calm as the rapidly converging winds hit the superheated air and spiral upward.

Even when a storm manages to become a hurricane, however, there's still only a slight chance that it will develop into what meteorologists consider a major storm—one with winds exceeding 111 miles per hour.

A hurricane that grows into a true monster with the power to level cities—that is, one with winds exceeding 155 miles per hour and a barometric pressure reading around 27.00 inches—is a rarity among rarities. And like so many other aspects of hurricanes, the process by which a devastating storm forms isn't fully understood.

When a hurricane does manage to reach this supernatural intensity, it usually doesn't maintain it for very long. Subtle changes in conditions can cause the hurricane to weaken quickly and dramatically. Even the strongest hurricanes can become their own worst enemies. Sometimes these storms form a second eye wall around the original one. This second eye wall acts like a noose, literally strangling the hurricane and throttling its strength, as though Nature herself were resorting to some desperate last-ditch method to control her own raging creation.

The tropical disturbance that formed east of the Bahamas during the last days of August 1935 would encounter those exceedingly rare, perfect conditions that foster rapid and unhindered strengthening. After it crossed the Bahamas, the warm waters and minimal upper-level winds allowed it to coil tighter and tighter until it became, for a while at least, one of the most powerful natural forces ever to roam the planet. Unlike most hurricanes that reach this intensity, however, it would hold on to its unworldly strength long enough to unleash it against men who were almost completely helpless before its power.

But when Fred Ghent called the Florida ERA office at the Hotel Matecumbe around 10:00 a.m. Saturday, the disturbance wasn't much more than a minimal tropical storm as it approached the Bahamas.

Ghent called to tell Ray Sheldon that he could take a couple days off with his new wife. The newlyweds planned to take the leisurely ferry ride to No Name Key, then drive from there to Key West for the holiday weekend.

Elsewhere, others were making their own weekend plans.

In Homestead two sisters, Myrtle and Sarah Hodge, ages 15 and 13, respectively, had been given permission from their parents to visit a young friend in the Keys. Despite the summer heat, Myrtle Hodge decided to take along a sweater, and the teenager stuffed a comb and a small makeup compact into the sweater pocket.

In Islamorada, Rita Berteau, the 14-year-old daughter of FEC section foreman Paul Berteau, looked forward to the arrival of the Hodge sisters. The girls had become friends when Rita stayed with the Hodge family while attending school in Homestead. Rita planned to attend a Labor Day softball game in Islamorada with her pals.

On Saturday, August 31, Bascom Grooms, Jr., 13, was trying to squeeze the last bit of fun out of the summer before the start of school on September 3. He'd spent the previous few weeks with friends in Tavernier, but now the end of his vacation was fast approaching. On Monday, he would have to board the train to go back to Key West, where his father, Bascom Sr., was president of the municipal electric company and one of the city's most prominent businessmen.

Things seemed about to turn around for Bascom's older sister Rosalind Grooms Palmer, who was 21. Her short, impulsive, and unhappy marriage to a naval officer she'd met in Key West a few years earlier was about to end. She'd lived briefly with her husband in San Diego, but suddenly returned to Florida during the summer of 1934 and took a job as a court stenographer in Key West. She didn't say much about her marriage, other than the fact that it was over and she'd started divorce proceedings.

Her failed marriage hadn't discouraged her from continuing her search for true love, however. She quickly rejoined her circle of friends, and she had no difficulty finding young men to take her out. The brown-eyed, athletic brunette with a fondness for white pumps was considered by many to be the most attractive woman in Key West

But Rosalind Grooms Palmer didn't take herself or her looks too seriously. Her impending divorce had only sharpened her wit, and she thought her legs were too skinny for her to be really attractive.

During the summer of 1935, she fell in love with George Pepper, the nephew of a prominent Tallahassee attorney named Claude Pepper who was beginning a career that would eventually make him a legend in Florida politics. Rosalind intended to marry George Pepper as soon as her divorce was final. She was looking forward to spending the holiday weekend with Pepper, who worked as a steward at Camp 3. The fun-loving Pepper, who was only a few weeks away from his 20th birthday, was known for racing up and down the narrow roads in the Keys.

In July the couple had visited a photographer's studio in Miami and posed in front of a backdrop painted to look like a departing train. George draped his arm around Rosalind's shoulders, and she gazed at him with an adoring smile. From a railing resembling the observation platform of a Pullman car hung a sign: "Honeymoon Special."

In Miami, Roland Craig was doing some grocery shopping Saturday when he overheard two other customers talking about a storm that had formed near the Bahamas. Craig immediately pricked up his ears. He hurriedly finished his shopping and called the U.S. Weather Bureau's Miami office.

"I asked them if that storm continued on its present course would it strike in along around Long Key, because Long Key is only four miles from my place," Craig said. "The man from the weather bureau office told me it would if it kept going like the present reports."

Alarmed, Craig immediately called his store in the Keys and made plans to return to the Keys early Sunday morning. He had a lot of work to do to get his property ready for the blow that he thought would arrive soon.

Sam Cutler was thinking about fishing as he drove down to Camp 3 Saturday morning. His job as an assistant administrator had required him to stay in the camps every Sunday since May, and he was hoping this would be the weekend when he'd finally get a break. He'd been invited to go on an overnight fishing trip Sunday and had mentioned this to Ray Sheldon, hoping the camps' administrator would take the weekend duty so he could get away. But Sheldon had been noncommittal, and Cutler knew his boss was thinking about going to Key West for the weekend with his new bride.

Around 12:30 p.m. Saturday, Cutler left Camp 3 to return to the Hotel Matecumbe. He thought again of his fishing invitation during the short drive back to headquarters, but he saw a familiar-looking car approaching from the opposite direction. It was his boss's Chevrolet. As the car passed him Cutler saw Gayle and Ray Sheldon in the automobile. Cutler knew they were headed to the foot of Lower Matecumbe Key to catch the ferry to Key West. He disconsolately resigned himself to spending yet another weekend in the camps.

At 1 p.m. Sheldon drove his car aboard the ferry, which was scheduled to arrive at No Name Key around 5:30 p.m. From there Sheldon would have a 43-mile drive to Key West.

As the ferry pulled out of its berth, the weather bureau issued another advisory on the developing storm. Using information from weather stations and observers and ships at sea, the advisory reported that the small "tropical disturbance" had attained "considerable intensity" and was about 60 miles east of the Bahamas.

This advisory was waiting for Cutler when he walked into the camps' administrative offices at the Hotel Matecumbe. The disappointment about his canceled fishing trip vanished as he studied the bulletin, which said the storm was "moving west-northwestward attended by strong shifting winds and probably gales near center. Caution advised southeastern Bahamas and ships in that vicinity."

Cutler went to a map on the wall and carefully placed a thumbtack at the approximate position of the hurricane. Then he sat down at his desk and started making phone calls. He stayed at the desk well into the night, carefully putting more thumbtacks into the map each time he received new information.

As Cutler fretted over the map, the usual payday weekend drinking binge was well under way among the 400 or so men who'd decided to stay in the work camps during the holiday. But the recent announcement that the camps would soon close gave the vets more sorrows than usual to drown.

"These men who didn't leave the camp for the holidays were drinking more heavily than I had seen them over a period of about a year since the camp began," said John Good, the storekeeper for the work camps.

By Saturday afternoon, the storm advisories had gotten the attention of newspapers. *The Miami Daily News,* an afternoon paper, carried the weather bureau's 1 p.m. advisory in a small box on its front page.

The *Key West Citizen* also was an afternoon newspaper, and as the departing sun sank slowly into the Gulf of Mexico and bathed the island city in its soft, flattering light, author Ernest Hemingway put down his pencil and settled into a chair on his porch to sip a drink and read the local paper—in private.

Handyman Toby Bruce had recently finished the six-foot-tall brick wall around the writer's property. It was a curious structure because the paving bricks Bruce used for the wall hadn't been intended for such a purpose, and besides, Bruce never claimed to know anything about bricklaying. He'd done the best he could, but the courses of brick were not straight. They rose and fell slightly, and the mortar between them was smeared on instead of smoothly applied and pointed. But Bruce's effort more than satisfied Hemingway. At last the author could relax on his porch without enduring the prying eyes of tourists, and he hoped that his disappearance from public view would also diminish his appeal as a tourist attraction.

Hemingway also was happy with the day's work he'd completed in his large studio behind his home. He'd finished one short story and started work on another.

But he was jolted out of his self-satisfaction when a small headline near the bottom of the *Citizen*'s front page caught his eye. "Storm Warning," it read. Beneath the headline was the U.S. Weather Bureau's 1 p.m. advisory saying that a "tropical disturbance" had formed east of the Bahamas. The *Citizen* reported that Gerald S. Kennedy of the weather bureau's Key West office said the disturbance was about 500 miles southeast of the city.

It didn't matter to Hemingway that the disturbance hadn't been classified as a hurricane or that it was hundreds of miles from his home. He pulled out his barometer and storm chart and started making calculations and plans.

He figured that, at its current speed and direction of travel, the storm could strike Key West around noon on Labor Day. He wasn't willing to gamble that the storm would not strengthen, or that it would not affect Key West even if it didn't make a direct hit on the city. He decided to get up early Sunday morning to start getting his house and boat ready for a blow.

Many miles up the Florida coast, Fred Ghent also was reading about the storm in one of Jacksonville's afternoon newspapers.

At about the same time that news of the storm was ruining Hemingway's good mood, the S.S. *Dixie* was leaving its berth in the New Orleans harbor and gliding down the Mississippi River toward the Gulf of Mexico. At the helm was Capt. Einar W. Sundstrom. The *Dixie* had been scheduled to sail from New Orleans at 11 a.m., but Sundstrom decided to postpone the departure by seven hours to wait for some passengers who were delayed when their eastbound train derailed in Texas.

Sundstrom had only recently been given command of the *Dixie*. When he was appointed master of the ship on July 5, 1935, he was, at the age of 50, the youngest ship's captain in the Morgan Line. Despite his relative youth, however, he was a seasoned sailor who'd been breathing salty air all his life.

"You've always got to be on guard against the oceans," he said upon taking command of the *Dixie*. "They may look peaceful for a long time. That's your good luck. But you know the time is coming when the sea is going to rise and hand you all it's got in the way of trouble—and that's plenty."

Sundstrom grew up in the small seaport of Brunswick, Georgia, and got his first job on a ship in 1901, when he was 16 years old. He went to work for the Morgan Line soon afterward. When the United States entered World War I Sundstrom became a lieutenant commander in the Navy and commanded the U.S.S. *Connelly,* a fuel and supply ship, through waters infested with German submarines.

Sundstrom returned to the Morgan Line after the war and in 1921 was given command of the *Tamaihu,* at the time the world's largest tanker. His excellent record at the helm of the Morgan Line's freighters prompted company officials to promote him to the command of passenger vessels.

The *Dixie* was the flagship of the Morgan Line's passenger ships. The 426-foot, 8,100-ton ship had been launched in Kearny, New Jersey, in January 1928. The *Dixie* was a state-of-the-art ship with luxurious accommodations.

First-class passengers traveled comfortably in staterooms decorated in American colonial style. They could stroll around the ship on a promenade deck that was partially enclosed in sliding glass windows. The ship also had such luxuries as lounges and music rooms with fireplaces, dance floors, and game decks, and a sun parlor. More than 120 crew members worked aboard the *Dixie.*

Two massive steam turbine engines provided more than 7,000 horsepower to the ship's single propeller, and the ship had a top speed of 16 knots. The *Dixie* also was equipped with the most advanced directional technology that was available at the time—a radiotelegraph, a radio direction finder, and a gyrocompass.

On Saturday, August 31, Sundstrom hastily penned a letter to his wife, Marie, at their home in the Long Island village of Little Neck, New York. The captain told his wife and grown daughters Florence and Lillian that he'd delayed the *Dixie's* departure from New Orleans by seven hours. Still, he said he expected to make New York on schedule by Thursday "if we have decent weather."

Sundstrom knew about the U.S. Weather Bureau's storm advisories and knew the danger of running into a bad storm in the Straits of Florida, where there's very little room to maneuver away from a blow. But storms at sea were nothing new to him. In 1932, while commanding the passenger liner S.S. *Momus*, he'd safely weathered a hurricane off the Florida coast. He thought he could avoid the worst of this disturbance as well. Besides, if he was going to meet his schedule he didn't have time to wait and see what the storm would do. He'd have to push the *Dixie* hard enough as it was to make New York on time.

Rough weather was the last thing in passengers' minds as the *Dixie* sailed into the Gulf of Mexico. Florence Steiler, a passenger from San Francisco, joined the carefree crowd on deck to take in the Gulf Coast sunset and enjoy the first caress of the salty sea breezes. There was a holiday mood among those leaning on the deck rails and pointing to the sliver of a new moon that was just becoming visible in the darkening sky.

"Little did anyone realize when we sailed down the placid Mississippi, with the new moon just showing, what lay in store for us," Steiler said.

Almost half of the passengers were from New York City and its surrounding suburbs. There were two newlywed couples on their honeymoons, and teachers returning from last-minute vacations before the start of the school year. There also was a smattering of passengers whose home addresses on Manhattan's Upper East Side and in suburban Westchester County were badges of their prosperity and social prominence.

A few were traveling with small but precious personal items. Musician Cal Calman had his 18th-century Storioni violin. Anna Belcher brought along a friend she couldn't bear to travel without— a little Boston terrier named Skippy. Her husband, Frank, a former opera singer who ran a tobacco shop tucked amid the theaters on Broadway, was just as attached to Skippy as his wife was and had tried to talk Anna out of taking the dog on the trip, but Anna won out. Skippy, however, would have to make the trip deep in the hold of the *Dixie* in the ship's kennel.

Ed Sheeran had planned to spend the Labor Day weekend with his wife in their comfortable home in Coral Gables. He left his job site at Lower Matecumbe Key late Saturday afternoon but decided to stop for a haircut. Around 8:30 p.m. Saturday he climbed into a barber's chair in Tavernier. When the barber finished, Sheeran went next door to McKenzie's Drugstore to see if he had any phone messages.

There were two. Fred Ghent had tried to reach him from Jacksonville, and B. M. Duncan, the state highway department engineer in Key West, had called to tell him that a tropical storm had formed near the Bahamas.

Sheeran had weathered many hurricanes since riding out the terrible 1906 blow, and he'd learned not to play guessing games with tropical storms. He immediately forgot about spending the holiday weekend at home. He had a lot of expensive equipment that could be destroyed by rough weather, and he wasn't willing to wait to start securing it and see if the storm was going to come his way. He rounded up as many of his work crew as he could find in Tavernier and told them to be back at the job site at Lower Matecumbe Key at six o'clock the following morning. Then he got into his car and headed back down the islands. He knew he had a busy couple of days ahead of him.

At 9:30 p.m. Saturday, the U.S. Weather Bureau bulletin ordered Coast Guard stations, lighthouses, and weather stations from Miami to Fort Pierce to display northeast storm warnings. Along the coast, lighthouse keepers and stationmasters lit two red lanterns and hung them one above the other. Sailors and coastal residents who saw these lights knew instantly that this meant that a violent storm was approaching, and its winds would begin from the northeast.

The weather bureau also issued an advisory. The storm had

reached the northern end of Long Island in the southeastern Bahamas and was moving west-northwest very slowly, "attended by strong shifting winds and squalls over a considerable area and probably gale force near center." The advisory said the center of the storm would reach Andros Island—another island in the Bahamas chain, about 170 miles southeast of Miami—sometime late Saturday night or early Sunday morning.

Gayle and Ray Sheldon arrived in Key West around 7 p.m. Saturday. They had a late dinner and decided to go for a stroll around 10:30 p.m. Gayle stopped to buy some postcards.

As Sheldon waited for his wife to pay for her purchases he happened to notice the same storm warning on the front page of the *Key West Citizen* that had jolted Ernest Hemingway out of his self-satisfaction.

The couple returned immediately to their hotel, and Sheldon called the weather bureau's Key West office.

At the bureau's two-story, concrete-and-stucco office on Front Street, meteorologist Gerald Kennedy answered the ringing telephone around 11 p.m. Sheldon told Kennedy that he was in charge of the veterans work camps on the Upper Keys and asked the meteorologist to update him on the storm.

Kennedy told Sheldon that conditions on the Upper Keys "did not appear very alarming" at the moment. The weatherman said he'd call Sheldon if anything changed during the night.

At that moment there didn't seem to be much to worry about. The disturbance was little more than a windy rainstorm when it crossed the Bahamas Saturday night. The highest winds that were reported reached only 46 miles per hour.

Sheldon climbed into bed around 1 a.m. He intended to stay awake just in case Kennedy should call, but he fell asleep.

As Sheldon dozed in the wee hours of Sunday, September 1, Kennedy received barometric pressure readings from observers stationed in Miami and along the Keys. Something was happening with the storm, and the meteorologist didn't like what he saw. The storm had reached the warm, energy-laden salt water of the Straits of Florida. When Kennedy compared his own barometric pressure reading in Key West with those reported from Miami, he discovered the Key West reading was considerably lower than the one in Miami. That meant the storm was closer to the Keys than it was to the peninsula.

"After our immediate observations at 2 a.m., conditions looked as though the storm might prove dangerous on the Florida Keys," Kennedy said.

Around five o'clock Sunday morning, the weatherman picked up his phone and called Sheldon's hotel to advise the camps' administrator to return to Islamorada on the next ferry.

"I intended to convey there was danger in that section," Kennedy said. "It was impossible to say just where the storm would strike and just how hard it would strike, but being familiar with hurricanes I thought it would be advisable to take every precaution in advance and thought he should be on the ground [at the work camps] as early as possible."

As Kennedy hung up the phone after talking with Sheldon, a few blocks away from the weather bureau office Ernest Hemingway was already out of bed to start preparing his boat and property for a blow. The author wanted to pull the *Pilar* from the water, but when he went down to the dock he encountered a long line of boat owners waiting to do the same thing. He had too much to do to wait. He went to a hardware store, bought heavy marine rope, and tied the *Pilar* securely to her moorings at the Navy yard. Then he started boarding up the windows of his house.

The rest of Key West wasn't taking any chances either. Throughout the day Sunday the sound of banging hammers could be heard all around town as residents nailed boards over windows or closed and secured hurricane shutters.

M. E. Gilfond, who was now in charge of Florida ERA operations in Key West, had never been in a hurricane, but since arriving
in Florida he'd talked to lots of people who had, and what he heard
made him very cautious. He boarded up all the buildings that were
the responsibility of his agency and sent some of his workers to scour
the city's streets and remove anything that could become a deadly
missile if it was picked up by a hurricane's winds. As a final safety
measure, he moved all his men into barracks at the U.S. Navy base,
where they'd be safer in the substantial buildings.

In Miami, store owner Roland Craig rolled out of bed before daylight. He picked up a younger friend named Jack Crow, and by 5 a.m.
the two men were en route to the Keys. Craig also knew he had a lot
of work to do in the next few days.

Around 5:30 a.m. Ray Sheldon called Fred Ghent in Jacksonville
to discuss the storm. Ghent told him to catch the next ferry back to
the camps. Shortly before 8 a.m. Sheldon drove his car aboard the
northbound ferry at No Name Key for the trip back to Lower
Matecumbe Key. His brief honeymoon hadn't even lasted 24 hours.
As the ferry chugged away from its slip and into Florida Bay, Sheldon
and his wife settled back for the four-hour trip.

Meanwhile, Ghent called the FEC dispatcher in New Smyrna,
125 miles south of Jacksonville. Ghent wanted the railroad to add
four or five passenger cars to its regularly scheduled southbound and
northbound trains to allow veterans to leave the camps—provided
that the Florida ERA wouldn't have to pay for them. The dispatcher
told Ghent that the extra cars would be added without charge.

Ghent hung up the phone thinking that he'd given the railroad
notice that the evacuation train might be needed. He assumed that the
train was already assembled and waiting to be dispatched.

As the sun climbed out of the Atlantic and bathed the Keys in its
soft light, Roland Craig and Jack Crow pulled into the ferry landing
at Lower Matecumbe Key, where Ed Sheeran and his crew were hard
at work securing their construction equipment. Craig parked his car

and the two men started walking down the railroad tracks and bridges to Craig Key. When Craig reached his store, he called a friend who had access to the weather bureau's latest advisories. The friend promised to keep Craig updated on the forecasts.

Meanwhile, Sheeran moved his big dredge, the *Sarasota*, into the 1,000-foot-long canal he'd had dug months earlier. The little man-made creek would provide the expensive dredge with some protection from winds and high seas.

Sheeran had ignored the danger of German gunfire to work on that bridge in France in 1918, but he knew better than to ignore the danger indicated by signs of an approaching storm. The 1906 hurricane had taught him two important lessons for staying alive in the remote Keys during the perilous late summer and early fall—pay attention to your barometer and don't try to outguess a storm.

On Sunday, September 1, Sheeran was keeping his eye on the weather, and he was seeing some ominous signs of trouble.

One sign of the approach of a hurricane is the long, rhythmic swells that start rolling in several days before the storm's arrival. The hurricane's winds create huge waves around its spinning eye. The waves are pushed out in all directions and become smaller as they move away from the storm center. Although the waves lose some of their size, they retain their energy and become swells, and they can travel for more than a thousand miles ahead of the hurricane when the storm is over open water. They also move much faster than the eye.

When the swells arrive at a coastline, the normal pattern of breaking waves is altered. Under normal conditions, as many as 12 to 15 breakers per minute roll onto a beach. But hurricane swells slow that rhythm dramatically so that only three to five waves per minute will be breaking on the beach. And the breakers caused by the swells will be much larger than the normal waves.

If the direction from which the swells approach the beach does not change, it's an indication that the center of the hurricane is approaching that stretch of the coastline.

The reefs that lie off the Florida Keys usually prevent breakers from rolling onto the beaches there, and so the swells produced by this hurricane may not have been visible from the islands. But fishermen who lived in the Keys noticed the swells and talked about them when they returned to their homes.

Barometers also usually indicate the approach of a hurricane well in advance of the storm's arrival. When the weather is calm in and near the tropics, a barometer's needle fluctuates very little from its normal reading of just under 30.00 inches, and its slight changes are predictable according to the time of day. An approaching hurricane stirs a barometer in an unusual manner. When the storm center is roughly 500 miles from the coast, the needle can become restless, constantly rising and falling by a few hundredths of an inch. The pressure readings may even climb a little higher than usual for brief periods.

When the hurricane's center is 300 to 500 miles away—a day's to a day and a half's travel time for a storm moving at 12 miles per hour— bands of wispy, snow-white cirrus clouds, known among sailors as mare's tails, often appear. These clouds often indicate the direction of the center of the hurricane.

The approach of a hurricane also causes unusually spectacular sunsets. Around the same time the cirrus clouds appear, the barometer begins to drop slowly but steadily—an even more ominous indication that a hurricane is drawing near.

On the day before a hurricane's arrival, the weather is often unusually good, with exceptional visibility. Distant objects stand out distinctly even though the air is thick with humidity. Those inexperienced with hurricanes often comment later that the weather seemed so calm and beautiful that it was impossible to believe that a violent storm was almost upon them.

When the FEC's southbound passenger train made its regular stop at the Islamorada station Sunday morning, Ed Sheeran had decided that the hurricane was heading for the Keys. The weather in the Upper

Keys was squally—gusty winds and intermittent showers. Word of the developing storm was spreading through the work camps, and the train, as promised by the FEC dispatcher who had talked to Ghent a few hours earlier, was pulling five extra passenger cars to take the veterans out of the Keys. Few, if any, vets got aboard, however. Although many veterans knew from newspapers that a storm had formed east of the Keys, no one had notified them that the regular passenger train had been expanded so they could leave the islands. Fred Bommer, Jr., a veteran from New York who'd been assigned to Camp 1, summed up the vets' attitude about the developing storm. "We all hoped it would blow the mosquitoes away and cool things off," he said.

The worshipers who gathered Sunday morning at Matecumbe Methodist Church had something on their minds besides the Reverend S. E. Carlson's sermon. After services they chatted briefly about the bad weather that might be coming their way, but they cut short their usual socializing. They knew there was a lot of work to do, and hurried to their homes to begin the familiar ritual of preparing for a hurricane.

At Lower Matecumbe Key, Cardy Bradford, who ran a small cafe at the ferry landing, talked about the storm with his father, Carson Bradford, Sr. The elder Bradford had made his usual Sunday trip down from Miami Beach. The men decided that Cardy's wife, Elizabeth, and their children should ride out the storm in Miami Beach. Carson Sr. cut short his visit, loaded the group into his son's car, and left.

The weather bureau issued another advisory at 9:30 a.m. Sunday. The warm waters off Florida were stoking the storm. The weather bureau said it had reached hurricane intensity and was moving westward at about eight miles per hour. The storm was expected to pass through the Straits of Florida and into the Gulf of Mexico late Sunday night or early Monday morning. The northeast storm warnings had been extended to Florida's west coast, and the lanterns had been replaced by the signal that is hoisted during the day—a solid red pennant over a square red flag with a square black center. The warning was now displayed from Fort Pierce to Fort Myers.

The storm was actually moving faster than the weather bureau forecasters realized, however. Its speed was closer to 11 miles per hour. The difference was important. It meant that the storm would travel almost 75 miles farther in a 24-hour period than forecasters realized. And unknown to the forecasters, its eye had started to drift a few degrees north of due west.

As soon as Upper Keys residents got home from church, they started getting ready for rough weather. The telephone lines hummed with conversation as the few dozen or so people who had telephones talked about their preparations and updated each other on the latest information.

At the Hotel Matecumbe, the news about the developing storm was making Sam Cutler uneasy. He recalled the conversation he'd had in Miami two months earlier, when meteorologist Ernest Carson told him that a hurricane in the Straits of Florida meant dangerous conditions on the Keys. Now the weather bureau said that a hurricane had formed in the straits.

Cutler continued making phone calls to gather more information, and he pushed more thumbtacks into the map charting the hurricane's track. "I had never been through a hurricane, and never knew what they were," he said. "I didn't feel that I was in a position to judge on a matter of that sort, but I was fearful for the safety of the men."

Ed Butters, the owner of the Hotel Matecumbe, said he could tell the storm was making Cutler edgy. "I knew that Sam was very concerned, but he was very concerned when the first weather report came out that there was a storm over in Havana, so I didn't put much stress on that," Butters said. "You know, some storms strike some people one way and some another way."

Despite his concerns, Cutler wanted to know more before making a decision about a potential threat to the safety of the veterans. Around 10 a.m. Sunday he went down to Camp 3 to talk to Ed Sheeran.

The fact that the weather bureau wasn't predicting that the storm would strike the Keys didn't impress Sheeran in the slightest. "I pay very little attention to weather reports," he said. "If I have a barometer beside me, I don't care for the weather reports. They are too far away from me."

The situation had a chilling familiarity to him, and he couldn't get the memory of the horrible 1906 hurricane out of his mind. The supervisors in charge of building the Overseas Railroad had been warned about the storm, but they refused to evacuate the construction workers from Long Key, and the men were killed.

Now it was happening again. Another powerful storm was heading toward the Keys, and once again hundreds of construction workers who had no experience with hurricanes were completely exposed to its merciless power.

"To hell with what they say," Sheeran said to Cutler. "Our barometer shows we are in a low area."

Sheeran told Cutler to get the vets off the Keys.

"It was squally and the barometer kept dropping," Sheeran said. "I asked Mr. Cutler if he'd ordered a train [to evacuate the veterans] but he said 'No,' as he could get one on three hours' notice. I told them they had a bad storm coming and they better have the men out of there because it was a bad place for them."

Cutler returned to the headquarters office in Islamorada feeling compelled to prepare for an evacuation. He sent a driver to Miami to pick up Eugene Pattison, another Florida ERA engineer on the camps' administrative staff. Around 10:30 a.m. he tried to call the FEC's assistant general passenger agent in Miami. He wanted to ask if two trains could be assembled to move the veterans out of the Keys. But Cutler didn't reach the agent. Instead, he talked to a clerk, who said he would pass along Cutler's message to his boss.

Cutler also ordered the camp canteens to stop selling beer. The last thing he wanted if the order came to evacuate was to have to round up a bunch of drunken, unruly veterans and herd them aboard a train, and he wanted to give the men plenty of time to sober up.

At about the same time that the canteens were cutting off beer sales, Roland Craig's phone rang. It was his friend, who told him that the weather bureau reported the storm to be about 200 miles east of Havana.

Craig pulled out his map and studied it. He decided that the storm was about 150 miles south of his island. "I knew it was closer to the Keys than it was probably thought," he said.

Paul Jeans, editor of Miami Beach's audacious penny tabloid, the *Daily Tribune*, was also studying maps and trying to guess where the hurricane would go. They showed high-pressure areas that Jeans thought might steer the storm in Miami's direction. Or so he hoped.

The *Daily Tribune* was engaged in a circulation war with the *Miami Herald* and the *Miami Daily News*. Jeans—short, bespectacled, daring, and deeply cynical—was driving his staff mercilessly to dig up spectacular, scandal-mongering stories that he published beneath giant, shrieking headlines. He justified his anything-goes approach to news-gathering by presenting the *Trib* and himself as noble defenders of the First Amendment, friends and protectors of the common man, and tireless crusaders fighting crime and corruption in Dade County.

Jeans, a Chicago native, could trace his journalistic roots back to William Randolph Hearst. After graduating from the University of Chicago, Jeans volunteered for the Army when the United States entered World War I, but he was turned down because of poor eyesight. He got his start in the brutal world of Chicago journalism as a correspondent for the Hearst-owned *Chicago American*.

During the last decade of the 19th century and the first decades of the 20th, Hearst newspapers masterfully exploited the prejudices, ignorance, fears, and fascinations of the masses. The news became a breathtaking, gaudy melodrama. "A Hearst newspaper is like a screaming woman running down the street with her throat cut," said Arthur James Pegler, who also wrote for Hearst and was the father of Hearst columnist Westbrook Pegler.

In Miami, Jeans worked for publisher Moe Annenberg, another

Chicago newspaper veteran who had jumped back and forth as circulation director for the *Chicago Daily Tribune* and its archrival, the *American*. Annenberg amassed his own fortune as the publisher of *Racing Form*, a nationwide newspaper specializing in inside information about horse racing. He moved to Miami Beach and started the *Daily Tribune* in 1934 with Jeans as editor. Under their direction the *Trib* became a throwback to the classic turn-of-the-century yellow journalism tabloids—right down to its one-cent price tag. The *Tribune's* stories sought immediate emotional involvement among its readers—fear, shock, disgust, anger, indignation, pity, and confusion. Sometimes it demanded all of these simultaneously.

For all of the *Trib's* self-congratulatory posturing as a noble defender of justice and truth, however, Jeans used some decidedly ignoble methods, shaping the truth to his liking and narrowly avoiding convictions for libel thanks to a skillful attorney named Victor Miller. Jeans, the self-proclaimed champion of the people's right to know, also had a well-known fondness for sleaze, and once quipped that his idea of the perfect newspaper headline was "Sex Fiend Slays Six in Penthouse Orgy."

The *Trib*—like its turn-of-the-century ancestors—delighted in exposing the misdeeds of the rich and powerful, and if there wasn't a banana peel for the big shots to slip on or a stairway for them to fall down, the *Tribune* *would* happily provide both and then give them a shove.

By late 1935, the *Tribune* was providing readers a steady diet of stories about corruption in city government and questionable behavior by some of Miami's leading citizens, as well as gory tales of crime and passion. Many of the stories the *Trib* published were quite true; others contained just enough truth to keep the newspaper a few steps ahead of a lawsuit. The newspaper's rapidly growing audience enjoyed the *Tribune's* colorful reporting, but Miami's city officials and business leaders detested the publication, and some people on the receiving end of the *Trib's* crusade started extracting harsh revenge. Police supervisors looked the other way as cops punched out *Tribune* reporters and smashed photographers' cameras.

As the Labor Day weekend arrived, the *Tribune* was offering readers its usual front-page stories of crime and corruption—the arrest of city officials for a scam involving property tax certificates and a deranged father who'd brutally murdered his daughters. Then the U.S. Weather Bureau's advisory that a hurricane had formed near the Bahamas rattled across the *Trib's* Teletype machine.

Jeans studied the advisory and weather maps. Other newspapers were publishing the weather bureau's prediction that the center of the storm would stay offshore as it moved westward through the Straits of Florida. But Jeans decided to play a hunch that would prompt Miamians to snap up copies of the *Trib*. What better way to get readers' attention than to tell them a hurricane was heading for the city? The newspaper's Sunday edition included a brief front-page story saying the storm would strike Miami and a map on page two showing the path it would take from the Bahamas straight to Biscayne Bay.

Once again, Jeans had embellished the truth, and once again he would get away with it, not because it was exactly accurate but because it was close enough.

The weather bureau's Sunday morning advisory ignited a flurry of activity at the U.S. Coast Guard's air station on Dinner Key in Miami. Like Sheeran, Coast Guard commanders weren't going to try to outguess the developing storm. They'd decided that small craft should clear out of the Keys immediately.

Around 11 a.m. Lt. William L. Clemmer and his crew climbed aboard their big General Aviation PJ-2 seaplane. Clemmer, who had earned his wings the previous year at Pensacola's Naval Air Station, allowed the two engines to warm up for a few moments, then he opened the throttle and the big seaplane lumbered across Biscayne Bay, slowly gaining speed until it lifted itself free of the water and became airborne.

Clemmer swung the plane toward the Keys. He was about to spoil a lot of weekend fishing expeditions—and save many lives in the process.

In a few minutes he was looking down at dozens of small boats scattered along the islands. The pilot headed toward a cluster of the small craft. When he was over them a crewman dropped a block of wood trailing a long, brightly colored streamer. The block splashed into the warm water near the boats. A hurricane warning printed on the streamer advised boaters to leave the area.

Clemmer dropped dozens of warnings, and soon the fishing boats were speeding back to their harbors. But the Coast Guard pilot had run out of warnings, and there were still more boats to be warned. He headed back to the air station for more.

Out on Florida Bay, the ferry carrying Ray and Gayle Sheldon back to Lower Matecumbe Key suddenly slowed. Capt. Charles Albury discovered that he had a problem. One of the propeller shafts had broken, drastically reducing the ship's speed. The ferry would have to limp along with only one propeller for the rest of the trip. It would be hours late arriving at Lower Matecumbe.

By noon Eugene Pattison was back at the Hotel Matecumbe, and he joined Sam Cutler for another meeting with Ed Sheeran to discuss the hurricane. Sheeran repeated his assertion that the storm was a bad one and that it was headed in their general direction. Memories of the helpless workers killed in the 1906 storm were still haunting Sheeran's thoughts.

Sheeran's edgy demeanor bothered Cutler.

"He was much perturbed," Cutler said. "He is a man of few words, but from his looks I knew he was very much worried."

Sheeran made a chilling prediction to Cutler and Pattison. Because so many of the veterans had no realistic idea of what a hurricane was like, he told the two men, a lot of them would be killed if they were not evacuated.

Lieutenant Clemmer was back in the skies over the Keys early Sunday afternoon. Coast Guard crewmen in Miami had hastily prepared more hurricane warnings, stuffing them into round cardboard ice-cream boxes and then waterproofing the boxes with a coating of paraffin. Clemmer dropped the improvised warnings all along the Keys to boats as far as five miles offshore. He thought about dropping warnings in the veterans work camps and then decided against it. The warnings might panic the vets, and besides, camp administrators had to be aware of the warnings and were taking appropriate precautions, Clemmer thought.

Satisfied that he'd warned everybody he could possibly find, Clemmer turned the nose of his big seaplane northward and headed back to Dinner Key, where Coast Guard crewmen were already getting the station ready for a blow.

In the lukewarm waters between the Bahamas and the tip of the Florida peninsula, the storm began gradually slowing, almost as though it wanted to take full advantage of the opportunity to stoke itself from the warm waters. By 1 p.m., as the holiday fishing boats were scurrying away from the Keys, the hurricane's winds had increased to 86 miles per hour. It had also turned slightly more to the north and was roughly 200 miles from Islamorada.

Up in Jacksonville, Fred Ghent was playing a round of golf at the city's municipal golf course when he was called to the clubhouse telephone at about 2:45 p.m. Sam Cutler—nervous, edgy, over-reacting Sam Cutler—was on the other end of the line urging him to send an evacuation train to the Keys.

John Good, purchasing supervisor for the veterans work camps, was in the office with Cutler and listened as Cutler explained the situation to Ghent.

Cutler told Ghent that there were indications that "very nasty weather" was headed for the Keys, and that he thought, "we would shortly have an exceptionally high wind," Good said.

"He told Mr. Ghent....the veterans should be moved out of the camps area and asked him what arrangements had been made...for their removal," Good said.

Ghent sidestepped Cutler's concerns, however. He told Cutler that Sheldon was on his way back from Key West and any decision about sending a train would be based on Sheldon's assessment of the situation. Cutler asked what he should do if something forced the ferry to turn back to Key West. Ghent dismissed Cutler's concerns, telling him that Sheldon would get back to Islamorada that afternoon. At that moment Sheldon's ferry was already almost two hours overdue.

In Islamorada Postmaster John Russell had reached his own conclusion about the deepening threat to the Upper Keys. Around 3 p.m. Sunday he moved his family into the citrus packinghouse that doubled as the family's hurricane shelter. The 12-foot-by-20-foot building was typical of many of the Conchs' hurricane shelters, which were reinforced with strong timbers and held together with huge bolts. Russell had even bolted his shelter to the coral island beneath it.

Other families were going to their own similar shelters near the middle of the island.

Around 4 p.m. the ferry carrying Ray and Gayle Sheldon pulled into its berth at the foot of Lower Matecumbe Key, a full three hours late. A long line of cars snaked back up the road, waiting to board the ferry.

But those drivers were going to be disappointed. Soon after the ferry docked, Charles Albury spoke with his boss on the telephone. The captain was ordered to tie up the ferry at Lower Matecumbe Key and stay there until the hurricane threat was over. After the captain hung up, a veteran from nearby Camp 3 asked him if the ferry would make its return trip to No Name Key that afternoon. Albury said the boat would stay docked until the storm had passed.

The veteran was fascinated by the prospect of experiencing a hurricane. "I want to see one of those tropical disturbances," he said.

Albury, a Conch who understood the power of hurricanes, was astonished at this naive wish. He turned and looked at the veteran. "I hope you are the only one that sees it," he replied.

As Albury was speaking to the inexperienced veteran, another advisory was released from the weather bureau. The hurricane was 275 miles east of Havana, moving slowly to the west or west-south-west, the bulletin said.

In the Gulf of Mexico, Captain Sundstrom had no way of know-ing that the weather bureau's calculations were still off the mark, how-ever. He was studying every weather bulletin as it came in on the Dixie's radio. As the Dixie steamed across the Gulf of Mexico toward Key West, Sundstrom believed the hurricane's eye was well south of him, and that soon the Dixie would be traveling in the opposite direction from the storm.

Most of the liner's passengers were still in a festive mood and happily enjoying their cruise. "It was a gay crowd that cavorted under the deck showers and played in the water and at other sports," said Florence Steiler, the passenger from San Francisco.

Ray Sheldon reached his office in Islamorada 15 or 20 minutes after the ferry docked at Lower Matecumbe. He met briefly with Cutler, Good, and auditor G. A. Malcolm. Cutler briefed Sheldon on his earlier conversations with Ed Sheeran, telling Sheldon that Sheeran thought the storm was a bad one and heading their way, and that the veter-ans should be evacuated immediately. Good and Malcolm seconded Cutler's opinion.

"The majority of us thought they would go ahead and order out the train so we could get the men out," Malcolm said.

But Sheldon wasn't impressed.

"[Sheldon] gave us to understand that he was in charge and would take care of the situation," Malcolm said.

A few minutes after the brief meeting, Sheldon telephoned Fred Ghent in Jacksonville. Sheldon dismissed the concerns of Cutler and Malcolm, telling his boss that conditions in Islamorada did not look dangerous. Ghent told Sheldon to call him if conditions did get bad.

Unknown to the administrators, however, the conditions were

indeed getting very bad. By 7 p.m. the hurricane had slowed to only 5 miles per hour, and the warm water had increased its winds to 104 miles per hour. The eye continued to turn northward, and it was now about 160 miles from Islamorada.

Something strange and terrible was happening to the hurricane. It was about to undergo "rapid deepening," a process that would quickly transform this storm from a minimal hurricane into a once-in-a-lifetime monster.

Scientists do not fully understand what makes this phenomenon happen to a few storms. It's a process that seems to defy some known principles of hurricane development. When a hurricane slows and its eye starts to turn to the north, there's a fair chance that the storm will weaken, because its winds will have more time to churn up deeper, cooler water. When the cooler water reaches the surface, the hurricane's primary source of fuel is dampened, and the storm can rapidly lose strength.

But once in a while, a hurricane's strength mushrooms when it slows and starts turning. Researchers think this could be caused by large, deep pockets of very warm water that occasionally form during the late summer. Instead of churning up cooler water as it slows and turns, the hurricane brings still more warm water to the surface, and its slower speed gives it plenty of time to stoke itself.

These warm-water pockets usually form in the Gulf of Mexico, and sometimes they pass from the Gulf into the Straits of Florida.

Scientists are still trying to figure out what happened to this hurricane between the afternoon of Sunday, September 1, 1935, and the afternoon of Monday, September 2. As it churned across the Straits of Florida, something turned it into a force of incalculable power. For this to happen, the storm had to have an unlimited supply of very warm seawater. It's possible that the hurricane crossed paths with a pocket of deep, warm water that had drifted from the Gulf of Mexico into the straits at exactly the right moment. Now there was nothing to weaken or tear it apart—no upper-level winds, no cool water. As many veterans on the Keys were stumbling to their shacks to sleep off a holiday bender, this storm was becoming the most powerful hurricane that would ever touch land in the United States—the storm of the century.

Later Sunday night, Sheldon called FEC district superintendent P .I. Gaddis in Miami to discuss possibly sending a train to the Keys to evacuate the veterans. Gaddis told Sheldon that the FEC's regular northbound evening train from Key West had just arrived in Miami. That train could be turned around and sent back to the Keys, arriving in Islamorada in about four hours, Gaddis said.

Gaddis said Sheldon told him that he did not want to order the train then, and that Fred Ghent's office in Jacksonville would take care of ordering the train when it was needed. Sheldon asked Gaddis again if a train could be in Islamorada four hours after it was ordered.

"Yes, now, if you order the train now," Gaddis said.

But Sheldon misunderstood what Gaddis had said to him. He hung up thinking that regardless of when the order was placed, a train could be in Islamorada four hours later. What Gaddis had actually said was that the train that was at that moment standing at the Miami station with steam up and ready to travel could be back in Islamorada in four hours. If the FEC had to put together another train later that would be pulled by another locomotive, it would take longer for the train to reach Islamorada.

It was a critical misunderstanding that would infect Ray Sheldon's thinking from that point forward. Every decision he made later about evacuating the veterans would be flawed because of it.

At 9:30 p.m. the U.S. Weather Bureau issued another advisory. The agency said the center of the storm was now about 260 miles east of Havana and moving slowly westward. The advisory noted that the storm probably had hurricane-force winds near its center and advised caution for vessels—such as the *Dixie*—that would enter the Straits of Florida during the next 36 hours.

Officials in Cuba were keeping a wary eye on the reports from the U.S. Weather Bureau, especially since the American agency said that the hurricane was heading straight for them. But some Cuban meteorologists were puzzled. Barometers in Havana were rising, an indication that the hurricane could be heading away from Cuba instead of bearing down on it.

Still, officials in Isabela des Augua, a small coastal town east of Havana, were taking no chances. Residents there were herded aboard a special evacuation train Sunday night that took them inland to higher ground and out of harm's way.

At Lower Matecumbe Key, Ed Sheeran's crew finished securing their construction equipment. Although the weather bureau still said the storm was not a direct threat to the Keys, Sheeran didn't buy it. He was convinced the storm was much closer to them than anyone realized and heading their way. He told his men to get out of the islands because things would start getting dangerous the following day.

Sheeran's prediction was uncannily accurate. The hurricane was actually less than 200 miles from Islamorada. Its winds were increasing by the hour, and its forward movement had slowed even more as it started turning more toward the north. By late Sunday night its winds had reached 120 miles per hour. It was creeping west-northwest at about 4 miles per hour, and its slow forward movement allowed it to continue feasting on the warm waters.

At the Hotel Matecumbe, Sheldon, his wife, and some staff members sat down Sunday night to play gin rummy while they waited for updates from the weather bureau. A few minutes after 10 p.m., the phone rang. William Hardaker, superintendent of Camp 1, put down his cards and picked up the receiver.

It was Ernest Carson, chief meteorologist at the U.S. Weather Bureau's office in Miami. Thinking that he was speaking to Sheldon, Carson read the weather bureau's latest advisory to Hardaker. The weather bureau said the center of the storm was about 260 miles east of Havana and advised caution for ships in the Straits of Florida. A northeast storm warning had been issued for the coast of southern Florida from Miami on the state's east coast around to Fort Myers on the west coast. Carson added that there would be enough time to get the men out of the camps by Monday morning. The weatherman said he'd call again if anything changed during the night.

Hardaker hung up the phone feeling relieved. We're off the hook, he thought. He repeated Carson's statement to the others. The rummy game broke up soon afterward. Hardaker had been uneasy about the hurricane, but now he was convinced the Keys were no longer threatened by the storm. "When I went to bed [I] told my wife it would miss us altogether and would probably hit up around Tampa or up in that section," Hardaker said.

As Sheldon was about to retire for the night, he told Pattison and clerk Robert Ayer, Jr., to sleep on cots in the office in case the weather bureau tried to call during the night. "Should the report be serious, notify me at once," Sheldon told Pattison and Ayer. "But if not, wait until in the morning." Sheldon didn't bother to explain what he meant by "serious," however.

At 3:30 a.m. on Monday, the phone rang again in the Florida ERA office at the Hotel Matecumbe. A sleepy Robert Ayer rolled out of his cot and answered the phone. It was Carson again.

The meteorologist told Ayer that the weather bureau had issued another advisory, and he read the bulletin to the sleepy clerk. "Tropical disturbance still of small diameter but considerable intensity moving slowly westward off coast of north-central Cuba, shifting gales and hurricane-force winds at center," Carson said. "Probably pass through Florida Straits Monday. Caution high tides and gales on Florida Keys."

The last sentence in the advisory should have been an eyebrow-raiser for anyone on the Keys: "Caution high tides and gales on Florida Keys." Ayer repeated the advisory to the drowsy Pattison. They decided it wasn't worth awakening the boss. Ayer went back to bed without bothering to write down anything that Carson told him.

The Labor Day sunrise a few hours later didn't throw much light on the camps. Intermittent drizzle fell from an unusually dark sky.

Albert Buck, the foreman at Camp 5, from Kinston, North Carolina, got out of bed around 5:30 a.m. and immediately grabbed his barometer. He had scarcely taken his eyes off the instrument since hearing about the storm Saturday. He watched it for an hour after he got up Monday morning. The needle fell steadily the entire time.

"The barometer showed that the storm was not going around us, but was advancing on us all the time, gradually," he said.

Around 7 a.m. Buck stepped outside and looked up at the threatening sky. Dark, sinister clouds seemed to be so low that they were almost within his reach.

"Monday morning, the clouds looked so muddy and so close until it looked like you could reach out and get hold of them," he said.

Others were also noticing ominous signs of trouble over the horizon. Seventeen-year-old Laurette Pinder looked out at the Atlantic. Unusually large waves were crossing the offshore reef, rolling onto Upper Matecumbe Key and breaking noisily onto the beach. And the water looked eerie. Instead of its usual clear, turquoise color, the breaking waves were laden with air bubbles and debris, giving it a cloudy, milky appearance.

Buck decided to go to the Hotel Matecumbe to see what his bosses had decided to do about the situation.

The dreary beginning to Monday, September 2, 1935, was, in a sense, the last time that the sun rose on the old Florida Keys. When the sun came up again 24 hours later, the islands would be forever changed.

At sea, the hurricane had taken full advantage of its leisurely weekend stroll across the warm waters between the Bahamas and the Keys. As Buck stood on the beach looking out toward the menacing clouds, the winds around the hurricane's center were howling at almost 140 miles per hour. The storm was now unquestionably a killer and it was continuing to strengthen.

Buck had correctly interpreted his barometer's ominous message. The hurricane had turned to the northwest. It was now heading directly for the Keys, and its small but ferocious eye was only a little more than 100 miles away. The hurricane also had roused itself from its leisurely pace and was moving at 12 miles per hour.

Ray Sheldon awoke around 7:30 a.m. Ayer filled him in on the latest advisories from the weather bureau—including the telephone call of four hours earlier warning of high tides and gales on the Keys. "I gave him the exact telephone message that came to me," Ayer said.

A few minutes later, Buck, the Camp 5 foreman, and clothing supply officer Junius T. Wigginton walked into the administrative office. As the men discussed the latest weather bureau advisories, someone pulled out a deck of cards. Soon a poker game was under way as men drifted in and out of the office. "Anything to pass the time," Wigginton said. "We were all just waiting on those damn weather reports."

As more and more people crowded into the offices, clerks gave up trying to get any work done. "It was impossible to do any office work because of the conglomeration of people," Ayer said. "Therefore, we were waiting for instructions. We were playing bridge on a desk in the office, next to Mr. Sheldon's office, waiting for instructions."

Sheldon played cards sporadically when he wasn't on the phone or pushing more thumbtacks into the map on the wall. He also rescinded Cutler's order from the previous day stopping the sale of beer at the camp canteens. But he also ordered O.D. King, who was in charge of the motor pool, to fill the gasoline tanks of the camps' trucks and have them ready in case he decided to use the vehicles to move the men.

But Sheldon wasn't ready to order an evacuation. He wanted to wait.

If the weather reports and predictions failed to impress Sheldon, they got the attention of a federal official far from the Keys. Perry Fellows, an administrative assistant for the WPA in Washington, was sipping his breakfast coffee Monday morning as he browsed the Labor Day edition of the *Washington Post*. He noticed a small but prominently displayed story directly beneath the masthead, in the center of the front page. The headline read "Hurricane Heads Toward Florida."

The lead paragraph was an attention-grabber: "Destruction, perhaps death, was feared in at least two sections of the Nation last night as summer began to give way to the season of autumnal equinox."

The story noted that the hurricane was moving through the Straits of Florida, and that big, storm-driven waves were rolling onto beaches as far north as Daytona Beach.

In Tavernier, young Bascom Grooms, Jr., waited for the regular southbound passenger train, which was due at 9:16 a.m. The teenager was feeling glum. He had to go back to school the next day.

But the Labor Day passenger load was unusually heavy, and the train was running far behind schedule as it waited for the crush of passengers to board at each station. It would be late morning before it arrived in Tavernier.

At 9:30 a.m. the U.S. Weather Bureau issued another advisory giving the hurricane's location about 200 miles due east of Havana, or just off Cuba's long northern coastline. The storm was moving slowly westward, the advisory said.

At the same time as the advisory was issued, *Miami Daily News* reporter William Johns picked up his phone in Homestead and called Ray Sheldon.

"I said, 'Well, how is your weather?' " Johns said. "He said 'It's raining and blowing like hell down here right now.'"

Johns asked Sheldon what he was going to do about evacuating the veterans in case the storm struck the Keys. "I have two trains waiting in Miami that can get down here on about three or four hours' notice, and in case it gets too bad, why, we will send for them," Sheldon told the reporter.

Johns hung up, called the newsroom of the *Daily News,* and reported what Sheldon had said to him. He told his editor that he'd be aboard the train if the evacuation were ordered. When he hung up the phone, he fully expected to be taking a train ride down to the islands soon. "I knew they were going to get an awful blow," he said.

Meanwhile, in Washington, Perry Fellows decided to go to his office even though he had the day off. The story about the hurricane approaching Florida bothered him and he wanted to make a few phone calls to get more information. When he arrived, he discovered that Aubrey Williams, an assistant to WPA director Harry Hopkins, also had come in despite the holiday.

Fellows briefed Williams about the story he'd seen in the *Post.* Williams said that he didn't want to wait to see if the storm got closer to the Keys. He told Fellows to call Florida ERA administrators to make sure that the vets were moved off the islands.

Fellows got on the phone. Around ten o'clock he reached Florida ERA administrator Conrad Van Hyning in Tallahassee and suggested that he contact the camps in the Keys to make sure the veterans were being evacuated. Fellows told Van Hyning that Williams wanted the men moved even if the storm didn't appear to be heading their way. Van Hyning replied that he'd talk to the administrators in the Keys.

But the telephone at camp headquarters was busy. Van Hyning decided to call M. E. Gilfond in Key West and ask him to relay Fellows's message to Ray Sheldon.

In the Straits of Florida, the *Dixie* had rounded the tip of the Florida Keys and was now steaming a course that was roughly parallel to the islands. The ship was running into the same rain that was pelting the Keys, and passengers were scurrying for cover.

Pan American Airways officials had been closely following reports on the hurricane since the weather bureau released its first advisory. By early Monday morning they'd decided to take no chances with the storm. The regularly scheduled flight from Havana to Miami would leave early to make sure the plane didn't run into dangerous weather.

"We figured the storm would go westerly and would cover an extensive area from Key West north and south, starting Monday morning," said George Brand, Pan American's chief meteorologist.

At the makeshift veterans hospital near Snake Creek, Elmer Darty, from Charleston, South Carolina, lay in a bed near the window of his second-floor room overlooking the porch. All morning he'd been glancing out to watch a vine that clung to the building. The wind first stirred the vine early that morning, causing it to tap ceaselessly against the window screen. Now wind-driven rain was splattering against his window, and the vine was flailing furiously against the screen.

Darty became uneasy.

Around 10:30 a.m. Sheldon spoke with Ernest Carson in the weather bureau's Miami office. Carson told Sheldon that hurricane warnings had been hoisted in Key West.

"That's it," Sheldon said to Carson. "We're getting out."

Carson thought that Sheldon meant that a train had already reached Islamorada and the men would be leaving immediately. Sheldon was still under the mistaken impression that two special trains were ready and could be in Islamorada in a few hours.

Even though Sheldon had decided to evacuate the veterans, he wanted to run his decision past Fred Ghent before the trains were called from Homestead.

In Jacksonville, Ghent took advantage of the holiday and snoozed until around 11 a.m. in his room in the Mayflower Hotel. About 30 minutes later he checked in briefly at his office, then went to lunch. He didn't bother telling anyone where he was going, when he would be back, or how to reach him while he was away.

A few minutes after Ghent disappeared for his lunch break, M. E. Gilfond finally got a telephone line through to Islamorada to pass along Van Hyning's message. Gilfond told Sheldon that Van Hyning wanted the vets moved off the islands.

But instead of agreeing to order the train as Van Hyning wanted him to do, Sheldon told Gilfond that he had been through "three or four" hurricanes, and that Van Hyning had nothing to worry about.

"I told Mr. Gilfond we were watching the barometer and the course of the storm, according to the weather bureau reports, and that, at the first sign of danger, we would order the train out," Sheldon said.

After hanging up with Gilfond, Sheldon tried to reach Ghent in Jacksonville. It was about 15 minutes before noon. Ghent was nowhere to be found.

Still, there seemed to be no reason to be overly concerned. Sheldon figured that he had at least 12 hours to get the men off the islands before the storm posed any threat to them.

In the work camps, the veterans weren't too concerned about the storm—yet. Jacob Herbert, who was from Los Angeles and stationed at Camp 1, said the men had been told they'd be taken care of.

"We were sitting around talking, and I was playing my mandolin," Herbert said. "I thought there would be nothing to it, probably flooding of shacks, but not floating away."

Down at Lower Matecumbe Key, an FEC freight train backed a tanker car containing 10,000 gallons of water onto a sidetrack near Camp 3. Normally, Ed Sheeran would have ordered that the water be pumped into the camp's storage tanks, but he decided not to follow the usual procedure. Still convinced that the hurricane was a bad one and was coming their way, he decided that the tanks probably would be destroyed. If he left the water in the railroad tanker car, at least they'd have water after the storm.

Sheeran's decision would save dozens of lives.

As the tanker car was being uncoupled on the sidetrack, Pan American's big seaplane bounced across the water and slowly climbed above Havana. The pilots turned north toward Miami. It was 11 a.m., about two hours earlier than they usually took off.

Soon the pilots were running into squalls, but they expected to encounter some rough weather with a hurricane in the neighborhood. Still, they were puzzled.

Usually when a hurricane was somewhere in the vicinity during one of their flights, they were able to make a pretty good guess about where its center was. But this hurricane was different. Its small size made its exact position impossible to determine. The Pan Am pilots had no idea where its eye might be.

Out in the Gulf of Mexico, Einar Sundstrom also was puzzled.

"It was about 11 a.m. Monday when the weather appeared squally," said John Laycock, a passenger aboard the *Dixie* from Baton Rouge, Louisiana. "We were still in the Gulf. I spoke to the captain about it."

Sundstrom told Laycock there was "some rough weather ahead." Still, Sundstrom said that the center of the storm was behind them, off the coast of Cuba. "The captain said he could pass safely through the strait," Laycock said.

But Sundstrom wasn't bothering to share his weather observations with the U.S. Weather Bureau, and in Miami, meteorologist Ernest Carson was frustrated. There were about a dozen ships at sea from New Orleans to north of the Bahamas, but only a couple of vessels— including the *Dixie*—were anywhere near the hurricane. Around 11:30 a.m. Carson tore a sheet of paper off his Teletype machine with information from a ship at Sagua la Grande, just east of Havana. Carson studied the data, then looked up at George N. MacDonnell, director of public health services for Miami. "I hope more information comes in with the one o'clock report," Carson said to his friend.

Carson and MacDonnell also wondered why the S.S. *Dixie* wasn't sending any data to the weather bureau.

A few minutes before noon, Sam Cutler left his office on the second floor of the Hotel Matecumbe and went down to the lobby, where he bumped into Paul Vander Schouw, the assistant director of the Florida Transient Division. Vander Schouw's agency would be taking over supervision of the veterans work camps in the state, and he had come down to the Keys to take a look at the camps. With him was Leila Baggs, the supervisor for the Transient Division's caseworkers.

Vander Schouw and Cutler had met a few months earlier when Cutler was a safety inspector. The assistant director had a lot of respect for Sam Cutler.

Despite the wind and blowing rain, Cutler offered to take Vander Schouw and Baggs on a quick tour. The group left the hotel and drove down to Camp 3. Cutler and Vander Schouw got out and walked around the camp, but the veterans' well-established reputation for crudeness prompted Cutler to advise Baggs to stay in the car.

"Mrs. Baggs stayed in the car while we went around because some of the...We just felt it would be better for her to stay in the car," Vander Schouw said.

Meanwhile, Lawrence Bow, the former assistant camp administrator and engineer working on the bridge at Lower Matecumbe Key, sat down at his desk to make some calculations about the hurricane. Bow had spent part of his childhood in the Keys and had lived in Florida all his life.

The readings from Bow's barometer at Lower Matecumbe Key were lower than those reported from Key West to the south and Miami to the north. The engineer did some figuring and calculated that the eye of the hurricane was about 90 miles due east of the work camps. Bow put down his pencil and called his wife in Miami to tell her that the storm would be worse at Lower Matecumbe than it would be in the city. He had no way of knowing it, but his calculations about the position of the hurricane's eye were on the money. At 1 p.m. Monday, the eye of the storm was about 80 miles southeast of Islamorada.

As Bow talked to his wife, Alligator Reef lighthouse keeper Jones Pervis was talking by phone to the U.S. Weather Bureau in Key West. Jones hung up his phone and went to the flagpole. He removed the red pennant and replaced it with a second square red flag with the black square at the center. The brisk, rapidly rising wind quickly unfurled the banners. It was a signal that grabbed the attention of anyone who had lived near the ocean for any length of time. The two identical red-and-black flags indicated hurricane-force winds were expected in the area within 24 hours.

Cutler, Vander Schouw, and Baggs returned to the Hotel

Matecumbe shortly after 1 p.m. for lunch. Cutler disappeared briefly and returned with Sheldon. The director sat down at the table and chatted for a few moments, but he was called away for a phone call around 1:30 p.m.

When Sheldon was out of earshot, Cutler turned to Vander Schouw and Baggs. He was deeply worried and wanted to tell them something in confidence.

"This thing looks bad to me and I want to go on record with you," Cutler said. "If I don't see you again or if anything happens, [I wanted] to get these men out of here."

Vander Schouw studied Cutler closely as he spoke. Cutler was calm and collected, and Vander Schouw did not detect any nervousness or excitement in his friend that might indicate he was making a hasty or ill-considered statement.

Upstairs, Sheldon was finally talking to Fred Ghent, who had returned from his nearly two-hour lunch break. Sheldon told his boss that hurricane warnings were up in Key West and he thought the evacuation train should be ordered.

Ghent said he'd take care of it. Sheldon hung up and returned to the dining room. He apologized to Vander Schouw and Baggs and said he had to leave them to arrange for the evacuation of the veterans. Sheldon disappeared back into his office, and Baggs and Vander Schouw left a few minutes later to return to Miami.

As the pair left the hotel the weather was becoming frightening. The ocean was creeping onto Upper Matecumbe Key, and small breakers rolled across the road in one low place as the rising wind flung salty spray across the windshield of Vander Schouw's car. He began to understand why Cutler was so concerned about the veterans.

"I was glad to get out of there," Vander Schouw said. "As it turned out at one point—I think Whale Harbor, where the road is quite low— the waves were already splashing across the road, so they splashed, the spray from them splashed clear across the windshield of the car, and I thought it was a very good idea to get out of there."

117

William Thompson, a veteran at Camp 5 from Brooklyn, New York, was beginning to get the same idea.

"I had a little puppy dog I had ever since I was there, brought it from Clearwater," Thompson said. "It was restless, would not stay in the hut. We had two pups, six or seven months old. Usually they would run and play. They would not play or anything."

By Monday afternoon, Thompson was getting uneasy.

"I had a feeling about the storm myself," he said. "It began to rain and the wind"...and by two o'clock Monday I really began to be scared. I began to think of getting away very seriously. I didn't want to wait for no train or anything after that...I started up to the road and the water was up to my knees and I went back to the railroad track."

In the Straits of Florida, Florence Steiler was becoming concerned about the worsening weather. The wind was blowing the rain so hard that she gave up the idea of staying on deck, and finally decided to return to her stateroom aboard the *Dixie*.

In Jacksonville, Fred Ghent placed a call to the FEC's train dispatcher. It was approaching 2 p.m. More than three hours had passed since Sheldon told meteorologist Carson that he was moving the veterans off the islands, and almost two hours had passed since Sheldon had been told that his bosses wanted the veterans moved off the islands regardless of where the hurricane went.

Still, Sheldon and Ghent thought they had time to evacuate the men.

The weather bureau's 1:30 p.m. advisory said the storm's center was at latitude 23 degrees, 20 minutes north and longitude 80 degrees, 15 minutes west and moving slowly westward. This position would have placed the hurricane's eye about 120 miles south-southeast of Islamorada, or 135 miles due east of Havana and only about 10 miles offshore from the northern coast of Cuba. The advisory predicted hurricane-force winds in the Straits of Florida and gale-force winds on the Keys through Monday night.

But the hurricane wasn't following the schedule that Ghent and Sheldon had laid out for it. It was actually almost 100 miles northeast of where the weather bureau plotted it. Even worse for the veterans, the storm was now quickly gaining strength, as it underwent rapid deepening in the tepid waters off the Keys. In 12 hours the storm's top winds had exploded from 121 miles per hour to 150 miles per hour, and its forward motion had speeded up a little. The eye of the storm would be just offshore of the islands at about sundown, but the sun's normally spectacular descent into Florida Bay would be invisible behind the hurricane's dark, malicious clouds and dense, driving rain.

A terrible evening was in store for the Upper Keys.

chapter four

It's Blowing Like Hell Down Here

F. L. Aitcheson was taking a bath at his home in St. Augustine when his phone rang just after 2 p.m. Monday. It was Fred Ghent in nearby Jacksonville. Ghent told the dripping FEC assistant superintendent he wanted to send a special train down to the Keys to get the veterans off the islands because of the approaching hurricane.

Aitcheson told Ghent he'd go to his office immediately to order the train assembled. He hung up, dried himself, hastily pulled on some clothes, and dashed to his car.

As Aitcheson hurried to his office, Ghent called camps administrator Ray Sheldon in Islamorada to tell him the evacuation train had been ordered. Ghent detected some edginess in Sheldon's voice, but Ghent was confident the situation was under control. Using the U.S. Weather Bureau's latest advisory, he calculated it would be at least ten hours before the hurricane posed a serious threat to the Keys. Ghent told his assistant he'd meet the rescue train in Hollywood, a small town between Fort Lauderdale and Miami.

Ghent then returned to the Mayflower Hotel and packed a suitcase. He stopped at a service station to fuel up his car, and, thinking of the long drive from Jacksonville to Hollywood, decided to have the oil changed, too. He saw no reason to be in any hurry. It never occurred to him that the weather bureau might be wrong, or that he might have misinterpreted the agency's advisories. But as he waited for his car to be serviced in Jacksonville, the eye of the hurricane was within 100 miles of Islamorada and its outer winds already were tugging and tearing at buildings on the Upper Keys.

"The winds started about one or two o'clock in the afternoon," said Etta Parker Sweeting, whose husband owned a store in Islamorada. "Eddie and I went to the post office to see if there was any mail for the business, for the grocery store. When we came back, we slowed down in front of the store and the paper was being peeled off of the roof. That's how hard it was blowing already."

The winds made it difficult to move as well.

"You could not walk around," said Joseph Fecteau, a veteran from Massachusetts who was timekeeper for the veterans at Camp 5. "You were just tossed about by the wind."

Some of the flimsiest buildings in the veterans camps were already coming apart.

"At two o'clock the timber was starting to fly around," Fecteau said. "Some of the small buildings were starting to go."

Wind can become a deadly weapon during a hurricane. In winds blowing at hurricane force—74 miles per hour—a person can lean forward into the wind at a 45-degree angle without falling. When the wind reaches 80 miles an hour, it is impossible to walk without the support of a railing or other structure. Boards, tree limbs, and other flying debris can kill when when wind speeds reach 120. A 130-mile-per-hour wind can lift people off the ground.

Down at the southern tip of Lower Matecumbe Key, First Mate Fritz Maggeson was securing the lines that held the privately owned houseboat *Rowena* to the docks. Maggeson had tied up next to the ferryboat *Monroe County*. As he worked on the lines, Maggeson called to some veterans and invited them to get out of the rising winds by coming aboard the *Rowena*. But the vets scoffed at Maggeson's offer. "They laughed at me and said if I would come up to Long Island Sound sometime they'd show me what a real wind was," Maggeson said.

At Craig Key, Roland Craig decided he didn't want to try to ride out this storm in the islands. Around 2 p.m. Craig told Jack Crow to go back to the ferry landing to get the car started and then wait for him. Crow started walking the railroad track to Lower Matecumbe.

But Crow soon realized he couldn't possibly reach Lower Matecumbe Key. When he started across the railroad bridge, a gust of wind blowing across the open water shoved him so ferociously that he almost tumbled into Florida Bay. Shaken, he returned to Craig Key.

"We knew then that we were sunk," Craig said.

As the veterans dodged flying debris, Aitcheson called A. I. Pooser, an FEC dispatcher, starting a series of relay telephone calls to the railroad's offices and dispatchers along Florida's east coast to ready the evacuation train. Pooser called dispatcher J. L. Byrum in New Smyrna Beach and told him to contact George R. Branch, yardmaster in Miami, and tell him to assemble the train. In Miami, Branch ordered a crew to get locomotive number 447 ready. The 160-ton locomotive needed to get up steam before the train could leave, but because number 447's boiler was fired by fuel oil instead of coal, it would take only about two hours to generate the steam needed to pull the train.

The rest of the train—six passenger cars, three baggage cars, and a pair of boxcars—had to be hooked up. But the yard's switch engine—which would be used to assemble the cars—wouldn't go on duty until 3 p.m. Still, the FEC workers in Miami swung into action, dropping other tasks to work on the evacuation train. While workmen finished repairs on one of the cars, another dispatcher started calling in crewmen from their holidays to operate the train.

Down at Camp 3, Ed Sheeran was very worried. The horrible memories of the 1906 hurricane wouldn't leave his mind. Now it all seemed to be happening again. The people in charge didn't seem to be taking the warnings seriously.

"The first storm—it happened the same way," Sheeran said. "Lack of judgment and lack of knowledge of the storm."

He had said for two days that the men should be removed from the islands, but he hadn't said anything directly to Ray Sheldon nor had he heard whether the evacuation train had been called. Now his barometer was falling rapidly, and he was getting ominous news from Key West, where his boss, B. M. Duncan, had installed himself in the U.S. Weather Bureau office on Front Street. Duncan was calling Sheeran every 30 minutes to update him on barometric pressure readings from Key West, Miami, and elsewhere. Sheeran's barometer was reading lower than those in Key West and Miami, and he was sure that meant the hurricane was headed toward them.

"I didn't know if we were getting the center or the edge or what, but I knew it was so close," Sheeran said.

Around 2 p.m. Sheeran decided he wanted some answers. With the rising winds whipping around Camp 3 he drove to the Hotel Matecumbe to see what was being done to get the vets off the Keys.

When Sheeran walked into Sheldon's office, the administrator was talking on his phone. He ended his call and turned to face Sheeran. Sheldon's demeanor had changed as the wind rose and his barometer fell. Sheeran could tell instantly that Sheldon was scared.

Sheeran got right to the point. "I told him I thought it was close to us," he said.

Sheldon placed a call and talked for a few moments. Then he hung up and turned back to Sheeran. The train would arrive at 5:30 p.m. he said. Sheeran nodded, told Sheldon he couldn't stay any longer, and left.

Sheeran knew the arrival of the storm's eye would be preceded by steadily increasing gusts of wind that would come closer together as it neared. When the wind began rising Monday morning, the gusts were about 30 minutes apart. As Sheeran drove back down to Camp 3 after his brief meeting with Sheldon, he noticed the gusts were less than 10 minutes apart.

The hurricane was undoubtedly getting closer.

As Sheeran pulled into the camp, a screaming siren was audible above the wind. Superintendent Ben Davis sounded the alarm to call the men to an assembly. Davis told them the evacuation train was on its way and they should get ready to board it. Some of the veterans spotted Sheeran, and asked him what was happening.

"All the boys gathered around and asked me about the storm and

I told them to be ready to jump the train as it could not wait for them," Sheeran said.

He also called B. M. Duncan to again compare his barometer reading with those in Key West. "I talked to Mr. Duncan and said the barometer was going down fast and the telephone wires were giving way and I wouldn't be able to talk to him anymore," Sheeran said. "We were getting about a 60-mile-per-hour wind."

Sheeran had already ordered his work crew to get out of the Keys. But the aging combat veteran who wouldn't run from Germans wasn't going to desert in the face of this threat. He would take his chances with yet another hurricane.

"I just didn't have the heart to leave while there was anybody on the Keys," he said. "I asked my men if they wanted to go, and we had everything tied up as far as our work was concerned. I refused to leave. I preferred to go down with the ship. If they went down, I was going with them. I preferred to stay with them."

At Tavernier, young Bascom Grooms, Jr., reluctantly boarded the southbound passenger train that would take him away from summer vacation and back to Key West for the start of school. The train was running late because of the holiday traffic. Grooms found a seat in a crowded coach and stared glumly out the window as the train made its stops at Plantation Key and Islamorada.

Down the tracks at the Hotel Matecumbe, Rosalind Grooms Palmer knew her kid brother was on the southbound passenger train. She thought about getting him off the train to join her at the hotel, but decided against it.

The train continued, making stops at the ferry landing at Lower Matecumbe, Craig, and the Long Key Fishing Camp. Things brightened up a bit for Bascom Grooms when the train stopped at Marathon. A girl he'd met a few times at birthday parties got aboard and sat down with him. The two chatted happily during the rest of the trip to Key West, unconcerned that the train was running hours late and oblivious of the worsening weather outside their passenger car.

At the Long Key Fishing Camp, caretaker and weather bureau observer James E. Duane, Jr., kept a wary eye on his barometer and the ocean, which became angrier by the hour. With him were 19 other people, including railroad maintenance workers and fishing camp employees who lived on Long Key. Also in the group was a new railroad section foreman who had arrived at the fishing camp with his wife and four small children only that morning. The group would ride out the storm where they were. The only way off the island was by boat or train. It was suicide to take a fishing boat out into the giant waves, and no one boarded the train when it stopped at the small depot at Long Key.

Duane was as alarmed about the barometer readings as Ed Sheeran. Such readings are one of the best indicators of a hurricane's intensity. As a storm strengthens, the barometric pressure steadily drops. The lowest barometric pressure is around the eye of the hurricane.

For most hurricanes, however, the lowest barometric pressure reading doesn't fall too far below 29.00 inches. When it does drop well below that, it indicates a serious hurricane that causes extensive damage if it makes landfall. Hurricane Fran, which struck North Carolina in 1996, had a low reading of 28.17 inches. Hurricane Andrew, which devastated South Florida in 1992—the third most powerful hurricane ever to strike the United States—had a reading of 27.13 inches. Camille, the second most powerful hurricane to hit the United States, had a reading of 26.84 inches when it struck Mississippi in 1969.

At 2 p.m. Duane's barometer read 28.90 inches, and the winds were steadily increasing. An hour later his barometer had fallen to 28.52 and the winds were blowing still harder.

At the Hotel Matecumbe, Fern and Ed Butters hadn't been too concerned about the weather advisories Monday morning. They'd been in the middle of the horrible 1926 hurricane that nearly wiped out Miami Beach, and it was hard for them to believe a hurricane could be more powerful than that one. They'd already put up the heavy hurricane shutters over the hotel's windows, but Ed decided there was no reason to postpone a trip he'd planned to Miami, about 80 miles away, to paint a boat he'd just bought and pick up supplies from wholesalers. He left with his son, Jack, Monday morning.

But when Ed learned of the U.S. Weather Bureau's 1:30 p.m. advisory, he decided he'd better check about conditions in the Keys even though the bulletin said the hurricane was well south of the islands just off the northern coast of Cuba. At 2:30 p.m. he ducked into a telephone booth in the lobby of a Flagler Street hotel and called his wife.

Ed asked Fern if he should cut short his trip and return.

The wind was beginning to unnerve Fern, but she didn't want to let her husband know she was frightened. "I tried to be nonchalant and say I didn't think it was necessary," she said.

But at that moment the wind pried a shutter away from a window and slammed it against the building with a loud bang. The sudden noise, coupled with her mounting anxiety, destroyed Fern's forced composure, and she jumped involuntarily as she clutched the telephone.

"Well, if you want to know the truth," she blurted to her husband, "it's blowing like hell here."

Hearing his pious wife use even mild profanity surprised Ed Butters as much as the banging shutter had startled Fern. He decided his wife's uncharacteristically strong language was an indication the weather was getting bad. "I'm on my way," he said. He ran back to his Plymouth and dashed away to secure the boat he'd been painting so he could return to the Keys.

Regaining her composure, Fern went downstairs to the hotel kitchen at 2:40 p.m. Hurricane or no hurricane, supper had to be prepared for the Florida ERA officials. She told her cook to have it ready by 4:30 p.m. Then she asked her father-in-law, Charles Butters, and her son-in-law Olin Perdue to double-check the preparations they'd made for the bad weather.

As Fern Butters tried to maintain order in the mounting chaos, FEC engineer J. J. Haycraft answered his telephone in Miami. A dispatcher told him to report for work to take a special train to the Keys to pick up the veterans. As the engineer hung up his phone he checked the time. It was 3:10 p.m.

In the roiling seas off the Florida coast, the hurricane began to lash the passenger liner *Dixie* with increasing ferocity. Around 3 p.m. the storm ripped away the ship's radio antenna. Captain Sundstrom ordered the passengers to put on life jackets as the ship tried to push its way northward through gigantic waves.

The winds were hurling rain and seawater against the *Dixie* with so much force that Florence Steiler was convinced the porthole in her stateroom wasn't properly closed. As the ship rolled and pitched in the storm, three inches or so of salt water sloshed back and forth across her floor. Steiler called for a ship's steward and asked him to close the porthole. She was astonished when he told her it was, in fact, tightly closed.

Steiler decided that she might be able to escape the pool of water on her stateroom floor by climbing into her bunk and lying down. But the *Dixie's* violent tossing pitched her out, and she landed on the floor with a splash. She climbed back into her bunk and managed to escape the water again. But once again she was tossed out. So she scrambled back into the bunk. And she was thrown out again.

Up on the bridge of the *Dixie*, Captain Sundstrom knew his ship was in great danger.

"We rounded the southern tip of Florida and were going up through the shoals, but all the time the wind kept blowing harder," said John Laycock, the passenger from Baton Rouge, Louisiana. "Throughout Monday afternoon we were fighting our way slowly ahead, pulling for deep water to get away from the shoals. The captain evidently thought he could make it."

Using the weather bureau advisories, Sundstrom and his crew had plotted the storm to be well south of the *Dixie*, and the captain had been assuming he was heading in the opposite direction from the hurricane. But the ocean was becoming more ferocious by the hour and his barometer was steadily dropping. That could only mean that the *Dixie* was much closer to the hurricane's eye than he wanted to be. Without knowing where the hurricane was or which way it was moving, Sundstrom couldn't steer the *Dixie* to the storm's weaker side.

The passengers aboard the *Dixie* tried to forget about their growing fear by singing. George Outland, an instructor at Yale University, sat down at a piano in the passengers' lounge and started playing "California, Here I Come" and other familiar standards. A crowd gradually gathered around him and started singing along. Outland would stay at his post for hours, banging away on the piano as the storm relentlessly battered the ship.

In Jacksonville, the mechanics finished servicing Fred Ghent's car. He got behind the wheel and started the 350-mile drive down the coast to Hollywood.

At the makeshift veterans hospital on Windley Key near Snake Creek, Elmer Darty, the veteran from Charleston, South Carolina, had been uneasily watching the rising storm all day from his bed next to a second-floor window. The wind rattled the window screens, and fierce gusts shook the entire building.

Darty expected the storm to shove the screen through the window and into his room at any moment. "When that building started to shake, then I started to shake," he said.

The three doctors for the veterans camps decided they would take no chances with their patients' safety. They would be sent to a hospital in Miami. At 3:15 p.m. Darty and three other patients were loaded into the back of an ambulance. But as the vehicle pulled away, Darty still wondered if he'd escape the storm alive. The fierce winds slammed against the ambulance, causing it to rock alarmingly.

"Our ambulance like to have turned over two or three times before we got to Snake Creek and across, which is about a quarter of a mile [from the hospital]," Darty said.

On the other side of the Straits of Florida, nerves in Havana were just as frayed. At Morro Castle, the ancient fort that had guarded the entrance to Havana Harbor for centuries, the stiff wind made the red-and-black hurricane warning flags stand out stiff as boards. One report circulating through the city said the storm would strike Havana around 6 p.m., and a day earlier police had knocked on doors throughout the capital warning residents of the approaching hurricane.

But Cuban weather observers disagreed about the hurricane's track, and conflicting reports spread through Havana. Barometers there had risen since late Saturday, an indication that the storm was either weakening or no longer moving toward the city.

Newspaper offices were swamped with calls from edgy residents who wanted to know if the hurricane was heading their way. At an army base near Havana, Cuban military officers huddled to discuss a bold plan to get a fix on the hurricane's position.

Back at the Hotel Matecumbe, Ray Sheldon decided not to wait for the arrival of the evacuation train to get his wife and the wives of several veterans out of the Keys. Around 3:15 p.m. Gayle Sheldon climbed into a pickup truck with another woman and her infant child. Sheldon told the driver to take them to Hollywood and wait there.

A few minutes later, Sheldon told Sam Cutler to go to Hollywood and arrange with city officials for the veterans' arrival.

Down in Havana, Capt. Leonard J. Povey, an American flying instructor in the Cuban army air force, climbed into a small fighter plane and took off on an unusual mission. Povey intended to find the storm and plot its exact position and direction of travel. It was a daring and dangerous plan, and it was probably the first time an airplane had been used to hunt for a hurricane.

Over the Straits of Florida, not far from where the *Dixie* was wallowing almost helpless in the monstrous waves, Captain Povey sighted the storm.

"It appeared to be a cone-shaped body of clouds, inverted, rising to an altitude of 12,000 feet," Povey said. "The waves in the sea below broke against each other like [they were] striking a seawall."

Povey discovered the storm was well north of the position given in weather reports. Havana was off the hook, but the Keys were undoubtedly going to be hit.

That fact was becoming increasingly clear to James Duane at Long Key Fishing Camp. Duane took another barometric pressure reading at 4 p.m. The needle read 28.42 inches and seemed in a free fall, dropping one one-hundredth of an inch every five minutes. The wind still blew from the north at well over 100 miles per hour.

As Duane jotted down his 4 p.m. readings, Ed Butters finished securing his boat in Miami and, with his son Jack beside him, began a mad dash back to the Keys. He buzzed through South Miami in his big Plymouth, ignoring speed limit signs.

Soon Butters had cleared the city and hit the long, straight stretches of road that would take him back to the islands. He floored the accelerator, and the Plymouth's speedometer needle climbed to 80 miles per hour and stayed there.

At Key Largo, Butters turned onto another segment of road that was unbroken by curves. Now Butters was traveling southwest and his big car fairly flew, aided by the hurricane's rising wind, which blew across the islands from the northeast. The tailwind whisked the Plymouth along as though a giant hand were shoving the car from behind. "I hardly had to touch the accelerator," Butters said. "I got it right in the stern of my car."

In the work camps, the veterans were fed an early supper and told to go to their quarters to await the train. The men exchanged nervous glances as they ate their sandwiches.

"Along about supper time the wind and rain increased," said Jacob Herbert. "We noticed it was darker than usual. There was no lights, and with the increase of rain, it kept getting darker and darker. There was three of us that started kidding about riding tidal waves."

But as the vets tried to maintain their composure by kidding each other, their camps were beginning to disintegrate.

"We got uneasy about four o'clock," said John Dombrauski, a

veteran from Huntington, West Virginia. "Roofs began coming out. It began taking the place down."

Dombrauski and Adam Rambowski, a veteran from Alexandria, Virginia, decided they weren't waiting for a train to get them out of the Keys. They hot-wired a pickup truck and headed north.

Camp 3 superintendent Ben Davis was beginning to wonder about the evacuation train. He got into his Dodge and drove through the storm to the Hotel Matecumbe to see Sheldon, who told him the train was on its way. Davis started to leave, then turned back to Sheldon. Davis said he'd put his top assistant in charge of the veterans on the train and follow in his car.

But Sheldon said he'd rather have Davis aboard the train to help control the men, and added that he didn't think it would be a good idea to have women riding with several hundred boisterous, drunken vets. Sheldon asked Davis if he'd allow George Pepper to drive his car out of the Keys to evacuate four or five veterans' wives.

Davis agreed. He pulled a trunk of personal belongings from the car to make room for passengers. Pepper and his fiancée, Rosalind Grooms Palmer, got into the Dodge with him, and the three drove back to Camp 3 so Davis could rejoin his men. Meanwhile, the women gathered at the hotel to await the return of Pepper and Palmer.

In Miami, engineer Haycraft grasped the handle on the big throttle of locomotive number 447 and gave it a pull, setting nearly a thousand tons of equipment into motion. The evacuation train slowly rolled out of the FEC rail yard. It was 4:25 p.m. It had taken a little more than two hours to assemble the train, call in a crew, and get under way—not bad for a holiday. With Haycraft were yardmaster Branch, conductor J. E. Gamble, and fireman Will Walker. It was a run that usually took the FEC's daily passenger train about two hours.

The train had scarcely left the yard when Haycraft had to bring it to a halt. A drawbridge had been raised to let holiday boat traffic pass. The train idled on the track for about 10 minutes.

As the train crew watched the passing boats, the U.S. Weather Bureau issued a new advisory at 4:30. The weather bureau meteorologists had realized that this small, elusive hurricane was well north of the position they'd been giving. The new advisory said the hurricane was "apparently" moving toward the Florida Keys.

Miami was being lashed by winds and rain from the hurricane's fringe. In North Miami, 12-year-old Harold Parson climbed into his family's Ford Model A sedan with his parents, who had vivid memories of the 1926 hurricane ripping the roof off their house and had decided to ride out this storm at the Williams Jennings Bryan School near their home. Parson's older brother would follow the family in his powerful new Ford V-8.

Parson's father turned east onto the street that would take them to the school. But he also was heading directly into the storm's winds and rain, and the engine of his Model A stopped almost instantly, drowned out by the water pouring through the car's grill. But his son crept up behind the Model A until his bumper touched his father's car. He shifted his V-8 into low gear and pushed his family's car to the school, where they dashed into the building.

At Camp 3, Ben Davis handed his car keys to George Pepper sometime around 5 p.m.

"I instructed Mr. Pepper to make haste, wished him luck and bid him good-bye," Davis said.

Pepper turned the big Dodge around and started back up Lower Matecumbe Key. He was only six miles from the Hotel Matecumbe, where the veterans' wives waited anxiously for him.

But the weather conditions were about to take a dramatic turn for the worse. At about the same time that Pepper and Rosalind Grooms Palmer pulled out of Camp 3, the winds suddenly increased in intensity. The hurricane's eye was now within 30 miles of the islands, and the storm's fiercest winds were beginning to claw at the Keys.

Service station owner O. D. King left the hotel in his car around 5 p.m. for the short drive to his home. Suddenly, his car veered off the road as though a giant paw had swatted it. King realized a gust of wind had swept him off the highway. Shaken but unhurt, he steered his car back onto the road and resumed his trip.

The winds were becoming more furious by the minute. The hurricane began tearing at larger buildings. And it started killing people.

At Camp 1 many veterans had gathered in the mess hall to await evacuation. Around five o'clock, camp superintendent William Hardaker told the men that the train was due any minute.

"It was already blowing hard and we piled out as fast as we could," said Lloyd Fichett, a veteran at Camp 1 from Terra Alta, West Virginia. "As we came out the door the corners of the mess hall had started breaking off and it began blowing harder each minute. By the time we got to the railroad tracks, it hit us with all its force. The canteen blew down and wood started flying in all directions. It was terrible."

At about 5:15 p.m. the evacuation train stopped at Homestead, 26 miles south of Miami, to load telephone wire and allow a repair crew to board. Engineer Haycraft and Branch, the yardmaster, decided to turn the locomotive around during the stop. While that was being done, *Miami Daily News* reporter William Johns and several veterans boarded the train. The vets told conductor Gamble they wanted to go back to the camps to get their personal belongings, so Gamble reluctantly allowed them aboard as well.

The train resumed its journey at 5:30. The locomotive's nose was now coupled to the front of the train so the locomotive was traveling backward as it pulled the cars southward. When the train reached Islamorada, Branch and the train crew planned to uncouple the locomotive and switch it to a sidetrack so it could be moved to the other end of the train. It would then be re-coupled so its nose pointed northward. That way, the locomotive's powerful headlight would shine on the tracks during its return trip.

Soon the train had left the peninsula and was on a stretch of tracks that followed a narrow strip of land known as Cross Key, which separated Blackwater Sound from Barnes Sound. Waves were already breaking across the tracks on Cross Key, Johns said.

"There is just a little stretch slightly wider than the track through there, and those waves were coming up I would say from, well, about three or four feet then," he said.

As the train left Homestead, Sheldon sat down to supper at the Hotel Matecumbe with several of his staff and Deputy Sheriff Louis Maloney. Sheldon told Maloney to make sure his deputies understood the veterans had to be loaded as quickly as possible.

As the men finished their meal, Ed Butters and his son burst into the lobby of the hotel. He'd made the 80-mile drive from Miami in just over an hour. He made another check of the shutters while Sheldon and his staff dashed from the hotel to Sheldon's Chevrolet and piled in for the short drive up the island to the Islamorada train station, where they intended to board the train to supervise the loading of the veterans. The downpour was so heavy they had to creep along slowly in second gear so the water would not drown out the automobile's engine.

As Sheldon left the hotel, the women waiting for George Pepper and Rosalind Grooms Palmer looked at each other with growing uneasiness. The storm was clearly worsening, and they wanted to get off the islands. But Pepper and Palmer hadn't returned.

Down at Camp 3, Ed Sheeran was astonished. He had been in the middle of six hurricanes, and he'd never seen winds strengthen the way they did between 5 p.m. and 5:30 p.m.

"The wind was blowing 125 miles per hour by five o'clock," Sheeran said. He went aboard the dredge Sarasota—which he'd tucked into the relative safety of the canal he'd dug months ago—to ride out the storm. With him were about 30 people, including some veterans and a few fishermen with their families.

Offshore, the Dixie struggled against the huge waves being shoved at it by the hurricane. The passenger liner climbed slowly up each mountain of water, balanced for a moment on its peak, then raced down the other side. The waves were so big the Dixie's propeller broke free of the water and raced wildly for a few moments as the ship's bow plunged down into the trough. Too much racing could damage the engines, and Sundstrom was forced to cut his speed to five knots to reduce the risk.

"The ship was hammered by such waves as I never saw in my life," said passenger Anna R. Chambers. "Great, towering, racing mountains of water that hurled themselves on us out of the dark and the murk."

The passengers clung to anything stable. "The deck never seemed to get level," Chambers said. "It was tilting always, forward or aft, to starboard or to port. If you moved around at all, you were climbing a hill or sliding down one."

The screaming winds were equally terrifying.

"That wind was like something solid hitting us," she said. "When that wind struck the ship, the *Dixie* staggered as if a charging loco-motive had hit the steel sides."

Captain Sundstrom and his crew were blinded by the wind-driven rain and giant waves that smashed against the *Dixie*'s bridge 55 feet above the ship's normal waterline. They had only a vague idea of where they were. They tried to get a rough estimate by counting the number of propeller revolutions to estimate the distance they'd traveled. Sundstrom knew his ship was being pushed toward the treacherous reefs that lie a few miles off the Florida coast.

To make matters worse, the rudder had been damaged and the ship was almost unmanageable. "Then it seemed all hell broke loose," said Laycock, the passenger from Baton Rouge. "The ship began to toss and rock helplessly, great waves breaking all around and over the superstructure."

The *Dixie* was exactly where Sundstrom did not want it—caught in the hurricane's dangerous semicircle, out of control and sailing straight for the eye of the storm. But there wasn't much he could do about it.

Around 5 p.m. the ferocious winds suddenly stopped hammering the *Dixie*, and the sun and blue sky appeared overhead. Sundstrom had sailed his ship smack into the eye of the hurricane. Huge waves converged on the Dixie from all directions, but at least the winds were gone—for a while. Sundstrom decided to take advantage of the lull by sailing the *Dixie* away from the treacherous reefs off the Florida Keys. He knew that when the backside winds reached the *Dixie*, his ship would be shoved back toward the coast.

At 5:30 p.m. the dark clouds, fierce winds, and driving rain again enveloped the *Dixie*. The liner was back in the teeth of the hurricane.

In Islamorada about a dozen men, including Sheldon and Maloney, waited for the train at the station. They became uneasy as the storm thrashed the structure.

"At six o'clock the wind was blowing so hard and the station building was shaking so violently that I did not see how it could stand much longer," said Robert B. Lee, the FEC ticket agent and telegrapher in Islamorada.

The Butterses were reaching the same conclusion about their hotel.

"I never knew a howling, raging wind to come so fast," Fern Butters said. "At six o'clock, we were forced to leave the hotel."

Ed Butters ordered his family into the Plymouth. He backed the automobile against a tour bus that had been parked behind the hotel beneath the gumbo-limbo tree. Eight people were packed into the car. Ed and Fern were joined by his father; their sons, Jack and Chester, their daughter, Loretta Perdue, and her son, Pete; and Sheldon's secretary, Mrs. L. A. Fritchmann.

They could hear the hurricane tearing at the hotel and out-buildings.

"We heard crashing and noise from the hotel, and a building blew down and landed beside the left front wheel of the car," Fern Butters said. "We watched it anxiously, fearing it might blow into the car."

Out at Alligator Reef, four miles offshore from Upper Matecumbe Key, lighthouse keeper Jones A. Pervis and his two assistants prepared the lighthouse for the blow. As they worked, assistant keeper James

Duncan looked out at the fearsome ocean and saw a monstrous wave bearing down on the 136-foot-tall lighthouse. Duncan shouted a warning. The men dashed into the tower and scrambled up the ladder as the huge wave submerged the lighthouse's lower platform and then rolled on toward the islands.

The lighthouse keepers were soaked and frightened, but alive. "How I held on and why I wasn't drowned, I can't say," Duncan said.

The mountain of water—a freak "rogue wave" piled up by the hurricane's winds—barreled on toward the Upper Keys, where Joseph M. Lydon, a veteran from New York City, was eating supper with friends in a cabin at Camp 1.

"We heard the wind, and there were things flying through the air, but we thought we'd be all right till the train got there," Lydon said. "Suddenly the wind tipped the whole cabin over—carried everything out to sea. I got washed away from the cabin somehow. The waves were terrible big things."

As the hurricane approached, the veterans had tried to bolster their courage by reminding themselves again that they were the same men who'd stood face-to-face with death in France, and they weren't going to be frightened by a little bad weather. But when their camps began to disintegrate around them and they saw their buddies sent sprawling, their sad bravado evaporated. They realized they faced an enemy far more deadly than the German soldiers they'd confronted when they were younger men.

"We'd been telling ourselves how much better this was than France," said Leroy J. McMullen, a veteran from Akron, Ohio who was discussing the storm with ex-boxer Jimmy Conway and three other veterans in another Camp 1 cabin. "I guess we shouldn't have been bragging. The next minute we were underwater. I guess a mountain wave hit us."

The men were washed across the railroad embankment. When the water receded, three of them had vanished. But the danger wasn't over for the two survivors.

"I saw a big beam swish through the air and hit Jimmy Conway in the back of the head," McMullen said. "He dropped as if a shell had hit him."

Conway, former contender for the heavyweight boxing crown, was one of the hurricane's first fatalities.

In Camp 3 at Lower Matecumbe Key, 75 veterans gathered in the mess hall to wait for the train. They looked at each other nervously as the hurricane shoved and tugged at the building as though it were testing the strength of the structure. Suddenly the howling wind found the grip it sought and ripped the roof off the building.

"Nearly everybody ran just like a bunch of rabbits," said James B. Lindley. "And when we ran out, we ran right into that wind, and after that I don't remember much what happened to the boys because the wind knocked me right on the banister of the mess hall, and I hit the ground, and I got up, and it knocked me down three times before I stayed down."

The vicious wind did Lindley a favor. The air was filled with flying timbers and other deadly debris. As Lindley clung to the ground he watched a board torn from the building whiz past him and impale Elmer Kreitzburg, a veteran from Baltimore. Other veterans helped the horribly injured Kreitzburg to a nearby automobile and tried to make him comfortable.

G. C. Sain, the timekeeper at Camp 3, was blown through two rooms and an outer wall when the mess hall collapsed. He grabbed the floor sill of the mess hall and held on for dear life. Timbers, stoves, iceboxes, and tables flew past his head. Sain felt safe for a while—until the water started rising. Eventually it reached his chin, and then it kept rising until it reached the floor of what had been the mess hall. The water lifted the floor from the sill and washed away the underpinnings. The sill dropped onto Sain's right foot. He was trapped.

"I finally succeeded in getting off my right shoe, and by this time I was entirely underwater," Sain said.

Sain grabbed a piece of two-by-four and worked it beneath the floor sill. With all his strength, he tried to use the wood as a lever to lift the sill off his foot. He couldn't budge it. Then he had another idea.

Sain timed his lifting to correspond with the waves pushing against the sill. The force of the waves, combined with his makeshift lever, provided just enough force to get the sill off his foot.

The pounding rain annoyed George Senison, a 39-year-old veteran from Bridgeport, Connecticut, because he'd planned to go fishing. Somehow, he'd managed to avoid hearing warnings that a hurricane was just offshore.

"I never even thought of a hurricane and had not heard any talk about one and I did not think there was any danger in staying there—until our shack began to shake," Senison said. "We four were in our shack waiting for the storm to blow over. I was going to go fishing and was monkeying around the shack getting things ready. I generally fished about two hours after supper most every night. On that evening it was raining....It kept raining more and more and the wind was blowing. The wind kept blowing harder and harder and began shaking the shack and things like toilet articles and mirrors began falling. I got nervous."

Then Senison could feel his cabin moving. He looked across the street and saw the roof leave the Camp 3 mess hall.

"We were all together leaning against the shack and holding on to each other," Senison said. "I heard William Clark holler that the roof was coming down. We all started away in the same direction and the roof came down on us. It must have hit every one of us. After the roof fell all I could hear was the grunting and groaning of the boys. I never saw any of them after that."

Senison clung to the roof of his shack as it sailed through the air and into the mangroves.

Not far away dozens of vets were sipping beers at Cardy Bradford's store when two men rushed in with news that the roof had been blown off the mess hall. The building shuddered under the wind's ceaseless pummeling as the newcomers breathlessly told their tale.

As the veterans described the destruction of the mess hall, store-owner Cardy Bradford was talking on the phone with his father in Miami Beach. The elder Bradford urged his son to get off the islands.

"You'd better come up," Carson Bradford said. "Get out of there."

Cardy Bradford could hear debris from the mounting destruction slamming against his store. All hell had broken loose outside, and he realized it was too late for him to make a run for the safety of his father's home. "Well, Dad, I don't think I can make it now," he said.

Suddenly, the loud crackling of splintering wood interrupted their conversation. Everyone in the store looked up in horror as one end of the ceiling sagged and the opposite end opened up like the lid of a box. Then the entire roof was lifted from the building and carried away.

In Miami Beach, Carson Bradford slowly lowered the telephone receiver from his ear. The line was dead. He had no idea what had just happened to his son.

The veterans scrambled frantically for cover as the store flew to pieces around them. Some made it to safety, but the flying debris cut down many of them.

"Just as I got outside the door, I was struck in the back of the head with what I think was a filling station pump," said Gay M. Postell, a veteran from Ducktown, Tennessee. "I went out."

John Dombrauski and Adam Rambowski made a couple of stops to see if anyone wanted to make a run for safety with them in their stolen pickup truck, but they had no takers. They reached the bridge across Snake Creek at about the same time the mess hall at Camp 3 collapsed. The bridge was already starting to break up, but they decided to take a chance. "We heard the bridge kind of wiggling as we drove over," Dombrauski said.

On Alligator Reef, Jones Pervis climbed the lighthouse tower at 6:30 p.m., as he did every evening. His duties as keeper required that he light the beacon regardless of weather conditions. But as he tried to ignite the lamp, the half-inch-thick glass protecting it shattered with a terrible crash and the lens was lifted off the tower and carried away. Pervis scrambled for his life as deadly shards of glass flew all around him.

At about the same time Pervis dodged flying glass, Fred Ghent reached Melbourne, roughly halfway between Jacksonville and Miami. He stopped at the FEC office, hoping for a message from Ray Sheldon about the evacuation train. But nothing had been heard from it since it left Homestead an hour earlier.

Down at Long Key, James Duane's barometer read 27.90 inches at 6:45 p.m. The wind, which had backed around to the northwest, performed astonishing feats of strength. A giant beam—6 inches thick, 8 inches wide, and 18 feet long—pulled loose from one of the destroyed buildings. The wind lifted the beam as though it were only a twig. The massive timber sailed 300 feet across the island until it slammed against Duane's house. The building was virtually destroyed, and Duane and the others scrambled through the storm to the hotel.

It was the start of a nerve-racking game of hide-and-seek that the terrified people on Long Key would play with the hurricane for the rest of the night.

At the quarry near Camp 1, a crane near the railroad track swayed violently in the vicious winds. Finally the boom gave way, lurching upward and buckling and pulling loose a thick steel cable that had anchored it. As the boom fell, the cable was hurled across the railroad tracks, taking down telephone lines and setting a trap for the approaching train.

Nearby, Mallie K. Pitman, a veteran from Gastonia, North Carolina, wondered how much longer his cabin could withstand the storm. Pitman was convinced the fearsome winds would send his trembling shack tumbling at any moment. Then, above the roar of the hurricane, he heard a single, wheezing blast of a locomotive's steam whistle. The evacuation train had reached Camp 1.

Pitman asked two other men in his shack to come with him to board the train, but they refused. "I think both of those boys had been drinking some," he said.

Pitman set out alone. The downpour was so heavy he couldn't see the train, but he pushed his way through the storm in the general direction of the railroad track.

The train crew hadn't intended to stop at Windley Key until the return trip, however, and the train crept slowly by. But suddenly the crew heard the scrape of metal on metal. Then, with a rattling shudder, the train was violently snatched to a stop. The crane's steel cable, three-fourths of an inch thick, had tangled itself among the cars. The train was held fast and nearly derailed.

The crew piled out into the raging storm to inspect the damage. It was 6:50 p.m.

chapter five

In the Heft of the Hurricane

As Mallie Pitman neared the railroad track, he saw, through the driving rain and howling wind, men moving frantically between two of the train cars. When he got closer he could see what they were doing. A steel cable from the trackside crane had snared the train and held it fast. It was not going anywhere for quite a while.

A crewman spotted Pitman and asked him to give them a hand. He could see they needed all the help they could get.

Pitman scrambled atop one of the cars with Edgar Boatmen, a veteran from Knoxville, Tennessee. The men seized the cable and started pulling. As they loosened the cable it fell between the train cars.

"It was tangled pretty badly, it was wrapped around and everything," Pitman said. "They kept pulling it after I finished. Myself, the conductor, and a veteran got on the opposite side and straightened it, and the rest of them pulled it. It was a pretty bad mess."

While the men worked to untangle the cable, a few more veterans and some Windley Key residents struggled through the hurricane hoping to board the train. But the fearsome wind made it all but impossible to walk. *Miami Daily News* reporter William Johns and the veterans who'd boarded in Homestead formed a human chain and dragged the others aboard.

At Long Key the old hotel trembled as timbers from the disintegrating fishing camp relentlessly battered the building. When James Duane, Jr., recorded his 7 p.m. barometer reading he saw the needle had tumbled to a chilling 27.78. The wind, which by now had reached about 130 miles per hour, was blowing from the northwest and pushing water out of shallow Florida Bay, piling it up against the rail-road embankment near the hotel.

On the Atlantic side, the powerful winds were sweeping the ocean away from the islands.

Duane had been in half a dozen hurricanes, including a typhoon that smashed into Japan in 1923. He'd never seen anything like this.

Neither Duane nor anyone else had any way of knowing that this storm had become so powerful so quickly. Only a day earlier the storm's strongest winds were blowing at 104 miles per hour. But for 24 hours, the hurricane had greedily gorged itself on energy as it drifted slow-ly across the unusually warm waters between the Bahamas and Florida, moving 4 miles per hour. There was nothing to stop its strengthen-ing—no upper-level winds to shear off its cloud tops and halt its devel-opment, no cooler waters to deprive it of its fuel.

By 7 p.m. Monday the hurricane had quickened its pace so that its eye was less than 30 miles offshore from the Keys. The winds around its center were screaming at better than 160 miles per hour. And, incred-ibly, it was still getting stronger.

But a hurricane's deadliest weapon is its storm surge, a mound of water that is piled up by its winds and pushed along just ahead of the eye. The size of the surge is directly related to the strength of the winds. A hurricane with 160-mile-per-hour wind can create a storm surge of more than 18 feet—enough to easily bury the low-lying Keys, where the highest elevation is 18 feet above sea level. Like the most powerful winds in a hurricane, the worst part of the storm surge is to the right of the eye in what meteorologists call the front right quadrant of the storm.

Keys natives have their own word for this part of the storm that packs the deadly one-two punch of peak winds and maximum storm surge. They call it the heft of the hurricane. And the heft of this storm would strike Islamorada at exactly the right moment to make sure that no one would escape aboard the rescue train.

By 7 p.m. the hurricane had destroyed the flimsiest buildings in the work camps and was beginning to weaken the more substantial structures. In Islamorada the train station could no longer withstand the furious onslaught and began breaking up. As the wind tore away chunks of the station, Ray Sheldon and the others waiting for the evacuation train realized they'd have to find shelter somewhere else.

The men left the disintegrating building, struggled through the storm, and climbed into a boxcar that was parked on a nearby siding.

With buildings being blown to pieces around him, Sheldon knew the men under his supervision were in serious trouble. As the hurricane raged outside, he prowled uneasily around the boxcar, saying repeatedly that he'd done all he could to get the veterans off the Keys. Some of the men agreed with him. Others looked away in grim silence.

A little farther down Upper Matecumbe Key, Ed Butters was flicking on his flashlight every few minutes to check his barometer. What he saw unnerved him.

The needle kept plunging, and by 7:45 p.m. it had fallen to the lowest reading his barometer could register—26.00 inches. Butters was terrified by the astonishingly low reading—but he was strangely fascinated as well. He couldn't stop the needle's relentless nosedive any more than he could stop himself from staring at the instrument. He realized that watching it fall was only adding to his terror. He decided he no longer needed the barometer to tell him what was plainly obvious—this was one hell of a hurricane.

Butters held the barometer aloft and shouted above the roar of the storm for the attention of the others in his Plymouth.

"I called five witnesses, and I threw [the light of] my flashlight on it," Butters said. "And I said 'I don't want to read that thing anymore.'"

With that, Butters rolled down the window of his car and flung the barometer into the storm.

Up at Windley Key the train crew finally freed the locomotive after working for 80 minutes in the driving wind and rain, and the rescue train continued its journey southward a few minutes after eight o'clock.

Seawater now covered the tracks, and engineer J. J. Haycraft could only creep along at a few miles an hour as the malevolent winds rocked the heavy train coaches.

As the rescue train crawled along the tracks, the northern edge of the hurricane's eye reached Alligator Reef. When the winds subsided, keeper Jones Pervis ventured out to check his lighthouse. About 50 feet above the normal sea level, the pounding of the hurricane had pushed a pair of heavy steel doors inward. Lighthouse windows were broken, allowing the vicious wind to rip interior wooden doors off their hinges. The light atop the spire was gone, but otherwise the structure was withstanding the blow.

A few minutes later the edge of the eye passed. Pervis and his assistants returned to their perch about halfway up the lighthouse ladder as the wind and rain resumed with renewed fury.

Somewhere lost amid the mountainous seas off Key Largo, Captain Sundstrom and his crew still wrestled with the storm for control of the *Dixie,* but the hurricane was steadily gaining the upper hand. At 8:12 p.m. the storm claimed its victory, slamming the ship onto French Reef like a wrestler pinning his opponent.

It was a terrifying moment for the passengers.

"The sound was horrible, even above the roar of the wind and the thunder of the waves," said passenger Anna R. Chambers. "A crunching, grinding sound, and the *Dixie* shuddered like a live thing that had received a death wound."

The impact sent passengers tumbling. Furniture and fixtures broke loose and careened wildly across the lower decks. Some slammed into Mrs. C. H. Colgin, a passenger from Brownsville, Texas. The impact pinned her against a bulkhead and injured her leg.

A frightened Florence Steiler dashed from her stateroom and into a nearby lounge. There, she found other passengers, clinging to chairs, with expressions of terror frozen on their faces. One young man— who'd perhaps had too much to drink—had grabbed a soggy pillow, lain down on the floor, and fallen fast asleep.

A crew member stepped into the room. His voice was calm, but what he said sent a shiver through the crowd. "Get up, and everybody on with their life belts," he said.

Steiler looked around at the other passengers. "The crowd was immediately electrified," she said.

As the seas smashed against the helpless liner, Ray Sheldon peeked through a crack in the boxcar and saw a flashing red light. The rescue train had at last reached Islamorada.

Sheldon climbed down out of the boxcar. As he pushed through the storm toward the train, seawater suddenly began to rise around his ankles, and by the time he reached the locomotive less than 100 feet away he was waist deep in salt water. Sheldon didn't know it, but the hurricane's storm surge was coming ashore. The raging, flailing beast had finally set its watery foot on land.

Less than a mile away, the people packed into Ed Butters's Plymouth could hear the hurricane dismantling the Hotel Matecumbe.

"The hotel sounded like it was going to fall apart," Fern Butters said. "The kitchen had exploded."

Suddenly, the back of the second story collapsed, and the debris tumbled onto the new fire engine the Florida ERA had parked behind the hotel. The rubble crushed the roof of the truck's cab, and Fern Butters heard a new scream. Somehow, the falling wreckage turned on the fire engine's siren. The eerie, mournful wail joined the storm's cacophony of chaos.

Then, still more screams, but Fern realized these were human. Charles Butters snapped on his flashlight and pointed it into the storm.

The light revealed three hotel employees struggling against knee-deep seawater. At the same moment Fern Butters felt dampness around her feet and instinctively looked down. The water was seeping into the car. As she felt it swirling around her ankles, Fern was almost overwhelmed with fear. She slumped limply against the back of the car seat. "Oh, God!" she murmured.

Ed Butters pushed open the car door, slogged through the water, and helped each of the employees to the Plymouth. There was no room for them in the car, however, and with the water creeping above his knees, Butters decided the automobile was no longer a safe refuge. He decided to move everybody to the railroad embankment—the highest ground they could possibly reach.

Butters put his younger son on his shoulders, and the others formed a human chain behind him. But as the group started toward the railroad track, Ed stepped into a deep hole and lost his balance. He felt a sharp, stabbing pain in his foot and realized that he'd stepped on a long nail that penetrated his shoe. He struggled back to his feet.

Fern Butters saw her husband go down and decided that making the railroad was impossible. "Ed!" she shouted above the hurricane. "Let's stay together and get into that old bus!"

A friend from Chicago had driven the bus to Florida two years earlier and asked Ed to let him park it at the hotel. It hadn't been moved since then. Now it offered emergency shelter from the raging hurricane.

The group climbed into the bus. Soon the seawater joined them.

In the Russell family's storm shelter, the winds were pounding at the door, causing it to vibrate so furiously that John Russell feared it was about to be torn from its hinges. Several men, including Bernard Russell, leaned against the door to brace it and stop the vibrations.

Bernard Russell noticed that muddy water was seeping beneath it and into the shelter. He knew the building was about three feet off the ground, and the fact that the water was muddy indicated it wasn't rainwater being blown under the door by the storm.

Bernard Russell dipped a finger into the water and touched his finger to his lips. The water was salty. His worst fears were realized. Upper Matecumbe Key was underwater.

John Russell had an awful decision to make. The shelter shielded his family from the killer winds outside. But if his family stayed there, they risked being drowned. The postmaster pondered a choice that probably would mean life or death for him and those he loved.

Back at what had been the train station, Ray Sheldon climbed into the cab of locomotive number 447. He was very glad to see the train and tried to put a cheerful face on his fears. "You're the man we've been looking for," he said to engineer Haycraft.

Sheldon checked his watch by the lights that illuminated the locomotive's pressure gauges and other instruments. It was 8:20 p.m. He asked Branch if they could take the train down to Camp 3. Branch said he thought they could continue southward. But the train master also had a problem—a steam-powered locomotive could travel only about 150 miles before it needed more water for its boiler. The locomotive's water tank would have to be filled before the return trip to Miami, and trying to do that in winds that were now blowing at better than 150 miles per hour would be a nearly impossible task. But they had to try.

Haycraft gave the locomotive's big throttle a tug to move the train to a nearby railroad water tower, but the train wouldn't budge. The brakes on the coaches had locked.

Branch and conductor Gamble climbed down from the locomotive, slogged through water that was now chest-deep, climbed back aboard, and worked their way through the coaches to find out why it wouldn't move. They discovered the wind had blown a 75-ton boxcar off the tracks, setting off the train's automatic braking system. Even worse, the water had risen above the train couplings so they couldn't unhook the derailed boxcar.

And still the seawater rose. Finally it reached the level of the locomotive's firebox and extinguished the flames that heated the boiler. Branch's worries about taking on water for the boiler and detaching a derailed boxcar didn't matter anymore. Without the fire the boiler couldn't produce steam, and without steam the locomotive was dead.

At the Russells' storm shelter, John Russell had made his difficult decision. He would move his family to higher ground. They tried to brace themselves for the onslaught. Bernard Russell put his arms protectively around his sister, Marjorie Spitz, and her toddler son, Raymond

Spitz, Jr., as one of the men opened the door. The hurricane roared into the shelter like a wet, savage beast pouncing on its prey.

Bernard Russell tried to steady himself and hold on to his sister and nephew as the furious winds and blowing water engulfed them. But the teenager was no match for the hurricane. Suddenly the woman and child were gone, ripped away from him and sucked into the howling blackness as though the storm had simply swallowed them whole in a single greedy bite. Stunned, he stepped backward into the shelter. But something else was terribly wrong. The door frame was tilting, and the floor was rising. Russell realized the hurricane was pulling the shelter away from the thick steel bolts that held it to the coral island. The building was slowly turning over.

The peak of the storm surge had arrived. In the next few minutes dozens of lives would be snuffed out as easily as the flames in number 447's firebox.

When a storm surge makes landfall, giant breaking waves riding atop the mound of water usually accompany it. A storm surge of 18 to 22 feet such as the one created by the Labor Day hurricane can have breaking waves 30 feet high. It is these breaking waves that cause much of the carnage when the storm surge comes ashore, smashing everything in front of them and sweeping away the wreckage like a giant wet broom.

At the same time that the waves riding the storm surge were ripping the Russells' shelter from its anchors, they were also slamming into the rescue train with an unearthly force. The cars, each weighing from 75 to 100 tons, were shoved off the tracks. Only the locomotive, weighing more than 160 tons, remained upright.

In the train's smoking car, reporter William Johns thought he was about to die.

"We had been stopped but 10 or 15 minutes when a wall of water from 15 to 20 feet high picked up our coaches and swirled them about like straws," Johns said. "We felt them going and I imagine everyone thought it was the end. I know I did."

Thousands of World War I veterans came to Washington in 1932 hoping to persuade Congress to approve early payment of a bonus for their wartime service. President Hoover ordered the eviction of the "Bonus Marchers" from government property.

FLORIDA EAST COAST RAILWAY, KEY WEST EXTENSION.

EXPRESS TRAIN CROSSING FAMOUS LONG KEY VIADUCT, FLORIDA.   21397

Henry Flager's Florida East Coast Railroad's Key West Extension opened in 1912. Handsome concrete viaducts spanned many miles of water between the Florida Keys, linking the islands.

The Roosevelt Administration sent hundreds of World War I veterans to work camps in the Keys to work on a highway that would link the Keys to the mainland. Critics of the program said FDR wanted to prevent them from gathering in Washington.

The Atlantic Ocean lapped the shore just yards away from rows of shacks at Camp 1. Each cabin,

One of the highway projects, the construction of a bridge at Lower Matecumbe Key, is depicted in this John Ambrose cartoon from July 1935. An artist and veteran from Louisiana, Ambrose drew elegant cartoons for the *Key Veterans News* depicting life in the camps.

as they were called, housed four vets. A piece of canvas stretched over the top served as a roof.

Fern and Ed Butters operated the Hotel Matecumbe on Upper Matecumbe Key. They and a dozen others survived the storm in an abandoned tour bus that was protected from the storm surge by a mangrove forest.

Bernard Russell, age 16 in 1935 (shown here around 1942), grabbed gulps of air as the storm surge rolled over him. Of the 80 members of his family who lived in the Keys, just 9 survived the storm.

A "Conch" family— The Edna and Edny Parker family posed for a photo taken sometime in the mid-1920s. Their daugher, Faye Marie, a hurricane survivor who would unveil the hurricane memorial in 1937, had not yet been born.

SPECIAL HURRICANE PICTORIAL SECTION

SUNDAY TRIBUNE

Vol. 1, No. 30—Section No. 2, MIAMI BEACH, FLORIDA, SUNDAY, SEPTEMBER 8, 1935

1,000 DEATH TOLL OF HURRICANE ON KEYS

Complete Story of Carnage in Pictures

The Miami Beach *Daily Tribune* correctly predicted that the hurricane would strike South Florida, but the tabloid's coverage of the tragedy was lurid and often wildly inaccurate. *Tribune* editor Paul Jeans greatly exaggerated the death toll and his reporters fabricated quotes for some stories.

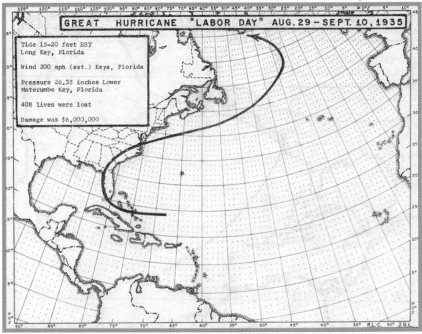

GREAT HURRICANE "LABOR DAY" AUG. 29 – SEPT. 10, 1935

Tide 15-20 feet EST
Long Key, Florida

Wind 200 mph (est.) Keys, Florida

Pressure 26.35 inches Lower
Matecumbe Key, Florida

408 lives were lost

Damage was $6,000,000

The Labor Day hurricane of 1935 formed from a tropical wave that blew off the west coast of Africa in August 1935. It became the most powerful hurricane ever to strike the United States and killed at least 408 during its rampage up the East Coast.

The S.S. *Dixie* was en route from New Orleans to New York with more than 350 passengers and crew when the Labor Day hurricane threw it onto a reef near Key Largo.

Swept off its tracks by the powerful storm surge, the rescue train lay helplessly on its side in Islamorada. The hurricane would mark the end of the Florida East Coast Railroad.

Rescue workers seached among the ruins of the work camps, which were torn apart by winds that may have reached 200 miles per hour. More than 250 veterans were killed.

Victims' bodies quickly decomposed after the hurricane, and rescue workers were forced to cremate most of them. Here, a National Guardsman discusses how to light a funeral pyre with representatives of the Florida ERA and Salvation Army and two clergymen.

The WPA built this art deco memorial to hurricane victims at Islamorada. The memorial, paid for by an American Legion post in Miami, was dedicated in November 1937.

The storm had no difficulty pushing the train off the tracks.

"It went over so easy that we thought that something was just lifting up and possibly something had blown under it," Johns said. "We didn't know exactly what it was."

As Johns felt the coach lifting off the ground he screamed in terror to the others. "She's gone, boys!"

When the coaches came to rest they stretched in an arc along the west side of the railroad tracks. A couple of the cars at the apex of the arc were carried about 150 feet.

"We came out of the swirl of water with a thump that tossed the inmates of the coaches across seats, against windows, and in crazy heaps on side walls that had suddenly become floors," Johns said. "Miraculously, none was hurt severely."

It took a few moments for the occupants to realize they were no longer moving. The foamy seawater swirling through the car gave them the impression it was still being carried along by the storm.

The worst of the storm surge sped quickly across the islands. "The wall of water passed as quickly as it came, else we would all have been drowned like rats in a trap," Johns said.

Johns and the others had no idea what had happened to them or where they were. The car leaned crazily, and for all the occupants knew, it was dangling over a ledge and could topple into the ocean at any moment. Rain and seawater blew through the smashed windows. "You couldn't see six inches to either side," Johns said.

The surging water also pushed over the boxcar where Louis Maloney, Wilbur Jones, and others had sought shelter after the train station was destroyed. "All of a sudden, bang, it went over," Jones said. "It was dark as hell."

The peak of the storm surge had passed, but the water didn't completely leave the island. The Conchs' fears about the railroad embankments and the causeways between the islands were coming true. They were blocking the path of the surge as it tried to flow around the islands, and the water piled up and spread out across Upper Matecumbe

Key instead of flowing into Florida Bay. It was still deep enough on the island to submerge the huge drive wheels of the locomotive.

Back at what had been the Russell family's storm shelter, Bernard Russell plunged into the watery, howling darkness as the structure disintegrated. The dozen other relatives who'd been in the shelter had simply vanished.

Russell struggled to keep his head above the water. The noise of the hurricane was deafening—a raspy, wailing, ear-splitting screech unlike anything he'd ever heard.

Something slammed viciously into Russell's back and began relentlessly pushing him downward until his head disappeared beneath the waves. The teenager involuntarily gulped a mouthful of salt water and figured he was about to die.

But just as suddenly he was released, and his head popped back above the water like a cork. Still, he couldn't move. Something held his left foot, and he couldn't pull loose. The waves continued to roll in, and Russell's head disappeared briefly beneath the water as each crest passed him. He had to time his breathing, cupping his hands around his mouth and hastily gulping air during the troughs of the waves before being dunked again by the next crest. He knew each breath might be his last.

Aboard the *Dixie,* Captain Sundstrom ordered that lifeboats be partially lowered on the side of the ship that was protected from the wind. Sundstrom had no intention of putting people into lifeboats unless the ship started to sink or break up, but he wanted them ready for immediate use if necessary.

But after standing near the lifeboats for about an hour, many passengers became bored. They drifted into one of the lounges, sat down, and started talking.

"The chief topic was death and whether one minded it," said Florence Steiler. The Reverend F. A. Wakeman, a Catholic priest from San Diego, started praying. Occasionally a passenger would interrupt the priest's prayers to ask for absolution.

Others, however, started singing "That Daring Young Man on the Flying Trapeze."

"All the while, the ship was rolling badly and those on the down side would be in water up to their knees, and then as the ship rolled back, the other side was drenched," Steiler said. "Suitcases, shoes, and personal belongings were washed from one stateroom across the alleyway into another stateroom. But no one seemed to care."

One passenger spotted a friend's expensive new shoes floating across the deck and called to her friend. "Who the heck cares about shoes now?" her friend answered.

On the Keys the hurricane continued its methodical slaughter.

Islamorada resident Jimmy Woods took shelter at his parents' house with his brother and three sisters. When the storm surge came ashore, the house was lifted off the ground. The family tried to flee, but Woods's mother couldn't move quickly enough to avoid the refrigerator that slid down the tilting floor toward her. The appliance slammed into her, breaking her back and paralyzing her from the waist down.

In the midst of the swirling chaos, Woods heard his 11-year-old sister, Ruth, pleading for help. "Lord!" she screamed above the hurricane's roar. "Save me!" Then she disappeared into the blackness.

Woods held his baby sister in his arms, trying to protect her from the storm, but too many missiles filled the air. A chunk of flying debris struck the child's head.

"It crushed her right against the side of my head," Woods said. "And she was dead. She was just killed instantly."

Before Woods could react to the tragedy, he was knocked unconscious by another piece of flying debris.

At the Hotel Matecumbe a thick tangle of mangroves lay between the old touring bus and the beach. The mangroves absorbed and dispersed the terrific force of the storm surge and kept the bus from being carried away.

Still, the water kept rising.

"We had constant flashes of sheet lightning, and all this with the wind howling like a banshee, the siren moaning, and the water rising everywhere," Fern Butters said. "You would have thought there would have been mass hysteria. Yet with everyone looking into the face of death, there were no hysterics. Everyone was quiet."

Outside the bus, the brilliant flashes of lightning briefly illuminated corpses floating past in the swirling seawater.

Nearby, Bertram Pinder decided that his house was about to go to pieces. He told his family they had to get out or be killed in the wreckage.

The Pinders gathered near the back door and steeled themselves for the dangerous dash through the storm that awaited them. But before they could move, the house suddenly shattered as though a bomb had hit it. "It was like the house just blew up," said Evanette Pinder.

The family was suddenly thrown into the swirling, merciless night. The wind and flood carried away Evanette Pinder, her husband, and their four-year-old daughter, but miraculously they all landed together in a lime grove, where they clung to the top of a tree. Hanging on to the prickly tree was like "trying to hold on to a cactus," she said. But it saved their lives.

Back at the ruins of the Pinder house, Dolores Pinder and her mother, Elizabeth, clung to the wreckage trying to keep their heads above water.

Russell Pinder was knocked senseless when a small water tank slammed into his head.

At the Hotel Matecumbe, Ed Butters stationed himself at the door of the bus to keep debris away and help anyone trying to struggle through the storm. He spotted the dazed, semiconscious Russell Pinder and helped him into the makeshift shelter.

Farther up the island, Rev. S. E. Carlson and his wife were locked in a life-and-death struggle with the hurricane. The surging water lifted the Methodist parsonage off its foundation and shoved it across the island. With water rapidly rising around him, Carlson grabbed an ax and starting hacking away at the ceiling of his home. If he could open a hole, he and his wife could climb up onto the rafters and perhaps escape the water.

The veterans suffered horribly as their flimsy camps disintegrated around them. In Camp 1 the winds picked up one veteran, hurled him through the air, and slammed him against a post with a sickening thud. He died instantly.

John Conway, another Camp 1 veteran from Marion, Iowa, watched three men clinging desperately to a telephone pole, but by now there wasn't much that was big enough or tied down tightly enough to withstand the hurricane. "The pole went into the air with the men hanging on," Conway said. "It blew far out to sea. Those men [were] goners."

Many vets were killed as they fled the wreckage of their camps.

"When the buildings began to crack, men ran out like scurrying rabbits, only to be picked up and blown in the air in every direction," said veteran Jack Clifford, who was from Hampton, Virginia.

Many who had somehow survived the storm surge were being beaten to death by windblown debris. Some were killed by flying coconuts or chunks of coral. Others were speared by boards or tree limbs. One man was killed when a steel spike buried itself in his skull.

Some men never knew what hit them. One moment they were alive and alert, thinking about their families, praying they'd survive and trying to hold on to their courage by reminding themselves they'd been terrified before when they were clinging to the mud in France as exploding German shells shook the ground beneath them. Then the next moment they were gone, their lives snuffed out as suddenly and easily as the flame of a candle.

Death came more slowly to others, who watched helplessly as seawater swirled around them. When the water started rising around their chins and filling their mouths, they knew they were going to die.

A few clung to life during a wild and terrifying ride across gigantic waves, carried along by the hurricane for miles until they were tossed, exhausted and half-dead, onto one of the many small, soggy islands that dot Florida Bay. A few were pitched onto Cape Sable at the tip of the Florida peninsula after riding the hurricane for 40 miles or more.

Some died quickly; others lingered horribly after the hurricane had passed and died slowly from thirst and untended injuries.

Some simply disappeared from the face of the Earth forever.

At Camp 5, John Ambrose, the talented artist from Louisiana who'd fretted that the veterans might not get to see a hurricane, clung to Lower Matecumbe Key with a hundred or so other men. But they were in the most poorly situated of the three camps on a narrow, low-lying section of the island that was only a few feet above sea level, and they were taking a deadly pounding from the storm.

Acts of courage and compassion penetrated the chaos. At Camp 1, veteran George Sherman of Little Falls, New York, spotted a puppy struggling for its life in the water. Sherman dashed into the surf, grabbed the animal, and hauled it out to safety.

At Camp 3, the veterans who had scoffed at Fritz Maggesen's offer to ride out the storm aboard the *Rowena* had realized that Long Island Sound had never seen a wind like this, and by 8:45 p.m. two or three dozen of them had piled aboard. The *Rowena* was standing up to the fierce blow, but Maggesen discovered that ceaseless tugging on the mooring lines was loosening the boat's steel ringbolts. It was only a matter of time before the ringbolts were pulled out of the boat, and when that happened the *Rowena* would be swept away to God only knew where. Maggesen told the veterans they'd better figure out a way to get aboard the *Monroe County*, then he and several volunteers ventured out into the watery chaos and started rigging new lines to hold the *Rowena* to the dock. Suddenly, above the roar, Maggesen heard a sickening crash. The lines securing the *Monroe County* had broken, and the ferry careened wildly away from the dock. The wind and waves hauled the helpless craft onto Lower Matecumbe Key and slammed it against the railroad embankment, where it began breaking up.

Then the raging winds and drenching downpour suddenly ceased at Lower Matecumbe Key. The hurricane's tiny eye had arrived at Camp 3. James Lindley, who had escaped the wreckage of the mess hall, poked his head above the railroad embankment during the calm.

"It quieted down just like that, just stopped," Lindley said. "The stars come up and the wind seemed to get warm, and it was just as still, a piece of paper wouldn't flutter in the air."

Arthur Mewshaw half waded and half swam through the seawater until he was within shouting distance of the *Sarasota,* where Ed Sheeran and others had taken shelter. He called for Sheeran and asked him what the men should do.

Sheeran warned Mewshaw that the worst of the hurricane was still to come and told Mewshaw to take the veterans to higher ground. About 100 men, including Mewshaw and camp superintendent Ben Davis, walked up the island to the tanker car that was parked on a sidetrack. They'd ride out the rest of the storm there.

Roland Craig, Jack Crow, and several others had ridden out the first part of the storm by moving from building to building on nearby Craig Key. When the eye arrived, Craig left his bungalow to look around.

"All my buildings on the east side [of the railroad tracks] were as flat as a pancake and all torn up and gone," he said.

As the veterans huddled behind the tanker car near Camp 3, they heard a strange, distant rustling. A few minutes later they discovered the source of the noise.

"We could hear this wave out there just rustling like somebody brushing leaves," Davis said.

They were actually hearing the Atlantic Ocean rushing to reclaim the seabed that the hurricane had forced it to abandon. During the first part of the storm, the fierce winds had piled up water on the bay side of the Keys, but pushed water away from the islands on the ocean side. Now, with the backside winds blowing in the opposite direction, the water that had been swept far offshore was charging back toward the Keys, piled high and moving with terrific force.

Soon the surge of water reached the reef, and the faint rustling became a deafening roar. It was a terrifying moment for the veterans, who could only watch helplessly as the salt water—whipped into snowy white foam and illuminated by the feeble light of the new moon—hurled itself at them.

"It started coming in over the reef, and then we watched it coming in, and it looked like white foam," Davis said.

The men tightened their grips on the tanker car and tried to brace themselves for the inevitable. As the roiling water drew closer they could feel the ground trembling from its massive weight. Then it was upon them, slamming into the tanker with a murderous impact.

The tanker disappeared briefly beneath the water, and the force of the wave ripped the main track from its bed and slammed the strands of steel against the railroad car sitting on the sidetrack. But the heavy tanker, loaded with 10,000 gallons of water, didn't budge. Then the wave was gone—and so were more than 25 of the 100 or so men who'd tried to cling to the tanker. Some of the men screamed in terror as the rushing seawater carried them away. Others rode the wave silently to their deaths.

The killer wave seemed to be towing the backside of the hurricane's eye. Immediately after the water was gone the winds resumed. They were even fiercer than before.

Aboard the *Rowena*, Fritz Maggesen looked around at the three dozen or so veterans now aboard the boat. Their fear was clearly evident on their faces. Maggesen had an idea. He pulled out his accordion and started playing "Over the Waves." A few veterans recognized the old sailing song and started singing along. Others joined in, and for a few moments the terror of the storm abated.

But the roar of the wind steadily increased, eventually drowning out Maggesen and his accordion. He suggested they start praying. Nearly all of the men agreed, but one veteran refused—not because he was an atheist, but because he didn't think it would be right. "I've been an old son of a gun all my life, and I'll go out the same way I've lived,"the man said. "It wouldn't be fair to the Lord to ask for mercy on my carcass at this late date. I'll just have to take the consequences."

Down at Long Key, James Duane, Jr,. continued to take his hourly readings even though it was impossible for him to report his information to the weather bureau with the telephone line gone. At 9 p.m. his barometer had fallen to 27.29 inches—well below the levels of three earlier terrible storms that had devastated parts of Florida. The 1919 storm that left Key West in ruins and then barreled across the Gulf of Mexico to strike Texas had a low reading of 27.37 inches, and the barometric pressure during the horrific hurricane of 1928 that killed almost 2,000 around Lake Okeechobee had fallen to 27.43. Even the 1926 hurricane that had nearly wiped out Miami Beach wasn't this intense. That storm's lowest reading was 27.61 inches.

At ten minutes past nine the torrential rains and raging winds suddenly stopped at Long Key as though an unseen hand had flipped a switch. The hurricane's eye was crossing the fishing camp. It was a bizarre contrast to the fierce winds of only a few moments earlier.

Stars were clearly visible—another indication of the hurricane's intensity. In many hurricanes, the sky remains obscured by clouds in the eye. Very intense hurricanes, however, often have small, cloudless eyes. The clear eye of Hurricane Andrew in 1992, for example, was only 14 miles in diameter.

The eye of this nameless hurricane was only about ten miles wide.

Duane and a few others cautiously ventured out to take a look at the ruins. Most of the camp's buildings had been reduced to piles of tangled lumber and debris. Amazingly, no one in the group was seriously injured, but Duane knew the backside of the hurricane would soon arrive, and with it would come even stronger winds. He ordered the others into the only remaining building he thought might withstand the awful blast that was sure to come—the cottage of Britain's Lady Ashley.

At Craig Key, Roland Craig ventured down the railroad trestle to the home of R. G. Jackson, who operated the railroad drawbridge. Jackson, a veteran of many hurricanes, advised Craig to ride out the rest of the hurricane on the lee side of the railroad embankment. Craig hurried back up the tracks to prepare for the backside of the storm.

While Craig was looking for a safe place, Fred Ghent was running into rain from the hurricane's outermost fringes a few miles north of West Palm Beach. Around 9:30 p.m. he stopped at the Florida East Coast Railway office there to check on the progress of the train. But there was still no word.

Ghent walked back out into the rain to his car wondering if the rescue train had encountered problems down in the Keys.

As the first pangs of uncertainty about the fate of the veterans stabbed at Ghent, Fern Butters stood in chest-deep seawater and thought about biblical references to water and flooding.

"I had great faith in what God could do," she said. "I was think-ing of how He rolled back the Red Sea, parted the rivers of Jordan, and how Jesus spoke to the waves and they were still."

She started to pray aloud.

"I mentioned all these things I had been thinking about and asked God, for Jesus' sake, to make the water go down," she said. She ended her prayer by lifting her arms out of the water and crossing them above her head.

Minutes passed. Nothing happened.

The heft of the hurricane continued to lash Upper Matecumbe Key, and the boisterous sea kept pounding relentlessly against the railroad causeways between the islands.

Then, suddenly, the water began dropping as though someone had pulled the plug of a bathtub. The railroad causeways had finally given way. The pent-up storm tide rushed into Florida Bay.

In the bus, the refugees realized that the water was going down.

As the water receded, Bernard Russell discovered he was atop a pile of debris. He worked his foot free and scrambled off the pile. He was certain he was the only living thing on the island. Then, above the tearing winds and slashing rain, he heard someone calling for help. He shouted a response and started feeling his way through the raging darkness toward the voice.

Elizabeth Pinder and her daughter Dolores kept their heads above water by clambering atop the wreckage of their home. But the sudden drop in the water created suction so strong that Elizabeth was suddenly yanked down into the wreckage, pulled through small openings deep into the pile of debris that had been her home. Moments later she was hopelessly entangled, alive but badly injured with many cuts and broken bones. Her daughter could only hold a coat over her mother's head to keep the pounding rain off her face.

Ed Butters heard calls for help above the roar of the winds. He and his father plunged into the storm. Moments later they brought three more refugees—a woman and her two children—into the bus.

Butters left the bus again to go into the ruins of the hotel to get blankets. He found Ruth Woods in the lobby. The storm had torn the clothing from her body, and the girl was shivering with cold, but the prayer she'd screamed at the moment her house was destroyed had been answered. She was unhurt. Butters carried her to the Plymouth and went back to the ruined hotel to find something to cover her.

A few minutes past 10:30 p.m. the sea suddenly started rising at Long Key. James Duane pointed the beam of his flashlight toward the ocean. He saw a terrifying sight. The calm continued, but out toward the reefs Duane could see a "wall of water, many feet high" racing toward the island.

It was the displaced ocean returning.

Duane and a companion sprinted for the cottage where the others waited, about 60 feet away. Before they could reach the door they were waist deep in water. Then the cottage floated off its foundation.

At Craig Key, Roland Craig and Jack Crow had just reached the railroad embankment when the wind suddenly resumed and the sea quickly rose around them.

"The wave come clean over the track, bringing all kinds of debris ...and throwing it on our heads, and knocked us into the water," Craig said. Craig and Crow scrambled atop the embankment and grabbed hold of the railroad tracks.

"I really, in fact, dug under the crossties and held onto the rail," Craig said. "I prayed a lot all night, and we stayed there until three o'clock and I never heard such a roar of wind in my life."

Not far away, Ivar Olson had pulled his small, sturdy boat out of the water and secured it at the southern end of Craig Key to ride out the storm. His boat had held together, and those who were with him were unhurt.

Olson had a barometer that bottomed out at 28 inches. The needle had dropped far below that mark long ago. Still, Olson kept an eye on the instrument, which also had a thermometer. During the lull he noted the barometer's needle dropped to the point on the thermometer that read ten degrees above zero Ceksius. Olson took note of the needle's position even though he had no idea whether his barometer was still responding properly to the astonishingly low atmospheric pressure created by the hurricane.

Down in Key West the fringe of the storm dumped torrential rainfall on the city. Bascom Grooms, Jr., ignored the deluge, however, and escaped his gloom about the end of summer vacation by going to an early showing of *West Point of the Air*. He removed his soaking shoes, settled himself into his seat in the darkened theater, and became absorbed in the drama starring Wallace Beery and Robert Young.

The youngster had no way of knowing that his sister Rosalind and her boyfriend, George Pepper, had never arrived at the Hotel Matecumbe to pick up the veterans' wives waiting to get off the island.

Around 10 p.m. Ernest Hemingway lay down for a couple hours of sleep. His home, like the rest of the city, was boarded up tightly. The winds hadn't reached hurricane force in Key West, but the rain hadn't let up all night. Hemingway expected the worst part of the storm to reach there in a couple of hours. The author put a flashlight and a barometer next to his bedside. He intended to get up at midnight to go down to the docks to check on his beloved *Pilar*.

Up at Camp 1 on Windley Key about 40 people, including mothers and their children, had crowded into the makeshift veterans hospital. The storm-driven sea had flooded the first floor of the two-story building, and the refugees were crowded into the second floor.

Around 10 p.m. the unrelenting pounding of the storm and the fear it inflicted were taking a toll on the mental stability of some refugees. Leo Moran, a veteran from Philadelphia, watched as the strain worked on Stanley Warman, one of his buddies, who also was from Philadelphia. The terrified man was sitting, dazed, on the floor.

"He was like a madman, eyes staring out of his head," Moran said.

Monroe County Deputy Sheriff T. F. Russell was among the refugees in the hospital. He'd watched the rescue train crawl past earlier in the night and assumed it would soon be returning from Islamorada to pick them up.

Russell announced he would lead a group from the hospital to the lee side of the railroad embankment, where they would wait for the train.

The deputy led a group downstairs and opened the door. Some of the refugees shrank back at the sight of waist-deep water swirling outside the building.

"Who wants to go with me?" he called above the hurricane's roar.

"I'll go!" Elva Loper shouted, and she took Russell's hand. Her husband, Dave Loper, also a deputy sheriff, took her other hand, and the three of them pushed into the storm.

A few others ventured after them, but most refused to leave.

As the vicious winds hammered the building, Elva Loper saw an astonishing sight.

"As we were leaving I looked back, and it seemed to me the hospital jumped about a foot off the ground," she said.

The building shattered, collapsing into a heap of rubble. A dozen people managed to escape the ruins. The rest were trapped inside.

Albert Christie, a veteran from Detroit, was trying to protect a little girl when the hospital disintegrated. The air suddenly was filled with wreckage, and Christie was battered from all sides. Something smashed against his head, and he lost consciousness.

"I don't really know [what hit me]," he said. "It was so dark you couldn't see. It was flying timbers that hit me, I guess."

When Christie came to, the child he'd been trying to protect was gone. Somehow, in his stupor, he'd managed to grab another child and keep her from being carried away.

"I was hanging on to a little girl," Christie said. "Mr. Van Ness came down with a little girl about six years old and I was trying to help her. He was outside trying to get her. That was the last I saw of her. When I came to, I was hanging on to another girl. Frances, I think her name was."

Lassiter Alexander, a physician who worked at the hospital, was one of those who pushed his way out of the ruins. With only the feeble light of a flashlight to guide him, Alexander struggled through the water toward the railroad embankment. He was repeatedly knocked off his feet by the wind and flying debris. An awful mélange flew past his head.

"Timbers and trees and the bodies of children were whirled through the air," Alexander said.

Alexander reached the small rock wall that had been built by Jimmy Conway, the ex-boxer, shortly after the camp was established. Conway's handiwork was withstanding the storm. Alexander scrambled over the four-foot-high wall and crouched behind it. He found about two dozen people huddled there.

At Long Key the sudden rush of water that had covered the island during the last part of the lull was only a hint of what was coming. At ten minutes past ten o'clock, Duane, standing in waist-deep water with the other refugees, checked his barometer. The needle had dropped yet again, to 27.02 inches. The wind was stirring again, this time from the southwest—the opposite direction from the earlier winds.

Five minutes later the backside winds were upon them. Duane glanced at his barometer. The dial read 26.98 inches. Then the hurricane—almost as though it had had enough of Duane's constant monitoring—snatched the instrument from his hands. The barometer disappeared beneath the wind-whipped salt water.

Lady Ashley's cottage, where Duane and his party had taken refuge, started to break up. Duane was suddenly sucked out of the building and thrust into a life-and-death struggle against the wind and water. He grabbed at something to keep from being pulled out to sea. It was the top of a coconut palm tree. Duane seized an armful of palm fronds and hung on. He watched the cottage begin to float away. His companions were still inside. Then something slammed into the back of his head, knocking him unconscious.

Up at the remains of Camp 1, the refugees who had taken shelter behind the small stone wall decided to try to reach the railroad embankment—the highest spot on the island. Once there they scrambled to the lee side of the embankment and started clawing holes into the marl that supported the tracks, burrowing into makeshift bunkers to protect themselves from the deadly debris that still filled the air.

Elsewhere, those who were still alive clung to anything that wasn't moving. At Camp 1, Lloyd Fichett crawled from the wreckage and struggled to higher ground, where he found a telephone pole that had withstood the onslaught. Fichett unbuckled his belt and used it to tie himself to the pole.

"A barrage of stones kept hitting me all over the body and then I partly lost consciousness," Fichett said. "I hung on through the night in a semi-dazed condition."

Charles Van Vecten, who had been visiting friends at Camp 1, clung to the railroad embankment with the veterans. The scene around him resembled a battlefield.

"I saw bodies with tree stumps smashed through their chests— heads blown off—twisted arms and legs torn off by flying timber that cut like big knives," Van Vecten said.

In Islamorada, Bernard Russell followed the voice in the blackness until he found his father. John Russell had a chunk of flesh torn from his buttocks, but he was alive. The teenager also found his uncle Clifton Russell wandering in a daze through the windy, watery chaos. The three men huddled together in the darkness to wait for daybreak.

At Camp 5, Melton Jarrell, from Forney, Texas, spent the night clinging to the railroad track. "A heavy sea came along and washed it up and as it settled back down it pinioned my left leg under it," Jarrell said. "After lying there for what seemed countless ages, suffering horrible agony I decided to try to cut my foot off but I couldn't get to my penknife. After that I passed out."

When Jarrell regained consciousness he found himself being washed away from the railroad track. "I was thrown upon a tree," he said. "It was a mangrove."

Jarrell seized the stubborn mangrove and hung on.

Elsewhere in Islamorada, fisherman J. R. Beckham rode out the storm in his new home with his wife and grandchildren and 13 other people who sought shelter there. Beckham had survived three earlier hurricanes and was confident his new house would withstand this storm.

"All of a sudden, it was like some great hand picked up the whole house and dropped it in the ocean," Beckham said. "When I came out of the daze, I was clinging to bushes. There was no sign of any of the 16 other persons we'd been talking with only a few minutes before. I crept from bush to bush and from stump to stump trying to find my wife and grandchildren. It didn't seem this could happen to me."

The winds and rains still raged at 11 p.m., but as the final hour of the awful day began, those who could still read their barometers saw a long-awaited sight—the needles were finally starting to climb. The worst part of the hurricane had passed and was moving away from the Keys. The storm's eye continued its northward turn and was now on a course that would brush Cape Sable at the tip of the Florida peninsula.

Around midnight, Ernest Hemingway got out of bed and, flashlight in hand, went out to his car to drive down to the docks. The rain was still falling in torrents in Key West, and the downpour drowned out the engine in Hemingway's car. He got out of the useless automobile and slogged through the storm to the naval base to check on the *Pilar*. With the winds and rain still lashing Key West, he decided to wait out the storm by his boat.

Around 12:30 a.m. Tuesday, Fred Ghent reached Hollywood, where he hoped to find the rescue train waiting for him. Instead he found only Sam Cutler. Ghent learned that FEC officials hadn't heard from the train since it pulled out of Homestead seven hours earlier.

Ghent and Cutler climbed back into Ghent's car and drove on to Miami. FEC officials there knew nothing about the train either, but said they intended to send a wrecker after it if they hadn't heard anything by 3:30 a.m.

Ghent continued south.

Aboard the *Dixie*, George Outland tired of playing piano for the passengers' morale-raising sing-along. The Yale professor organized a poker game with eight other passengers. As the winds and waves continued to thrash and rock the *Dixie*, the players hunched over their cards in one of the ship's lounges.

Elsewhere on the ship, many other passengers tried to find a dry spot to catch a little sleep.

At about 12:15 a.m. Tuesday, Captain Sundstrom got his first bit of good news in a long time. The *Dixie's* weak SOS had finally been picked up by Tropical Radio in Hialeah, Florida, and relayed to the U.S. Coast Guard in Jacksonville. Tropical Radio was broadcasting the SOS to all ships at sea.

Then the Coast Guard station in Key West picked up the SOS. The Coast Guard radioed a message to the *Dixie* that a cutter was on its way. Other ships in the area changed course for the *Dixie's* position, which was mistakenly being given as aground on Carysfort Reef.

Around 2:30 a.m. Tuesday, James Duane shook the cobwebs from his head and discovered that he was still in the coconut palm tree. He looked around at a scene that was illuminated by terrific flashes of lightning. The floodwaters had receded, and Duane was about 20 feet above the wreckage of Long Key Fishing Camp.

The cottage where his companions had taken refuge had been blown back to the island, and their incredible luck had held. They had all gone through the storm with no serious injuries.

At about the same time Duane was climbing down from the palm tree on Long Key, Fred Ghent pulled into Homestead. A drenching, windblown rain was falling when Ghent arrived at the FEC station.

Ghent ran into a section foreman who had just returned from Florida City, only a few miles to the south at the tip of the peninsula. The foreman told Ghent that the road linking the peninsula with Key Largo was underwater. Ghent decided to stay the rest of the night in Homestead.

On the Upper Keys many grim, battered, soaking-wet survivors huddled in the darkness behind whatever meager shelter they could find as the departing storm continued to batter them. The veterans at Camp 3 who'd survived the storm wave by hanging on to the tanker now crouched behind the car that saved their lives.

Near the ruins of the Islamorada train station, someone managed to shove an ax between the slats of the overturned boxcar that had protected Deputy Louis Maloney, Wilbur Jones, and others from the fury of the storm. The men used the ax to chop an escape hole.

Ray Sheldon spent the night in the locomotive cab with the engineer, fireman, and conductor. Back in the coaches no one had been seriously injured when the storm surge shoved the train off the tracks. The passengers settled down in the overturned cars to wait out the rest of the storm.

Around 2 a.m. the winds peaked at 45 miles per hour in Key West. Ernest Hemingway watched his boat until about 5 a.m., when the needle on his barometer stabilized. The weary author decided to call it a night and trudged home through the debris-strewn streets as a dreary, windy, rain-soaked dawn gradually materialized.

Hemingway discovered that a few trees had been blown down on his property, but otherwise his home had gone through the storm unharmed. He went back to bed.

As the first light appeared on the Upper Keys Tuesday morning, Ray Sheldon climbed down from locomotive number 447 to look around. What he saw was almost beyond comprehension.

chapter six

A Terrible Sunrise

The feeble, storm-shrouded sunrise Tuesday morning gradually revealed the horrible night's work done by the hurricane. As each layer of darkness peeled away, the awful landscape came clearly into focus.

The eye of the hurricane was now in the Gulf of Mexico as the storm spun its way northward, heading for a second landfall somewhere on the Florida Panhandle. Although the hurricane was weakening, the winds around its center were still blowing at a furious 130 miles per hour Tuesday morning, and the backside of the storm was lashing the Upper Keys with torrential rain and winds exceeding 60 miles per hour.

John Russell had been badly injured, and somehow lost his shoes. Bernard Russell searched through the gloomy dawn until he found two sponges and some twine. He and his uncle Clifton Russell tied the sponges to John Russell's feet. The trio started looking for shelter.

They found the derailed evacuation train with only the locomotive and its tender still upright. The coaches tilted crazily against the denuded brush and rubble left behind by the storm. Pieces of buildings, automobiles, seaweed, and human bodies had been swept beneath the leaning train cars.

But the steel coaches were intact, and they offered shelter from the pouring rain and fierce wind. Bernard Russell and his uncle helped John Russell into one of the baggage cars, and then they climbed in after him.

"We curled back in that for protection, because there was stuff blowing and raining like mad, and that's where we stayed until we could get some help," Bernard Russell said.

While they waited for the storm to subside, they wondered if any of their relatives were still alive.

William Johns, the *Miami Daily News* reporter who'd boarded the train in Homestead, tried to get out of the overturned passenger car where he'd spent the night. But the wind was still blowing so hard he could barely walk. He gave up and climbed back into the wrecked train.

As the dawn materialized, Edney Parker was trying to figure out where he was. He and his family had taken shelter in his brother's house. The storm swept the structure off its foundation and carried it away, and they'd spent the night wondering where the hurricane had taken them. For all they knew, they'd been washed to another island.

"Then it was not very light, but we knew it was day," Parker said. "I crawled out and located a road that ran from the ocean to the bay, and being so familiar with the place, I knew where I was at."

Still, it took a few moments for Parker to get his bearings. The storm had obliterated most of the landmarks. Finally he discovered that the hurricane had torn the house from its foundation and deposited it almost a mile away.

"I went back and told [my] wife we were still on Matecumbe," he said. "We were south of the hotel, about three-quarters of a mile, and I didn't know who was left. I didn't see a sign of a house anywhere, and no trees."

Parker and his wife discussed what they should do. As they talked the wind-driven rain continued to soak them in the ruined, roofless remains of the house. They decided to look for shelter.

Parker gathered his family and walked to the highway. "I realized it was the highway because it was a tar and asphalt road. There was a little piece of Mr. King's filling station left, and Mr. King was in it. We went there and got under shelter, standing in water to our ankles all day."

Parker and his family joined a small group of refugees who'd also taken shelter at King's filling station. Among the group were the veterans' wives who'd been waiting at the Hotel Matecumbe for George

Pepper and Rosalind Grooms Palmer to pick them up. No one had seen Pepper and Palmer since they'd left the hotel with Ben Davis around 4:30 Monday afternoon.

The departing hurricane blew over a scene of stark and total devastation. Buildings had been swept away or reduced to piles of lumber. The normally lush vegetation was gone; only bare, broken branches remained. Instead of leaves, the branches were covered with shreds of clothing. The tattered rags whipped in the wind like pathetic flags of surrender.

The Matecumbe Methodist Church was gone, and so was the Matecumbe School. Only 10 of the school's 65 students were still alive.

Just offshore, about a quarter-mile from the beach, was an astonishing sight—a 3,000-ton Danish freighter hopelessly aground. The ship, the *Leise Maersk*, had been picked up by a giant wave, carried over the reef, and deposited almost on Upper Matecumbe Key. The dazed crew members could see the overturned train from their ship.

The concrete foundation was the only reminder of the small hospital at Camp 1. Soon after daylight, Lassiter Alexander, who had clung to the railroad embankment after the hospital was destroyed, struggled to his feet. His back had been painfully injured when the building collapsed. To his surprise, he saw his car. He managed to walk the 100 feet or so to it, then opened the door, eased himself into the vehicle, and lay down on the backseat.

Corpses were scattered everywhere. They were dangling from palm trees, floating in the surf, entangled in the mangroves. High overhead a corpse clung tenaciously to a telephone pole. The lifeless body of a toddler lay curled on the ground, his head resting on his hands as though he'd lain down to take a nap. An elderly man who died during the storm sat in a chair amid the roofless ruins of his house.

A piano had been slammed into the railroad embankment. The body of a young woman sat next to the piano.

Arms and legs protruded from mounds of debris. A puppy crouched next to one of the piles, gratefully licking a motionless hand.

The hand belonged to George Sherman, the veteran who'd dashed into the deadly brine to rescue the struggling animal. Sherman had been killed later when a large, jagged splinter of wood, propelled by winds far in excess of 160 miles per hour, was driven through his skull.

From some of the piles of rubble came the weak, pitiful calls of helpless survivors hoping to hang on to life until someone found them and dug them out.

Not far from the derailed train stood a battered but intact remnant of the home of Leo Johnson. The storm had deposited a large rowboat between two cypress trees near Johnson's house. The oars were still in their locks, both pushed forward as though the boat was about to land. On the seat next to the oars was a child's teddy bear, looking exactly as though it had rowed the boat through the storm to safety and then, too exhausted to move, slumped against the railing to rest.

The raging winds and water had killed the ex-servicemen in droves. In one place the storm swept the bodies of 39 veterans into a windrow like so much windblown sand.

The flimsy work camps—the veterans' end-of-the-line, edge-of-the-cliff refuge from the economic chaos of the Depression and the emotional turmoil of their own confused lives—were simply gone, blasted to splinters and blown into oblivion. Dozens of veterans had died at each of the camps, but Camp 5—only a couple of feet above sea level, so close to the ocean that normal high tides had sometimes invaded the kitchen—had been turned into a slaughterhouse. Fewer than a dozen men of the 125 or so who'd been in the camp when the storm began were still alive Tuesday morning.

"I would rather face machine-gun fire than go through an experience like that again," said veteran George Senison of Bridgeport, Connecticut, who was at Camp 1.

Long-standing landmarks were obliterated or smashed almost beyond recognition. The post office, which had been a daily gathering place for Islamorada residents, was reduced to only the three porch columns, part of the front wall, and the foundation. The roof and much of the second floor of the Hotel Matecumbe had been sliced off and carried away.

Behind the ruins of the hotel, Fern and Ed Butters and the others who'd taken shelter in the bus looked around them in disbelief.

"The wind shrieked and howled all through the night, and as it abated and daylight came, devastation was all around us," said Fern Butters. "We could hear the screams of neighbors as they searched for loved ones, and they could not find them or they were so badly injured when they did find them."

Ed Butters and some of the other men left the bus to look for survivors. Soon they returned with a dozen and helped them into the vehicle. Some were injured. Butters and the others went into the ruins of the hotel, found a couple of rooms that were still dry and relatively intact, and put the injured there.

Charles Butters tried to provide something for the group to eat. He found an oil stove still in working condition and dragged it into the lobby of the hotel, out of the rain. He set out drinking glasses, pots, bowls, and other containers to catch rainwater and scrounged through the ruins of the hotel for canned food. He lit the stove and soon had a pot of coffee and hot boiled tomatoes for the survivors.

The men brought more survivors, some of them gravely injured. Bertram Pinder appeared and asked Ed Butters if he could borrow a saw. His wife, Elizabeth, who had been sucked into the ruins of their house when the floodwaters suddenly drained off the island, was still alive and would have to be cut out of the wreckage.

Someone took a sheet from the hotel and stuffed one end down into the gasoline tank of Ed Butters's Plymouth and used it to start a fire near the bus.

All that remained of the Caribee Colony was a bathtub—a single plumbing fixture—surrounded by the splintered stumps of palm trees. Nearby was a storm-mangled automobile belonging to Caribee manager Wade Dumas. The car's roof had been torn off and the windshield frame flattened. Both doors were wide open.

There was no trace of Dumas and his wife, Marie.

Other wrecked automobiles were strewn along the road. Some had been pushed into piles of debris or overturned in ditches. One car had been left resting on its rear bumper, its radiator pointing skyward.

The railroad track was impassable. About 40 miles of track between Tavernier and Marathon had been destroyed. In some places the wind and storm surge had lifted one side of the crossties and tracks upright so that they looked like a big picket fence. The concrete railroad bridges and viaducts had easily withstood the hurricane, but tracks that were 30 feet above normal high tide had been ripped off the bridges and carried away by the storm surge.

Even the ground beneath the survivors' feet was unrecognizable. In some places the scouring force of the storm surge had scrubbed off the thin layer of topsoil, exposing the islands' coral foundation.

Survivors desperately clawed and tugged at piles of rubble searching for missing family members, or wandered aimlessly through the ruins, too stunned to comprehend what had happened to them. Some of the wanderers were so dazed they didn't realize that the hurricane had torn every stitch of clothing from their bodies.

Nearly everyone who was still alive had injuries of some type. Most had had their ears and the backs of their necks scrubbed raw by windblown sand. Others who spent the night climbing up and down telephone poles to stay above the flood or clinging to lumber floating on the raucous seas had splinters painfully imbedded in their arms, legs, and torsos.

A veteran too seriously injured to walk sat helplessly in the driving rain, leaning against the foundation of a ruined house and pleading for help.

Near Snake Creek a group of veterans huddled behind a railroad tanker car. Somehow they got a fire going and made coffee.

At Lower Matecumbe Key, Fritz Maggesen surveyed the damage to the *Rowena*. The roof had been torn from the houseboat's cabin, and a timber ripped from the wreckage of Camp 3 had been driven through the *Rowena's* hull and into the engine room. And there wasn't a square inch of paint left on the vessel. The hurricane's winds had sandblasted the boat clean. But with the timber removed from the hull and the hole patchd, the *Rowena* would be seaworthy enough to make it to Mami for major repairs—as soon as the seas quieted down. Maggesen checked his lines again and settled down to wait.

Aboard the *Sarasota*, Ed Sheeran was sizing up the situation. He knew that dozens of veterans had been killed, and many more probably had been injured. He took no satisfaction from the fact that he'd tried to warn the people in charge that this would happen if those men were left on the islands.

But the men under his care were safe. Most of them had left the Keys when he told them to. Those who stayed had taken shelter and survived. Some of his construction equipment had been damaged, but thanks to his preparations the damage was repairable, and for the most part the $400,000 worth of equipment he was responsible for was OK. Once again, Ed Sheeran had outfoxed the raging elements.

In Islamorada a dazed Ray Sheldon and six other survivors began walking north. They trudged through a bizarre landscape of destruction that held no resemblance to what had been there before the storm. They got as far as Snake Creek. Both the highway and railroad bridges were gone, and Snake Creek was a swollen, raging torrent as the backside of the departing hurricane now pushed water from Florida Bay back into the Atlantic. With the bridges destroyed and the railroad impassable, those who were still alive from Snake Creek south to Lower Matecumbe Key were completely cut off from the rest of the world.

Sheldon and his group returned to the ruins of the Hotel Matecumbe to wait for help. There was nothing else they could do.

The outside world had no idea of what had happened in the Keys. Tuesday's newspapers published front-page stories about the plight of the *Dixie* and fretted about whether the ship would be pounded to pieces before its passengers and crew could be rescued.

"Fate of 800 Veterans on Matecumbe [Is] Mystery; Train Is Trapped," read the *Miami Daily News* headlines of Tuesday afternoon.

Aboard the *Dixie,* passengers were seeing daylight for the first time in what seemed like ages. Florence Steiler ventured onto the ship's main deck early Tuesday afternoon. She was amazed at the damage.

"The devastation was almost incredible," Steiler said. "Furniture was broken and piled up in heaps. Windows smashed, three lifeboats torn off, the galley and dining rooms complete wrecks."

With the galley a shambles, the ship's cooks couldn't prepare hot meals. But the crew still tried to reassure the passengers as best they could, and plenty of food—even if it was sandwiches, soda crackers, and fruit—was one way to do it. Everyone got all they wanted to eat. With the deck furniture swept away or smashed to bits, a few passengers simply sat down on the deck, leaned against the ship's superstructure, and sipped soft drinks as they watched the heaving ocean.

No one outside the Keys—not even the weather bureau—had the foggiest idea how powerful this hurricane had been. Weather bureau officials told the Associated Press that the storm "can not be compared with the great hurricanes of 1926 and 1928. The hurricane area is much smaller and the winds are of far less velocity."

The weather bureau's description of the hurricane was comically inaccurate. The two earlier storms were indeed very bad—the 1926 hurricane nearly wiped out Miami Beach, and the 1928 storm pushed Lake Okeechobee out of its banks and killed almost 2,000. But meteorologists would soon determine that the storm that had just swept through the Keys was the most powerful hurricane ever to strike the United States.

Even the Conchs, who had weathered many violent storms, were astonished by the unearthly intensity of this hurricane.

"Nobody expected what we had," said Edney Parker. "Nobody seemed to have any expectation of what we were going to have. We were prepared only for gales."

The murderous storm surge and the railroad causeways that piled up the water on the islands were responsible for the death toll, he said.

"I think the railroad officials, the weatherman, the camp officials, and all the natives were fooled, and fooled bad," Parker said. "I don't think they knew what was going to happen. We never dreamed anything was going to happen such as that." It would be a full day before the rest of the world learned what had happened to a 40-mile stretch along the remote Keys.

At Long Key, James Duane, Jr., and his band of storm survivors crawled out of the wreckage of the fishing camp and looked around at the chaos. A couple of the buildings had stayed more or less intact, but the hurricane had shoved them around like toys in a child's sandbox. The rest of the cottages, the hotel, and the boardwalks had been chewed up and tossed into a wild tangle of lumber, coconut palm trees, and seaweed. The railroad track had been ripped from its bed and haphazardly woven into the jumble of wreckage.

But, unbelievably, no one at Long Key had been killed or even seriously injured. The group took shelter in the surviving cottages to rest and wait for the rains and winds to subside.

Out near French Reef off Key Largo, ships were braving the still-ferocious ocean to come to the aid of the *Dixie*. The passenger-carrying freighter S.S. *Platano* was among the first to reach the grounded passenger liner. The *Platano* had been en route from Cortez, Honduras, to New York when the ship picked up the *Dixie*'s SOS signal. Without hesitation, Capt. C. D. McRea had sent his vessel charging through the storm-tossed seas at full speed when he picked up the distress call.

The *Platano* reached the *Dixie*'s reported position on Carysfort Reef Tuesday afternoon, but the liner was nowhere in sight. Had the ship been pounded to pieces by the storm? McRea hoped *Dixie* captain Einar Sundstrom had been wrong about where his ship had grounded. He ordered his freighter to come in dangerously close to the reef-lined shore and search for the passenger ship. His hunch paid off. He spotted the *Dixie* on French Reef.

W. H. Depperman, a passenger aboard the *Platano* could make out the stranded ship "through squalls of rain and mist from moun-tainous waves." The *Dixie* was visible "intermittently...about three miles off our starboard bow."

Three other vessels eventually arrived to aid the *Dixie*—the *Limon*, the *Gatun,* and the *El Occidente*. They dropped anchor to wait for the seas to subside so they could begin taking passengers off the *Dixie*.

Aboard the stranded passenger liner, there was nothing for the weary, relieved passengers to do but try to find a quiet, dry spot to settle down and wait to be rescued. Their fears of being dumped into a raging ocean were gone, but they'd still have to endure discomforts until they could get off the ship.

On the Keys the survivors scrounged for food, clothing, anything they could find to make themselves even a little more comfortable. A group of survivors talked about their experiences during the awful evening as they stood around a fire next to the FEC locomotive at Islamorada.

Down at Camp 3, Elmer Kreitzburg, who'd been impaled by a board when the mess hall was destroyed, had clung to life for almost 24 hours with the two-by-four still protruding from his body. But he became steadily weaker. Around 6 p.m. Tuesday he died.

As darkness fell Tuesday, some of the survivors gathered at the ruins of the Hotel Matecumbe. Ray Sheldon, tired and dazed, was among them. He spent the night at the bedside of 18-year-old William Baker, who had been seriously injured in the storm.

At Lower Matecumbe Key, Ed Sheeran's decision not to unload the railroad tanker containing 10,000 gallons of fresh water had proved to be a lifesaver. The heavy car had withstood the backwash of the Atlantic Ocean as it swept over the island and saved the lives of dozens of men who managed to hang on to it, and later it provided a source of drinking water when everything else had been destroyed.

179

Sheeran was exhausted. He had been wearing the same clothes for three days. "I was about whipped," he said. "I didn't have a thing left."

The following day, Sheeran's boss, B. M. Duncan, ordered him to go home to Coral Gables. "I had to borrow a shirt to come home in," Sheeran said.

Early Wednesday morning, William Johns climbed out of the wrecked train and walked down to the Hotel Matecumbe. The *Miami Daily News* reporter found Sheldon, and the two talked as they walked along the highway. Johns asked Sheldon why the veterans hadn't been evacuated from the Keys before the hurricane struck.

"He told me that he had been in touch with Washington, trying to get permission from Washington to move those veterans, and he was instructed to stay there to await further developments," Johns said. "Now, the man had gone through an awful lot. Maybe he was excited, and maybe it [wasn't] the truth." Johns did something very unusual for a newspaper reporter—he didn't include Sheldon's quote in a story he wrote later about his experience in the hurricane.

"I'll tell you the reason I never wrote that in my story," Johns said. "I believed at the time when Sheldon told me that, that he was possibly mistaken.....He was worried, and scared, and trying to do the best he could down there. But he actually did say that to me."

In the coming months, Ray Sheldon would be repeatedly answering the same question that Johns had just asked him.

chapter seven

Just a Catastrophe

At daybreak on Tuesday, September 3, Fred Ghent left Homestead with a small crew of Florida ERA workers and headed south into the Keys. He still had heard nothing about the train sent to evacuate the veterans.

The road into the islands was a battered pathway across a vast lake. Mangled tufts of palm trees, mangroves, and other vegetation protruded from the water, their tops looking as though a grazing sea monster had chewed them off.

Ghent had to stop a few miles south of Tavernier, where downed trees blocked the way. He left his work crew to clear the road and drove back to Homestead, where he dispatched a quick report to his superiors giving his impressions of what he'd seen and started rounding up help to send to the Keys.

Ghent also talked briefly to a reporter for the *Miami Daily News*. The afternoon newspaper was preparing stories about the hurricane for that day's edition. Ghent sidestepped the reporter's question about what had happened to the veterans waiting to be evacuated, saying he "would rather not express an opinion."

Others were realizing, however, that something was very wrong in the Florida Keys.

A few minutes past 7 a.m., Roy Hurley, a veteran from Sandusky, Ohio, boarded the FEC train in Miami to return to Camp 1. As he entered the passenger coach, he spotted two women he'd met a few days earlier—a nurse and a hairdresser, both from Key West.

Hurley sat down and immediately struck up a conversation with them. They'd chatted for a few minutes when the conductor stepped into the coach and called for the passengers' attention. As heads turned his way, the conductor announced that the morning train to Key West was suspended indefinitely because several sections of track in the islands had been washed out by the hurricane.

"That was the first actual news that told me that there was something wrong down there," Hurley said. "Of course, I [suspected] it right along."

The hurricane had lost some of its punch after inflicting the savage beating to the Keys, but it was still a very powerful and dangerous storm. By Tuesday morning the eye had crossed Florida Bay, brushed Cape Sable at the tip of the Florida peninsula, and was moving northwest. It had expanded some—an indication that it was weakening—but its strongest winds around the eye were still blowing at better than 130 miles per hour.

Although the eye was well offshore in the Gulf of Mexico, the fringes of the hurricane were raking Florida's west coast with strong winds and heavy rainfall. And even though it was weakening, it managed to take the life of one more veteran. Edward Kettner, a 58-year-old bus driver who'd served in the U.S. Navy during the Spanish-American War and World War I, was driving across the state from West Palm Beach to Fort Myers. Near the small town of LaBelle, Kettner lost control of his empty bus in the blinding rainfall. The bus veered off the road and overturned, throwing Kettner from the vehicle. A passing motorist found his body lying by the roadside.

Coast Guard commanders wanted very badly to get search-and-rescue planes aloft to assess the damage to the Keys and help survivors, but winds were still gusting at 50 miles per hour or better at the air station on Dinner Key, and all planes were grounded. High seas prevented cutters from coming to the aid of the *Dixie*.

Roy Hurley and the women from Key West left the train depot and walked to a nearby filling station, where they met a young man who was filling up his car with gasoline to drive down to the Keys. He agreed to give them a lift, and the four headed south into the islands.

The evidence of the hurricane's handiwork became steadily more dramatic as they drove deeper into the Keys.

"It seemed as though every house in Tavernier was blown in one spot," Hurley said. "They weren't smashed up so much, they were lifted bodily."

There was more gruesome evidence as well.

"I saw three bodies up alongside of the railroad tracks, and one on the railroad track," he said.

Hurley realized that he recognized the people who'd been killed. Two of the victims were a married couple who ran a saloon, and another was a man he knew as Harry who worked at the hospital at Camp 1. The bodies were already starting to decompose.

In Miami, Elizabeth Bradford had been worried sick about her husband since the phone line went dead Monday night. After spending an awful night of uncertainty, she was determined to get back to Lower Matecumbe Key and find Cardy Bradford.

She called Pan American and other airlines trying to charter a plane to fly down to the islands. They all refused. No one was willing to challenge the powerful and freakish winds of the departing hurricane.

Finally someone told her a pilot named Charles Collar might be willing to make a flight to the Keys. Bradford dashed to the Miami airport, catching Collar as he was about to leave after checking to see how his amphibious airplane had weathered the storm.

Bradford begged Collar to fly her to Lower Matecumbe, but he refused. She didn't give up, however, and finally the pilot relented.

Collar had second thoughts as he tried to get airborne, however. The winds whipping across the airport shoved his airplane around and nearly caused him to crash.

Collar coaxed his plane higher until he'd gained enough altitude for the flight. He turned the nose of the amphibian toward the Keys.

By mid-afternoon, Roy Hurley and his three companions had reached the north bank of Snake Creek. That was as far as they could go. The highway and railroad bridges linking Plantation Key to Windley

Key were gone. Hurley walked to the edge of the creek, which was now a racing torrent well out of its normal channel. He joined a group of people gazing helplessly toward the opposite shore, where two men were trying to communicate to them with shouts and gestures.

"I tried to talk to two men across the gap, but the wind was blowing pretty hard and you couldn't hear what they were saying," Hurley said. "So by signs they told us they had counted 78 dead, and 30 that had broken legs and arms."

Among those who stood on the north side of Snake Creek was Fred Ghent, who had driven back down from Homestead after preparing his report and talking to the *Miami Daily News*. Eugene Lowkis, a veteran from Brooklyn who had been in Miami during the holiday weekend, happened to be standing next to Ghent when someone asked him if many of the veterans in Camp 1 had been killed.

Lowkis heard Ghent respond, "I don't think so."

Ghent shouted and waved to the two men on the opposite bank, then returned to his car and headed back toward Homestead.

At about the same time Ghent was leaving the Keys, a rescue party led by Homestead Mayor Preston Bird rolled out of the town. But it was slow going over the debris-strewn road, and it would be dusk before the group reached Snake Creek.

When the Homestead group arrived, 25-year-old Henry Day, a strong swimmer, tied a rope to his waist and plunged into the water. He got about halfway across the racing creek and paused to rest on one of the abutments that had supported a bridge. Before he could continue, two men sculled past him in a small rowboat they'd found and fished out of the creek. More Homestead rescuers arrived with small boats and outboard motors, and soon the little craft were chugging back and forth across Snake Creek.

The first rescue boat brought six-year-old Dorothy Van Ness across. She and her family had sought shelter in the ill-fated hospital at Camp 1. The child's face and legs were cut and scratched from her ordeal. Someone asked her where her father was.

"Papa is gone," she answered. "My big brother is gone, too. So is Katherine, and so is Gene. All are gone except me and Mama."

Laura Van Ness arrived in another boat a few moments later. The child ran to her mother, who burst into tears as she embraced her daughter.

The girl's sad tale was a story that would be repeated many times in the coming days. Entire families had been wiped out. A few, however, were lucky.

J. R. Beckham, the fisherman who spent Monday night crawling from tree stump to tree stump searching for his wife and grandchildren, crossed Snake Creek in a small rescue boat and climbed aboard a truckload of refugees bound for Homestead. When he arrived, he saw another truck with more refugees. He waved for it to stop, ran up to it, and peered inside anxiously. He was delighted by what he saw.

"There were my wife and two grandchildren," he said. "My wife was unhurt, and the two children only slightly injured. God was certainly good to us."

Miami Daily News reporter William Johns was among the survivors ferried across Snake Creek late Tuesday. Johns then caught a ride back to Homestead, where he wrote a dramatic first-person story about his experience aboard the ill-fated evacuation train.

Reporters and photographers from Miami's other two dailies, the *Herald* and the *Daily Tribune*, were pushing through the wreckage of the Keys for stories and photos. One of the *Herald* newsmen was veteran cop reporter Henry Reno. In a few years, Reno and his wife, Jane, would become the parents of a baby girl named Janet, who would become the nation's first female attorney general.

Above the islands, Elizabeth Bradford and Charles Collar were peering intently down at the Keys looking for something familiar. But the winds had ripped away landmarks, and the floodwater distorted and concealed so much of the islands that they had no idea which one was Lower Matecumbe.

As the sunlight faded, Collar told Bradford that he'd have to land somewhere for the night. They finally recognized Snake Creek, and Collar put his amphibian down there.

At Dinner Key, the Coast Guard was preparing for an all-out rescue effort as soon as weather conditions permitted. Ground crews cleared storm debris away from hangars and got two seaplanes ready to take off at daybreak Wednesday. A crew also loaded radio truck number 1455 with equipment—spare parts, medical supplies, a small boat, an outboard motor, and rifles and side arms. By 10 p.m. Tuesday the seas had calmed enough to allow three Coast Guard boats loaded with food and supplies to cast off from Fort Lauderdale and head for the Keys.

In Key West, Monroe County Sheriff Karl Thompson met with Major William Albury, commander of the 2nd Battalion, 265th Coastal Artillery of the Florida National Guard. Thompson asked Albury to assemble his troops and take them to the hurricane-devastated Upper Keys as quickly as possible.

By Tuesday night Homestead was swamped with hurricane survivors. The Sunday school building of the First Baptist Church of Homestead was converted into an emergency hospital and refugee shelter. Residents took more hurricane refugees into their homes.

As the survivors found refuge in Homestead, Fred Ghent talked by telephone with an Associated Press reporter. His description and interpretation of what he'd seen and heard earlier on the northern bank of Snake Creek was quite different from the impressions of Roy Hurley and others who'd witnessed the same thing. Ghent told the reporter that the two veterans standing on the southern bank of the creek "did not appear to be greatly perturbed and gave no signals that he interpreted as meaning any men had been killed."

Ghent also told the AP that he didn't think there had been "any great loss of life" at Camp 1.

The Coast Guard truck and its crew of six reached the northern bank of Snake Creek about 2:30 Wednesday morning. An hour later, National Guard troops from Key West landed at Lower Matecumbe Key. The rescuers had their work cut out for them.

As the sun came up Wednesday, Coast Guard lieutenants Carl Olsen and William Clemmer were at the controls of their big amphibious airplanes. Olsen took off first. As soon as his Douglas Dolphin was airborne, Clemmer gunned his engines and the PJ-2 bounced across Biscayne Bay and lifted off.

Olsen swung his plane southward to search around the Keys. Clemmer turned westward to have a look around Cape Sable.

At 5:55 a.m. the radio crackled at the Coast Guard air station at Dinner Key. It was Olsen, who was looking down at the devastation between Tavernier and Grassy Key. The pilot reported that he saw "a scene of utter desolation, not more than three houses remaining upright."

The veterans camps simply didn't exist any more. The only way Olsen could even tell where the camps had been was from "a few pieces of lumber hanging in the mangrove trees."

And at last the fate of the evacuation train was revealed. Olsen told an astonished radio operator at the air base that something had shoved the train off the tracks at Islamorada, leaving only the locomotive upright.

As Olsen reported his grim findings, Bernard and Clifton Russell climbed out of the overturned train car where they'd spent Tuesday night and looked around in disbelief. The Keys were bathed in a typically gorgeous sunrise, but the day's beautiful beginning was a cruel contrast to the scene illuminated by the rising sun.

Daybreak brought with it the steamy, stifling heat that always follows a hurricane. Hundreds of corpses were strewn for miles along the islands. The humid heat was already accelerating the decomposition process, and the breezes off the ocean now carried the pungent and unmistakable odor of death.

The stench summoned blowflies—big, green, buzzing insects—that start the next stage of decomposition. The wind fanned the fumes of death up and down the Keys.

As the sun sparkled on the perfectly calm turquoise waters of the Atlantic Ocean, Bernard and Clifton Russell joined other survivors shuffling numbly through the nightmarish landscape of storm wreckage, swelling corpses, and buzzing flies, searching for friends and family members. They found a relative who'd been pinned in the top of a palm tree by a heavy timber, injured but alive.

But Bernard Russell also discovered two small legs protruding from a pile of debris. He pulled away some of the rubble and discovered the body of a three-year-old cousin. He marked the spot and walked away. On Monday morning more than 60 members of his extended family lived in and around Islamorada. Two days later his family and his home had been swept away in the blink of an eye. It was too much to comprehend.

Bernard and his uncle helped the injured John Russell out of the overturned train. They tied him to a board for stability and laid the board across the bed of a pickup truck. The truck wouldn't start, so, with the help of other survivors, they began pushing it northward, joining a stream of storm survivors walking toward Snake Creek.

Soon, Bernard, John, and Clifton Russell would learn that only eight other members of their family were still alive.

More people continued to arrive to search for friends and relatives, clear the wreckage, or simply gawk at the carnage. Members of a CCC company from Miami started building a temporary footbridge across Snake Creek while National Guard troops from Miami and West Palm Beach set up a roadblock at Tavernier to keep out sightseers who were already clogging the road between Florida City and Key Largo.

Two people who got through the roadblock were Herbert Harper—who was Elizabeth Bradford's brother-in-law—and Gifford Bunnell, a friend of the Bradfords'. When they met Elizabeth Bradford and Charles Collar at Snake Creek, the four climbed into Collar's plane to resume their search for Cardy Bradford.

They found him, alive and unhurt, amid the ruins of Camp 3. When the roof came off their café, Bradford and a veteran had taken shelter in an automobile parked nearby. The hurricane had picked up a corrugated tin garage and dropped it over the car, where it stayed for the rest of the storm and shielded Bradford and the veteran.

On the morning of Wednesday, September 4, the rest of the world was getting its first look at the horror on the Upper Keys. Miami newspapers published stories of the death and destruction, accompanied by full-page photo spreads.

One of the most haunting pictures was a *Miami Herald* portrait of eight-year-old Robert Adams of Plantation Key, who spent Monday night clinging to the railroad track near his home. Friends who found the terrified boy Tuesday had to pry his hands loose from the track. They took him to their damaged home and began massaging his hands. In the *Herald* photo, the boy's sunken eyes are wide with terror as he stares intently into the distance.

The news of the tragedy also had started the nation's major newsreel producers rushing to Florida. Newsreel cameramen descended on the Coast Guard air station demanding to be flown to the Keys to shoot footage.

Lieutenant Olsen said he could take only one photographer and told the others to choose one from among their group. A cameraman named Lyons from Universal Pictures was chosen, and he agreed to share his footage with the companies who'd sent cameramen to the air station.

Down at Long Key, James Duane and the other survivors started walking south along the ruined tracks of the Florida East Coast Railway. Duane hoped to meet a repair train dispatched from Key West to check the condition of the tracks—unless the tracks had been destroyed for the entire length of the line. He had no way of knowing how far down the Keys the hurricane damage extended.

In Washington, Roosevelt Administration officials were getting the first inkling of what had happened in the work camps. By nightfall Wednesday in a soggy Washington, where a steady rain had been falling for two days, they would be scrambling to head off what could easily become a public relations fiasco for the President and his men.

The day began with wildly varying estimates in newspapers about the death toll in the Keys.

The *Miami Herald* cautiously reported that 25 to 100 were dead, but added that the newspaper had received "widely conflicting reports" about the death toll. The *Miami Daily News* published a list of about 30 people thought to be dead or missing. The Miami Beach *Daily Tribune* saw no reason to be cautious about estimating the number of victims, however. The emerging picture of what had happened in the Keys was so awful that even *Trib* editor Paul Jeans would have difficulty exaggerating it.

Still, he would try.

"Death Toll on Keys Over 700," the *Tribune* headline screamed to its readers Wednesday morning.

The *Tribune* also eagerly—almost gleefully—pointed an editorial finger at a scapegoat to blame for the exaggerated death toll it was reporting. The *Trib*'s lead editorial said the U.S. Weather Bureau was responsible for the loss of "nearly a thousand lives" because it hadn't accurately reported the hurricane's position or correctly predicted its track in the Straits of Florida.

An editorial cartoon showing a blindfolded weatherman pointing to a map of Florida and chanting "Eeny-meeny-miney-moe" accompanied the opinion piece. The cartoon was titled "Where, oh, where, has my hurricane gone?"

Citing the American Red Cross as its source, the *Washington Post*'s lead story said 100 were dead, but did not distinguish between veterans and residents. But Coast Guard reports—including Lieutenant Carl Olsen's description of dozens of bodies floating in the surf and entangled in the mangroves at Camp 5—were beginning to reach officials in Jacksonville and Washington, and it was becoming clear that conditions in the Keys were far grimmer than the newspapers were reporting.

Soon after copies of Wednesday morning's *Post* landed on doorsteps in the District of Columbia, George Andrews, a Federal

Emergency Relief Administration engineer in Washington, took a phone call from R. G. Unkrich, assistant administrator of the Florida Emergency Relief Administration in Jacksonville. "We have possibly 300 men lost," he told Andrews.

Unkrich's grim report started the telephone lines buzzing between Florida and the District of Columbia. That afternoon, Marvin Porter, a Florida ERA engineer who'd rushed to Miami to supervise rescue operations in the Keys, talked briefly with George Andrews.

"It looks bad," Porter warned Andrews.

Andrews told Porter that Charles Forbes, a public relations specialist, had been dispatched to Florida and would arrive there the following afternoon. He then transferred Porter's call to Col. Lawrence Westbrook, assistant director of FERA.

"What is the number of the known or estimated dead?" Westbrook asked.

"There are 300 estimated dead," Porter answered tersely. "That's the best we can do on that."

"Our people alone?" Westbrook asked incredulously.

"Our people," Porter said.

Meanwhile, Steve Early, one of FDR's secretaries who'd made the trip to Hyde Park, New York, with the President after Congress adjourned, was talking with Marvin McIntyre, another Roosevelt secretary, and Gen. Frank Hines, director of the Veterans Administration. Knowing that the hurricane had hit the Keys, they assumed some of the men in the work camps had been injured and perhaps even a few had been killed. After the three laid out plans to care for the injured and bury the dead, McIntyre called Westbrook.

"I've been talking to Mr. Early and General Hines," McIntyre said. "The general has instructions from the President with regard to the veterans in the camps down there, about taking care of the injured and arranging about funeral services and all that. You don't mind, do you?"

"No, not at all," Westbrook said, adding that he'd just gotten an estimate of the death toll from Marvin Porter in Florida. "He said he believed 300, at least, were lost. Another hundred were injured, the remainder surviving. They are evacuating those people rapidly."

McIntyre was stunned.

"My God!" he exclaimed. Regaining his composure, he asked the question that would echo for months through the halls of power in Washington.

"Between us, Colonel," McIntyre said. "There is no blame that can be attached to the administration or to your office, is there?"

"No," Westbrook said. "It is just a catastrophe."

"Nobody suggested that there was any undue risk, or anything?" McIntyre asked anxiously.

"No," Westbrook said.

But Westbrook was wrong. A furious flurry of accusations was already erupting, and some of the accusers were pointing at Roosevelt and his aides. At about the same time that Westbrook and McIntyre were concluding that federal officials couldn't be blamed for the veterans' deaths, U.S. Representative J. Hardin Peterson, a Democrat from Florida, was demanding some answers.

Peterson had returned to his home in Lakeland after the long session of Congress ended. He was in Lakeland when rescuers learned of the huge death toll in the work camps.

Peterson discussed the aftermath of the hurricane with Arthur Boring, who lived in nearby Plant City and was commander of Florida's American Legion posts. Both men were incensed that the veterans had been left in the path of the storm. Peterson fired off an angry telegram to WPA director Harry Hopkins demanding to know why the veterans were not evacuated from the Keys before the storm struck. "They had plenty of notice, and I want to fix the responsibility," he said.

In the Keys, Lt. William Clemmer of the Coast Guard was following the hurricane's path of devastation across Florida Bay and Cape Sable searching for people who needed help.

The cape, at the tip of the Florida peninsula, had been scrubbed bare of buildings and vegetation. Near the tiny bayside settlement of Flamingo, Clemmer spotted about two dozen survivors clinging to the wreckage of a houseboat. The Coast Guard pilot carefully set his seaplane down in the shallow, debris-strewn water.

Three were badly hurt and needed medical attention as quickly as possible. Promising to return, Clemmer and his crew loaded the three injured survivors aboard the PJ-2 and flew them to Snake Creek, which had become the staging area for rescue operations.

Clemmer took off again, but he'd scarcely gotten airborne before he was setting the amphibian back down on Florida Bay, this time in about a foot and a half of water. He'd spotted more survivors at Upper Matecumbe Key.

Clemmer and a crewman waded ashore to size up the situation. Sixteen people needed help immediately. One was barely alive, and others undoubtedly would die soon if they didn't get medical aid. Clemmer knew his PJ-2 was designed to carry a maximum of 12 passengers, but he realized that making two trips wasn't an option because some of these people wouldn't be alive when he returned. He decided he had no choice but to cram all 16 survivors into his plane and get it into the air somehow.

The seaplane sank lower and lower as the injured were helped aboard. Then the crewmen closed the hatches. Clemmer gunned the engines, and the PJ-2 began slogging heavily through the water, struggling to pull itself into the air. Clemmer winced as he felt the overloaded plane sliding along on the muddy bottom of Florida Bay. If the amphibian struck a piece of coral or submerged debris, it would rip the bottom out of the hull. But finally, to his relief, he felt the seaplane lift itself free of the grasping mud and water. He was airborne.

Clemmer decided his passengers' injuries were too serious to be handled by first aid workers at Snake Creek. He turned the amphibian northeast toward the Coast Guard air station at Dinner Key.

Although the eye of the hurricane was now many miles away, the storm's backside winds were still kicking up choppy seas in Biscayne Bay. Clemmer carefully settled the PJ-2 and its bulging cargo of humanity into the bouncing water and glided to a stop. The water was too rough for him to taxi the airplane up the seaplane ramp and into the Coast Guard hangar. The hurricane victims were loaded onto a small motor launch, taken ashore, and transported to hospitals.

But Clemmer wasn't finished. He'd promised to return to the wrecked houseboat near Flamingo. As soon as his airplane was refueled, he was in the air headed back to Cape Sable. This time he loaded 10 more injured survivors aboard the PJ-2. In the fading light Clemmer brought the amphibian in for one more landing on Biscayne Bay. It had been a busy day for the Coast Guard pilot and his crew. They had plucked 29 lives from the ruins of the hurricane.

Clemmer and Olsen weren't alone in the skies over the Keys Wednesday. A Pan American chartered plane carrying a correspondent for the *Chicago Daily Tribune* flew low over the islands. Col. Robert McCormick, the *Tribune* publisher and President Roosevelt's old nemesis, was sharpening his sword for an attack on FDR and his New Deal programs.

While *Tribune* correspondent Spearman Lewis peered down at the devastation on the Keys, Ernest Hemingway and two friends, Bra Saunders and Sully Sullivan, loaded food and other supplies onto the *Pilar* in Key West and headed the boat northward to pitch in with the relief effort for the Upper Keys.

Hemingway was astonished by what he found as he approached Lower Matecumbe Key.

"The foliage absolutely stripped as though by fire for forty miles and the land looking like the abandoned bed of a river," he later wrote. "Not a building of any sort standing."

Hemingway and his companions counted 69 corpses in the waters around Lower Matecumbe. The appalling body count reminded him of his days as an ambulance driver in France during the war.

When the author arrived at what had been the ferry slip at Lower

Matecumbe, he saw two corpses that he recognized—the bodies of two women who ran a filling station and sold sandwiches near the ferry landing. But it took him a few moments to realize who they were. Their bodies had already become swollen and grotesque and covered with blowflies.

Hemingway was amazed at the power of the hurricane.

"Indian Key absolutely swept clean, not a blade of grass, and over the high center of it were scattered live conchs that came in with the sea, craw fish, and dead morays," he wrote. "The whole bottom of the sea blew over it."

The author was infuriated by the deaths of the veterans. "The veterans in those camps were practically murdered," he said.

By Wednesday afternoon word reached Fern and Ed Butters that help had arrived at Snake Creek.

"We were all in a state of shock, I think, and we started the five-mile trek to Snake Creek where a boat was waiting to take us across," Fern Butters said.

Her husband limped along, his foot sore and swollen from the nail he'd stepped on during the storm, and Fern Butters struggled to walk on a badly sprained ankle.

"When we reached the place where the boat was waiting, we had walked by the bodies of the dead and had recognized many," she said. "At the embankment there was a pile of bodies stacked up with a piece of canvas over them, but all of their feet were exposed, and so many were children's feet, that finally it was just too much for me. The last thing I remembered was falling toward the embankment. Someone must have caught me, for when I came to, we were in the boat being taken across [Snake Creek]."

Ed and Fern Butters were treated at a first aid station in Tavernier, and then taken by ambulance to Miami.

"A wilder ride I have never taken," Fern Butters said. "I guess we all looked in such terrible shape that they thought we should be gotten there in a hurry. I was not aware of it, but my face looked like a minute steak after it had been run through one of those mincers."

The ambulance took Fern and Ed Butters to a Red Cross station in the Everglades Hotel. As they sat in the lobby, a woman who knew Fern walked through calling her name.

"She failed to recognize me when I rose from my chair," Fern said. "She looked astonished. I was still not aware of the way I looked—face beaten by the wind and sand for two days and a night, a speckled tweed skirt and maroon turtleneck sweater, my whole body raw and sore from the wet clothes, wind, and rain. I neither laughed nor cried when I saw myself in the mirror. I guess I was still in a state of shock."

Miami hospitals were filling up with other hurricane victims. Red Cross physician William DeKlein reported that 57 survivors were being treated for "major" injuries that included serious wounds, fractures, and illnesses caused by prolonged submersion in water. At least two of the survivors had been paralyzed by broken backs.

Others were suffering from simple shock and exhaustion. At Jackson Memorial Hospital a young woman sat in a wheelchair trying to pull her skirt down far enough to conceal her muddy ankles. She'd been visiting in Islamorada when the hurricane struck. A reporter from the *Miami Daily News* asked her to talk about what had happened to her during the storm.

"I thought it was the most beautiful place I ever saw—Islamorada," she said. "I came down from Brooklyn, and the sea was so pretty and blue. And then suddenly Monday night it was sort of a hell turned inside out. The sea was gray and muddy and the wind was like something solid that moved over the land and knocked things down."

Around 3 p.m. Wednesday, rescue workers from Homestead reached Lower Matecumbe Key. Among those who arrived at the ruins of Camp 3 was Father Alfred McDonald, a Catholic priest who had once pleaded with the veterans to attend his masses. The first thing the priest did was administer the sacrament of last rites to seven dying veterans. Not long after that, officials in

Miami received orders for 240 plain pine boxes in which to bury the storm victims.

By 2 p.m. Wednesday the seas had finally settled enough to allow passengers to be taken off the *Dixie*. Still, it was a hair-raising experience—sizable swells were still rolling across the Straits of Florida.

The passengers put on life jackets, and *Dixie* crew members carefully helped them climb down a rope ladder and into a waiting lifeboat. The crewmen called encouragement as the lifeboats were filled. "Don't drop this sweetheart!" a crewman called as he helped a child down the ladder. A nimble young man impressed the crew as he quickly descended. "Hey, here comes an athlete," someone said.

When Florence Steiler's turn came, she carefully picked her way down the ladder and gratefully sat down on a lifeboat seat. Her ordeal was almost over.

A small motorboat took Steiler's lifeboat in tow. "The ride over was like having a continuous trip on a roller coaster," Steiler said.

The motorboat towed Steiler's lifeboat to the S.S. *Atenas*, one of the ships waiting to take on passengers from the *Dixie*. Steiler faced the difficult task of climbing up a rope ladder while wearing the bulky lifejacket. When she reached the top, *Atenas* crewmen pulled her aboard.

Steiler was greeted by a ship's stewardess, who hugged her and asked, "What can I do for you?"

"Honey," Steiler answered, "just give me a bath."

In the Gulf of Mexico the hurricane continued churning northward. The winds ahead of the storm's eye pushed much of the water out of Tampa Bay, then the winds to the south of the eye shoved the water back with such force that Tampa's seawall along Bayshore Boulevard was six feet underwater Wednesday and neighborhoods near the bay were flooded. The relentless battering of storm-driven waves finally caused the seawall to collapse.

Added to the seawater flowing in the streets near the bay was more than five inches of rain that fell on Tampa and St. Petersburg between Tuesday afternoon and Wednesday afternoon. The winds also peeled the roof off the U.S. post office in Tampa's Ybor City neighborhood.

In Cedar Key, a small island hamlet north of Tampa Bay, most of the town's 1,200 residents took shelter in schools and other larger buildings as the storm approached Wednesday afternoon. As the hurricane came ashore for the second time in less than 48 hours, W. M. Pepper, Jr., editor of the *Gainesville Daily Sun*, parked his car in the center of the little town's business district.

The heft of the storm was still strong enough to land a punishing blow. At 3 p.m., Pepper watched the rising, windblown waters of the Gulf of Mexico invade the streets of Cedar Key. "Up, up, that water is coming, the top layer vanishing into salt spray," he wrote. "What will go next? There, to the left, goes a roof. The car is swaying badly now....The car feels like it is going to fly."

Knee-deep salt water soon rushed through Cedar Key. "Main Street...looks like a turbulent river now," Pepper wrote at 4:45 p.m.

Farther inland, winds toppled trees in Gainesville, throwing a huge pine into the building that housed the Engineering Department on the University of Florida campus. The hurricane dealt a savage blow to poor, sparsely populated Taylor County, where it demolished the homes of 350 families and heavily damaged another 175 homes.

As evening approached, a dazed and exhausted Ray Sheldon reached Miami. But there would be no rest for the camps supervisor. Fred Ghent, thinking, no doubt, of the intense scrutiny he would undergo in the wake of the tragedy, was waiting for Sheldon with a court stenographer to take his statement about what had happened. Sheldon, still numb and disoriented from his awful experience, sat down and started talking. His first words were an explanation of why he had waited until Monday afternoon to call for an evacuation train.

It was only partly factual and it left out many details about the information that had been available to him.

Sheldon told Ghent that he had been "in constant communication with every available source of information regarding the storm" and added he'd called the U.S. Weather Bureau at noon Monday to check on the status of the hurricane.

That much was true. But his next statement simply was not.

"The weather bureau stated there was absolutely no danger, from the reports they had received, to the Florida Keys," Sheldon said.

In fact, Sheldon had been warned by the weather bureau that the Keys would be hit with at least gale-force winds and dangerously high tides regardless of the path of the hurricane's eye. He didn't mention that the weather bureau's Key West office had advised him early Sunday morning, September 1, that conditions probably would become dangerous on the Florida Keys even if the hurricane followed the weather bureau's predicted course and passed through the Straits of Florida into the Gulf of Mexico.

Sheldon also didn't mention the weather bureau's advisory of 3:30 a.m. Monday, September 2, warning of "high tides and gales" on the Keys, nor did he say that the weather bureau called the work camps' headquarters at the Matecumbe Hotel minutes later to inform camp officials of that advisory and its implications for the islands.

The statement laid the foundation for an alibi that would absolve Ghent and himself from any responsibility for the vets' deaths. The alibi—blaming the weather bureau for not providing adequate warning about the danger that the hurricane posed to the work camps— would persist throughout the investigations that would follow.

By Wednesday, Roosevelt Administration officials were scurrying to respond to the catastrophe. Roosevelt's secretary Stephen Early told General Hines, the VA director, that the President was very upset and wanted an immediate investigation to determine whether anyone in his administration was responsible for the veterans' deaths.

Early may have been keeping tabs on events in Florida, but the secretary was carefully avoiding making any record of his thoughts on the disaster or what was going on behind the scenes. It was a marked departure from his usual habits.

Throughout his years as Roosevelt's personal secretary, Early kept an unofficial White House diary in which he made brief notations of daily events, FDR's appointments, and his own thoughts. When natural disasters struck—such as an earthquake in Montana or spring flooding on the East Coast that drove thousands from their homes—Early usually made note of the events in the diary and discussed in a few words the administration's response to help victims.

But Early's entry for September 1 through September 8 makes no mention of the hurricane in Florida or the deaths of the veterans.

Around 6:30 p.m. on Wednesday, September 4, General Hines summoned his assistant, Col. George E. Ijams, and told the colonel to get down to Florida immediately.

Ijams would be the personal representative of President Roosevelt, and he would be responsible for making sure the injured veterans were properly cared for and the bodies of those killed were either sent home or to Arlington National Cemetery, whichever the family preferred. Capt. Harry Farmer, also attached to the Veterans Administration, accompanied Ijams.

General Hines had one more important meeting Wednesday. The administration had had a thorny relationship with the American Legion, one of the most vocal veterans groups, almost from the moment FDR took office, and the President hadn't helped his standing with the veterans group a few months earlier by vetoing a bill that would have allowed early payment of the bonus.

With another election year approaching, Roosevelt could not afford a repeat of the outrage that followed the deaths of two vets during the 1932 eviction of the Bonus Marchers from Washington. It wasn't unreasonable to assume that the voters' fury would be multiplied beyond measure if they believed hundreds of veterans had been killed in a hurricane because of governmental carelessness. That anger could linger for months and cause disastrous results for FDR and the Democrats in

November 1936—especially if the American Legion and Republican political operatives had a full year to fan the flames of voter outrage. Hines sought to head off some of that potential backlash. Around 11:30 p.m. Wednesday the general went to Washington's Union Station to meet a train from Huntington, West Virginia, carrying Frank Belgrano, Jr., the national commander of the American Legion. Hines spent about 90 minutes with Belgrano, discussing the tragedy on the Keys and, as he later phrased it, "Roosevelt's wishes in the matter." Belgrano—who hadn't yet talked to his Legion colleagues in Florida—told Hines that he would cooperate.

While Hines and Belgrano discussed the tragedy, the hurricane lost more strength as it moved farther inland, but it was still packing a punch. By nightfall the storm had crossed into south Georgia and was heading northeast toward Macon. In Valdosta, the barometer dropped to 28.90 inches—the lowest reading ever recorded there. More than five inches of rain fell in Thomasville, and Quitman was drenched with almost six inches. The winds also tore down a power line that fell on a store in Quitman and set the building ablaze.

As the storm created an unusually windy and rainy night in Georgia, George Ijams and Harry Farmer were trying to find a flight out of Washington to Florida, but the relentless rainstorm soaking the District of Columbia had grounded all planes. Ijams and Farmer finally gave up and boarded a train for Miami at 3 a.m. Thursday.

chapter eight

An Act of God

Editor Paul Jeans undoubtedly was pleased with the edition of the Miami Beach *Daily Tribune* that hit the streets Thursday, September 5, 1935.

The *Tribune's* front page had all a tabloid editor could hope for— tales of bravery, a whiff of scandal in high places, and a gruesome photo. And it was all related to the same story—the hurricane that had blasted the Keys three days earlier, exactly as the *Trib* had predicted. The headlines told of the daring rescue at sea of the passengers aboard the wrecked S.S. *Dixie* and hinted that a cover-up scandal was developing in the deaths of the veterans in the hurricane. The tabloid's front page also included a photo of dead veterans lying amid the wreckage of Camp 3, and on page 2 was a photo of a stack of coffins and a headline saying the death toll from the hurricane was more than 800. *Tribune* stories repeatedly described nude, disfigured corpses and declared the "rotting bodies" to be "mute evidence of government indifference."

In an editorial the *Daily Tribune* claimed that two rescue trains had been assembled Sunday in Miami and were waiting to evacuate the veterans, but that U.S. Weather Bureau meteorologist Ernest Carson had told federal officials in Washington that the veterans were not in danger and the camps didn't need to be evacuated. The anonymous writer crowed that the *Trib* had accomplished "the greatest scoop ever scored by a Florida newspaper" by correctly predicting that the hurricane would strike the Keys.

As usual, the reporting was a blend of lurid facts and cynical fantasy, and the outrageous claim that Carson had told officials in Washington not to remove the veterans from the Keys bordered on libel. But by Thursday morning, it was becoming clear that a terrible tragedy had occurred in Florida. The *Washington Post* of September 5, 1935, reported that as many as 500 people may have died in the Keys. A *Post* editorial said the veterans' deaths were a "tragedy," but offered only backhanded sympathy for the victims, referring to them as "drifters, psychopathic cases or habitual troublemakers."

As Thursday dawned in the Keys, conditions were becoming more horrifying by the hour. Blowflies rose in thick, noisy clouds when rescue workers approached a corpse. The pungent stench of decomposition carried for miles up and down the Keys. The men who'd come to the islands to try to help were struggling to overcome their own revulsion at the awful task confronting them.

Around 8 a.m. Thursday a Coast Guard patrol boat cast off from Lower Matecumbe Key with a gruesome cargo—the bodies of 38 veterans that had been recovered by their surviving comrades before the National Guard took control of rescue operations. About 90 minutes later the patrol boat reached the rescue staging area at Snake Creek, where the corpses were to be unloaded, placed into pine boxes, and hauled to Woodlawn Cemetery in Miami. But the shallow water prevented the boat from getting close enough to unload the bodies directly onto the shore. The Coast Guard officer in charge of the vessel cut its engines, dropped anchor, and waited for help from the men standing on shore.

Minutes passed and no one moved. The rescue workers on shore grimly studied the patrol boat. "The stench was something that made men turn and leave the vicinity," said John Teets, a Red Cross field representative helping with the rescue work.

Finally Dade County Sheriff Dave Coleman got fed up. "Either you come down here and help get these bodies off," he roared at the men standing motionless on the shore, "or get the hell out of the country! One or the other!"

Teets, a physician, and a few other men waded tentatively into the shallow water and waited for someone to start unloading the corpses. But the men aboard the cutter were no more eager to handle the bodies than the workers onshore. An argument erupted over how to get the corpses off the ship. Finally a large man wearing a VFW cap offered a solution. "We'll throw 'em overboard into the water, you grab 'em down there," he said. "Anyhow, they need washing off."

The men aboard the cutter dropped the first body into the water. Teets and the physician reached for it. The victim's scalp came off in Teets's hand. The decomposition was now so advanced that it was almost impossible to handle the bodies.

The rescue workers had more to contend with than the horrible task of recovering bodies.

The workers were composed of military personnel, state and federal government workers, Red Cross workers, and volunteers. The lines of authority were hopelessly tangled and confusion reigned—and tempers were short.

The main conflict was between a colonel representing Governor Sholtz and Sheriff Coleman, who was out of his district but had been sent as a Red Cross representative. "The colonel was taking charge, countermanding here, making new orders there," Teets said.

But the others decided to make Sheriff Coleman the director of rescue operations, and the indignant colonel immediately sent a telegram to Sholtz. Then National Guard troops arrived at Snake Creek, and their officers started giving orders as well.

At the same time, a Red Cross representative in Tallahassee told reporters that his agency was in charge of rescue work in the Keys.

David Sholtz had had enough. The governor boarded an airplane and headed for Miami to take charge of rescue operations.

"Behind it all was politics," Teets said. "Veterans had been killed, President's representatives were coming, governor's retinue already on the ground, Colonel Ijams arriving. There were political aspects. Investigations. And the press criticizing unto high heaven."

The press also was squabbling. A nasty dispute had erupted among five newsreel companies over the rights to copies of the film shot by the Universal cameraman whom Olsen had flown down to the Keys Wednesday. Angry telegrams and phone calls bounced from New York to Miami to Los Angeles and back. Charles Ford of Universal Newsreel refused to share the footage. The Coast Guard was asked to referee.

In Washington the telephone lines were humming again Thursday morning at the offices of the Federal Emergency Relief Administration as administrators there sought more information about the catastrophe in the Keys—and began laying plans for political damage control.

Lawrence Westbrook, an assistant director of FERA, had a long conversation with Fred Ghent in Florida. Westbrook was especially interested in the hurricane warnings issued by the U.S. Weather Bureau. He wanted to know when Ghent had learned the hurricane was heading toward the Keys. Ghent said he'd had a report around 1 p.m. or 1:30 p.m. Monday that the storm was still about 200 miles away.

Westbrook was intrigued. "The storm actually hit on Monday afternoon, didn't it, and you had a report between one and 1:30 that it was 200 miles from the Keys?" he asked.

"Yes," Ghent answered.

"And you got that report from the weather bureau?" Westbrook continued.

"Yes," Ghent said.

"Is there a published report on that?" Westbrook asked.

"That the storm was 200 miles away? Yes. I'm sure there is," Ghent said.

Ghent explained to Westbrook how he and Sheldon had decided to order the evacuation train for the veterans. Westbrook wanted more information about the weather bureau's advisories.

"Did you say that between one and two you had a warning that the storm would hit the Keys?" Westbrook asked.

"No," Ghent said.

"Then you acted on your own initiative on the assumption that if the storm did come your direction it would take about 20 hours to get there," Westbrook said.

"We had no information that the storm would hit the Keys at all," Ghent said.

Ghent's evasive response was technically accurate. As of 1 p.m. September 2, the weather bureau hadn't said specifically that the eye of the storm would cross the Keys. But Ghent's answer was still misleading. At least 36 hours before the hurricane's landfall—beginning with meteorologist Gerald Kennedy's warning to Sheldon at 5 a.m. on Sunday, September 1—the weather bureau had warned that dangerous conditions were likely in the Keys .

Westbrook was left with the impression that the weather bureau had given no hint of danger to the Keys, and that the Florida East Coast Railway had promised to have a special train waiting to be called on a moment's notice.

Both of these impressions were wrong.

Westbrook also took a call from Marvin McIntyre at the White House. The secretary got right to the point. McIntyre told Westbrook that Roosevelt wanted "a complete report as to whether there was any unnecessary delay in getting the train off, or with the weather bureau." McIntyre said FDR wanted assistant WPA director Aubrey Williams to send "an outstanding man" to Florida to work with Ijams.

McIntyre said he thought Harry Hopkins should dispatch Williams to Florida immediately. He added that he expected veterans' groups to react angrily to the death toll in the work camps.

"The Veterans of Foreign Wars will start something," McIntyre warned. "They will want to know why something wasn't done to warn those people or to take care of them."

"The weather bureau reported the storm at 1:30 p.m. Monday afternoon to be 200 miles away," Westbrook responded helpfully. "I think it will be pretty hard on them."

McIntyre's ears pricked up. "What about the weather bureau?"

"I wasn't the least bit concerned because it only travels 10 miles an hour and it was reported 200 miles away," Westbrook answered.

Westbrook found his most useful—and imaginative—informant in Julius Stone, the former Florida ERA director who had boasted in the *New York Times* about his New Deal transformation of Key West.

The two men discussed the weather bureau advisories suggesting the hurricane could make landfall near Havana. Because the weather bureau's erroneous information caused Florida ERA officials to delay evacuating the veterans, Stone thought there could be only one possible reason for the disaster on the Keys. "I think you will have to call it an act of God," he said.

Westbrook leaped at Stone's suggestion. "That's right," he said eagerly. "That's about the conclusion we had made."

Stone tried to reassure Westbrook that the Federal Emergency Relief Administration hadn't taken an unnecessary risk by putting the work camps in the Keys. "No hurricanes have hit there within the last 25 years, and there was no reason to expect one," he said.

Stone had somehow forgotten the four powerful hurricanes that struck the Keys between 1906 and 1919, killing hundreds, as well as the hurricane in 1929 that destroyed railroad tracks near Key Largo and kept trains from running for 10 days.

Westbrook added his own absurd notion that the vets had been safer in the isolated camps than they would have been in a city. In a city there would be more danger from flying debris, he reasoned.

The men were apparently unaware that dozens of vets had been beaten to death and impaled by flying lumber when the camps blew to pieces during the storm.

But Westbrook was now satisfied that nothing could have been done to protect the veterans from the storm. "That thing blew a train 50 feet off a track," he said.

"In the face of such violence no building that we could reasonably have constructed would have stood," Stone said. "It is just one of those things."

Westbrook told Stone that WPA director Harry Hopkins had been on the verge of going to Florida to investigate the veterans' deaths but had decided instead to send his assistant, Aubrey Williams.

Stone said there was no reason to go to so much trouble—especially since the veterans hadn't done much to ingratiate themselves with the administrators who were in charge of their work program.

"There isn't anything more that [Hopkins] could or should do," Stone said. "The fact of the matter is those fellows had a very bad name."

"Who had a bad name?" Westbrook asked.

"The veterans," Stone answered. "There will be some remarks made at headquarters that we would not want to repeat over the telephone."

"What are they?" Westbrook asked.

"If the thing had to happen, it might just as well take them,"

"Who would say that?" Westbrook asked.

"Everyone I have heard talk about the accident," Stone said, and suggested that Hopkins should simply order Florida ERA director Conrad Van Hyning to prepare a report about the disaster and be done with it. "That's what I'd do, but I don't think this thing merits too much attention."

"I think that is right," Westbrook said. "I think Harry thinks Aubrey ought to go, but I hope he will not."

"I do not think it would do a bit of good," Stone concluded.

Meanwhile, FERA engineer George Andrews was seeking information about the weather bureau's hurricane advisories from a reluctant R. G. Unkrich, who was Conrad Van Hyning's assistant in Florida.

Andrews wanted to know when Florida ERA officials received their first warning about the hurricane. Unkrich sidestepped the question, adding that his agency was trying to learn more about what had happened. He added that the Florida ERA didn't have time to answer a lot of questions and that he had been asked not to make any statements about the disaster.

Andrews pressed. "What time did you receive the first warnings of the storm?"

Unkrich dodged again, saying he had been spending the Labor Day weekend at a lake and had heard Sunday, September 1, that a hurricane warning had been issued for Fort Pierce—about 200 miles up the coast from Islamorada. Florida ERA officials were told Monday that the hurricane was headed toward Havana. "By 11 o'clock we decided that even though there was only a remote possibility that the storm would hit the Keys, it was planned to take them up to Hollywood and run them back the next day," he said.

Andrews wanted to know who had ordered the train, but again Unkrich avoided the question, saying only that he thought it had left Miami around 4:30 p.m. Monday.

Andrews asked Unkrich if he had copies of the weather bureau's advisories. Unkrich told him he was only aware of what had been published in newspapers and passed along by telephone.

"Can you get the official weather bureau reports down there, showing just what time they were sent out and just what they stated?" Andrews asked.

"It will take quite a little time to get them," Unkrich said. "We have not much communication left, and it will take some little time."

"If you have anybody you can put on that, put them on that job and get all the reports together," Andrews ordered, and hung up.

Florida ERA engineer Marvin Porter was no more enthusiastic about talking. Again, Andrews asked when Florida ERA administrators had received the first warning from the weather bureau.

"I am checking up on it," Porter said. "I am not in a position to say right now. I am checking up on what time the train left and when the requisition was made for the train."

"How soon will you have that?" Andrews demanded. "Can't you put somebody on it now and let them call the weather bureau and read off the time their warning went out?"

"I am having somebody do that right now," Porter said.

Andrews kept pushing. "Hopkins is hot on that right now," he said.

The task of getting copies of the advisories was handed off to J. P. Hallihan, a WPA engineer who went straight to the weather bureau's acting director, Charles C. Clark. Hallihan also submitted a list of questions to Clark about the weather bureau's performance during the storm.

With the advisories finally in hand, Lawrence Westbrook drafted a statement exonerating Florida ERA officials from any blame in the veterans' deaths—even though the investigators sent to look into the tragedy hadn't even reached Florida.

"There is every indication that the officials of the Florida State Emergency Relief Administration took every precaution in the light of the information at their disposal," Westbrook wrote. "Nothing in the weather reports up to this time could have given officials in charge of the camps any cause for serious alarm, but in order to be on the safe side, a train was ordered at 1:30 p.m. to evacuate the veterans' camps, but of course it arrived too late."

Later that day, WPA director Harry Hopkins met with reporters and criticized the U.S. Weather Bureau's advisories. Hopkins's comments were based on Westbrook's written statement, and Hopkins also included one of Julius Stone's remarks to Westbrook from their earlier telephone conversation.

"Our information from the weather reports showed that the storm was jumping all around there and nobody could tell where it would hit," Hopkins told reporters "Wherever we had a camp, at Key West or anywhere else, had the storm hit it, it would have been wrecked."

Hopkins added that the weather bureau's advisories hadn't been alarming enough to prompt anyone to move the vets off the islands.

"I don't think anyone reading the weather reports—and I have been reading them—would necessarily have evacuated those people,"

Clark was furious about Hopkins's statement and angrily denied that his agency was responsible for the deaths. Alexander J. Mitchell, the retired director of the Florida Weather Service, was also enraged by the insinuation that the weather bureau had somehow been at fault.

Mitchell sent a telegram to President Roosevelt calling Hopkins's comments a "discreditable libel."

In Hyde Park, President Roosevelt announced that veterans killed in the hurricane would be eligible for burial at Arlington National Cemetery. But when Colonel Ijams's train arrived in Jacksonville Thursday night, he learned that public health officials in Florida were going to order that the bodies be cremated. Ijams protested. He had "specific orders from the President to collect and identify those bodies," he insisted.

And still, the storm continued to cause havoc on the East Coast Thursday. In Gastonia, North Carolina, Maggie Gamble was killed when the storm's blinding rainfall prevented her from seeing an oncoming train at a railroad crossing.

Virginia had been primed for disaster by steady rain that had been falling for days, soaking the Old Dominion—as well as Maryland's Eastern Shore—until the ground just couldn't absorb any more moisture. When the rains reached Virginia, the James River leaped out of its banks and put downtown Richmond underwater.

Tornadoes spawned by the storm began touching down across Virginia and the Carolinas Thursday morning. E. F. Arrington, a farmer near Danville, Virginia, had to battle a twister for the lives of his wife and daughter. The winds tried to carry away his child, but Arrington seized her in midair and pulled her back to the ground and held her there with one hand. With his other hand he tried to keep his wife from being carried away, but the storm twice yanked her from his grasp. Each time Arrington caught her in midair.

The farmer finally threw his wife and daughter to the ground, lay down on top of them, and grabbed a fencepost.

In Farmville, Virginia, a tornado killed Mrs. Preston Simanski and her daughter-in-law, and in Courtland a twister destroyed the home of Nathaniel Turner, killed his six-month-old son, and seriously injured his wife, who was carried about 200 yards by the wind.

The same tornado also damaged venerable Hampden-Sydney College, tearing the roof off the administration building, uprooting six ancient oak trees, and plucking about 20 tombstones from a campus cemetery. The winds swept the stones into piles and hurled one high into a cedar tree.

The storm was still battering the East Coast when an angry Governor David Sholtz arrived in Miami late Thursday. He was in no mood to wait until he'd cooled off to call a meeting of representatives of the agencies doing rescue work in the Keys. Sholtz immediately summoned them to the McAllister Hotel. Around midnight Thursday the governor called the meeting to order. He looked around at the 15 people in the room. Dade County Sheriff Dave Coleman was there, and so were Marvin Porter and Conrad Van Hyning of the Florida ERA. Field representative John Teets attended for the Red Cross.

Finally Sholtz spoke.

"The governor announced that *he* was the boss, and asked if there were objections," John Teets said. "There were none."

When the meeting broke up, the men attending the conference had sorted out their differences, devised a clear plan, and assigned responsibilities for cleaning up the awful mess in the Keys.

As the meeting ended in Miami, the storm was continuing its destruction in New Bern, North Carolina, where it set a lethal trap for residents of Contentnea Street. The storm blew into the city shortly after midnight, and began taking down electrical poles and strewing live wires through the neighborhood, setting several houses ablaze.

Seeing that one of the downed power lines was about to set fire to his daughter's house, David W. Thompson, 55, ventured into the storm to try to move it. He was electrocuted, as was his 48-year-old wife when she tried to pull him away from the wire.

A few houses away, Carlton Smith wrestled with his wife to prevent her from running out into the storm—and certain death—to go to the aid of her dead parents. Then Smith smelled smoke.

He dashed into the bedroom where his two children slept and discovered that the fallen wires had started a fire.

As Smith extinguished the small blaze and hustled his children from the room, W. C. Hurley fought through the storm hoping to find someone to help him extinguish the fire in his home. But Hurley received a near-lethal jolt of electricity when he stepped into a pool of water charged by a fallen power line. His life was saved when Sam Smith—no relation to Carlton Smith—pulled him out of the water.

By Friday morning floodwaters were running through the streets of towns in Delaware, and on Maryland's Eastern Shore flooding forced about 1,000 people to leave their homes.

In Federalsburg, Maryland, the water steadily rose around a telephone office building. But operators Reba Pusey and Mollie Wheatley realized rescue workers were dependent on them for communications. So the women stayed at their switchboard.

"We are dead tired," Pusey told local reporters. "We had to wade up to our waists to get in here yesterday, and both Miss Wheatley and I knew we would be trapped by the flood."

Telephone linesman Charlie Marine swam through the floodwater to check on the women, then returned with linesman Edgar Ireland to bring them coffee and sandwiches.

The storm finally ended its deadly rampage Friday.

"With surprising suddenness, the tropical hurricane swept away from the Maryland coastal section today and swirling storm clouds broke to let the sun peep through," the Associated Press reported from Ocean City on September 6. "The Coast Guard station here announced the cheering news to the apprehensive city that 'the danger is all over.' The wind, which had dashed towering seas against breakwaters and over the jetties, shifted suddenly to the northwest. The abnormally high tide reacted by beginning to recede."

The U.S. Weather Bureau monitored the storm for several more days as it barreled northeastward past Long Island and Canada's

Maritime Provinces. Incredibly, it began intensifying again as it rolled across the Atlantic. By September 7 it had regained hurricane strength with winds of better than 90 miles per hour. Then, at last, it began to weaken and die as it turned to the northwest toward Greenland. On September 10 the weather bureau made its last notation of the storm, noting that it still had winds of about 40 miles per hour.

It would be months before rescue workers and government officials could come up with a realistic determination of how many people had been killed. The official death toll is 408, but so many victims were literally blown into oblivion that the actual number of deaths could easily be higher.

The best estimate of veterans killed is somewhere between 250 and 260—almost two-thirds of the men who stayed in the work camps during the Labor Day weekend. With so many vets coming and going from the camps during the holiday, it was difficult for officials to know exactly how many men were blown off the Keys never to be seen again and how many who'd taken holiday leave simply decided not to return to the islands after the hurricane.

As the storm headed back into the wilds of the Atlantic Ocean, which had spawned it, the political tempest it left in its wake was beginning to intensify. And Colonel McCormick's *Chicago Daily Tribune* was stoking it.

"Lay Vets' Deaths to Neglect," blared the *Tribune* headlines on Friday morning, September 6, 1935. The *Tribune*'s lead story reported that Roosevelt Administration officials were bracing themselves for "a scandal of shocking proportions."

Filing his story from Hyde Park, *Tribune* reporter Willard Edwards wrote that unnamed sources close to the President were saying FDR thought someone in the Federal Emergency Relief Administration was, at the very least, "guilty of extremely bad judgment."

An accompanying story from the *Tribune*'s Washington correspondent warned "a congressional inquiry and far reaching political repercussions appear[ed] inevitable" and reminded readers of an incident that was no doubt troubling the Roosevelt Administration. "Republican senators here believe it will be even more serious in its consequences [than] Mr. Hoover's ousting of the bonus army with machine guns and tear gas."

The story hinted that Republicans would make sure voters had every gory detail of the tragedy explained to them before the elections of November 1936.

As Chicago readers read the *Tribune's* prediction of scandal, President Roosevelt and Stephen Early met with reporters for a news conference at FDR's home in Hyde Park Friday morning, September 6. The President entered the room with a chipper quip about the pale complexion of one of the reporters and suggested that another reporter take him outside for a sunbath. "They have a good nudist colony across the river," Roosevelt joked.

Roosevelt mentioned his appointment of Stewart McDonald to the post of federal housing administrator, and answered a question about a recent meeting with New York Mayor Fiorello La Guardia. Then a reporter asked FDR about the hurricane.

"The papers were interested in the Florida hurricane deaths—why no precautions were taken," the reporter said. "Anything you can tell us along that line?"

"Nothing more," Roosevelt said. "No more news than we have."

The President was startled when another reporter told him that rescue workers in the Keys would begin cremating bodies instead of following his instructions to ship them to families or Arlington National Cemetery for burial.

"I do not think so," Roosevelt said. "Certainly they are doing everything by order."

Stephen Early also was surprised. "I didn't—" he began, and then stopped. "Actually burning?" he asked incredulously.

A reporter held up a copy of that day's edition of the New York *Daily News* and read aloud the story's headline: "Florida Burning

Dead." The story reported that rescue workers had started cremating bodies in the Keys against the wishes of federal officials.

When reporters from the *Daily News* and Associated Press got into a half-serious debate about how the story had been written, Roosevelt saw an opportunity to steer conversation away from the hurricane.

"I will have you both up here before an investigating committee," FDR joshed, prompting an outburst of laughter from the gathering. "We will get Colonel Ijams to subpoena you both and we will get the truth."

Soon after the President's press conference, Col. George Ijams, Governor David Sholtz, and Capt. Harry Farmer climbed into Lieutenant Olsen's Douglas Dolphin for a look at the carnage in the Keys. As the trio cruised over the islands, the odor of decomposing bodies wafted up to them. Sholtz told Olsen he wanted to go ashore to get a closer look at what the rescue workers were dealing with.

Coast Guard Lt. William Clemmer also was airborne Friday heading for Cape Sable with J. C. Stoddard, who owned a waterfront vacation cottage at the tip of the Florida peninsula. Stoddard's daughter and son-in-law had gone to the isolated cottage for the Labor Day weekend, and Stoddard hadn't heard from them since.

Stoddard made the sad discovery that his cottage—and his daughter and son-in-law—were simply gone. The hurricane had passed Cape Sable during the early morning of Tuesday, September 3. The spot where Stoddard's cottage had stood was now clean, bare sand.

"The cape had been swept so bare that not one piece of wreckage from his home could be found," Clemmer reported.

Around 4:45 p.m. Friday, Lieutenant Olsen eased his seaplane down onto the waters of Biscayne Bay. His VIP passengers had been shaken by what they'd seen.

Sholtz met with reporters soon after he landed. The governor, who had been among the rescue workers who'd gone into the shattered towns around Lake Okeechobee after a hurricane killed almost

2,000 in 1928, said he was "shocked beyond words" by conditions in the Keys.

Sholtz also told reporters that rescue workers would begin cremating the badly decomposed bodies in the Keys instead of trying to ship them out for burial.

In Washington, WPA director Harry Hopkins and Federal Emergency Relief Administration officials were trying to smooth over the furor caused by Hopkins's earlier disparaging comments about the weather bureau.

Hopkins tried to put some distance between Washington officials and Florida ERA administrators, telling reporters the veterans were "technically in the care of the Florida relief administration," with the obvious implication that federal officials in Washington therefore were not responsible for the death toll.

After talking with reporters, Hopkins left Washington for Hyde Park to talk with his boss about the situation.

That same day, the Federal Emergency Relief Administration issued a statement saying Hopkins's earlier comment that he would not have evacuated the veterans based on the wording of the hurricane advisories was not intended as a criticism of the weather bureau's competency. FERA "regrets the misunderstanding caused in some quarters by Mr. Hopkins' statement clearing Florida ERA camp officials of negligence in not evacuating the camps before the storm struck," the statement added.

In Florida, Hopkins's assistant Aubrey Williams was about to begin his probe into the conduct of the administrators who'd been hired by his agency. Williams talked briefly with reporters Friday.

"Everybody seems to have done what they thought was the right thing at the right time," Williams said. "But we mean to follow this thing relentlessly and let the chips fall where they may. If any of our men are to blame we want to know it."

By Friday afternoon, news editors had had almost four days to sift through accounts of the hurricane. As the week drew to a close, stories began appearing in newspapers across the country about local veterans who'd been killed in the storm.

"Grady C. Lewis, Concord Mechanic, Listed Among Dead in Florida," read a small headline in North Carolina's *Charlotte Observer*, while Norfolk's *Virginian-Pilot* reported "Portsmouth Man Probable Victim of Florida Storm."

Editorial writers also had had time to ponder the news of the hurricane's death toll and the comments from officials in Washington.

The *Washington Post* questioned the competency of the administration that had hired the men in charge of the veterans' work program. "Plans that make no allowance for these unforeseen and often inexplicable actions of nature are obviously too shallow to make much impress upon the growth of a nation,"the editorial concluded.

On the Gulf Coast—where hurricanes are a routine fact of life— newspapers weren't buying the notion that the weather bureau was responsible for the tragedy.

"We do not hesitate to say...that it is simply nonsensical to impute the blame for the disaster to the weather bureau," the *New Orleans Item* said on its editorial page of Saturday, September 7. Hopkins's comments indicated he was "entirely ignorant" about hurricanes. "All of us in the hurricane belt know that nobody can tell exactly where a hurricane center is going to strike the coast until half a day or less before it gets there," the editorial said. "But everybody knows a day or two before that the blast may center any-where on a line 100 or more miles long."

The *Tampa Daily Times* called Hopkins's statements about the weather bureau "ridiculous" and said work camps administrators were to blame for the veterans' deaths.

The *Pensacola News* unequivocally supported the weather bureau. "When the weather bureau gives warning of a hurricane to a community in plenty of time for the people of that community to prepare for a blow, its work is finished," said the *News*. "It cannot be expected to hunt up the individuals in that community and personally warn them to get out or suffer the consequences."

Other newspapers speculated about possible long-range consequences from the investigations being launched. Even papers less inclined to blatant Roosevelt-bashing than the *Chicago Daily Tribune* were commenting on the possibility of dire political consequences for the Roosevelt Administration.

"The tragedies [the hurricane] wrought [in Florida] are numerous; and in the still unsettled question of why the evacuation of the veterans was delayed, there is the possibility of a national scandal," said an editorial in Norfolk's *Virginian-Pilot* in its edition of Sunday, September 8.

The Sunday edition of the *Miami Beach Daily Tribune* again shrieked that 1,000 had died in the hurricane and published another front-page photo of a dead body from its seemingly inexhaustible supply of gruesome pictures. Again, the paper blamed the weather bureau for the veterans' deaths.

On Monday, September 8, *Chicago Daily Tribune* reporter Spearman Lewis proclaimed that Roosevelt Administration officials were trying to recover from a "colossal blunder" that could threaten Roosevelt's political survival.

"The heat is on and a national scandal that might well imperil the New Deal's next political campaign must be smothered," Lewis wrote. "The administration seems willing to forego for the time being any serious effort to fix responsibility for the delayed evacuation train."

Spearman's story included a quote from Colonel Ijams hinting that tension might be building between the WPA and Federal Emergency Relief Administration on one side and the Veterans Administration on the other.

"I was sent here to bury the dead and serve the living," Ijams said. "But I find an increasing public tendency to pin the responsibility for the delayed relief train on the Veterans' Administration. We merely rounded the men up in Washington and turned them over to the FERA and WPA, Florida division. Any responsibility is theirs and I shall look into that phase of the catastrophe when I have completed my original assignments."

The colonel was working diligently Saturday to accomplish those tasks. While workmen used jackhammers and a steam shovel to dig a large trench grave in Miami's Woodlawn Cemetery big enough for the veterans' coffins, Ijams worked his way through a long list of preparations for a memorial service planned for Sunday evening at the city's Bayfront Park. If his boss in Hyde Park was going to be deprived of the opportunity of laying the hapless veterans to rest amid military pomp and splendor at Arlington National Cemetery, then he was going to make sure they got a proper send-off in Miami. Ijams, with the backing of President Roosevelt, rounded up an Army general and a Navy admiral to attend the service.

At the cemetery the bodies in the pine boxes were so far gone there was little morticians could do. Rescue workers—including police officers from Miami and Miami Beach—had made an extraordinary effort to identify as many of the bodies as they could. The Veterans Administration had even sent fingerprint records to Florida to help identify the victims. It may have been the first time that fingerprints were used to identify victims of a catastrophe.

But by the time the bodies reached the makeshift morgue at Woodlawn, there wasn't much more that could be done with those that hadn't already been identified.

"The bodies were considerably swollen, all of the faces looked absolutely alike and not recognizable," said Arthur Bilsbrough, a Florida ERA engineer. "They were in a bad state of decomposition and it was impossible to identify [them] other than by physical defects or by marks such as tattoos, missing teeth, bridgework, gold, and so forth."

Morticians filled the pine boxes with a special preserving compound to reduce the odor. Each wooden box then was placed inside a metal casket and soldered shut.

Meanwhile, Ijams set about finding enough American flags to cover the coffins. Many of the flags in the Keys had been blown away by the storm, but the resourceful colonel had been sending telegrams seeking flags since before he arrived in Miami, "and within two days I had enough flags to bury the whole state of Florida," he said.

He also came up with a replica of the Tomb of the Unknown Soldier, and roses—hundreds and hundreds of roses.

Down in the Keys, a sad and simple ritual was being performed on the banks of Snake Creek. Heeding the orders of Governor Sholtz and state health officials, National Guardsmen and other rescue workers had built a funeral pyre of 36 pine coffins interlaced with driftwood, lumber from the nearby wreckage of Camp 1, and railroad ties. Clergymen from all faiths conducted services and a small detachment of National Guard troops fired a salute. Then a man, dressed in bib overalls and a jacket despite the heat and wearing a Salvation Army cap, raised a bugle to his lips.

The brief, mournful strains of "Taps" floated across the ruined island. As the notes faded away, a soldier stepped forward with a blazing torch, touched it to the pile of coffins and stepped back quickly as flames greedily enveloped the gasoline-soaked pyre.

In New York City, chartered trains carrying passengers from the *Dixie* were arriving.

The mood had been lighthearted as the trains chugged northward from Miami. During stops along the way, some got off long enough to buy local newspapers, then reboarded the train and eagerly read stories of their hurricane experience as their journey resumed. Some of them happily shouted the words to "Dixie" to the accompaniment of an accordion played by Harry Burk of New Orleans.

When the train stopped in Washington, 11-year-old Eleanor Shields of Philadelphia stepped off for a few minutes to stretch her legs. She was wearing a lifejacket emblazoned with "SS Dixie" in large letters.

When the trains reached the Pennsylvania Station passenger

platforms beneath the streets of Manhattan, however, all the pent-up emotions—excitement, fear, awe, despair, hope, overwhelming relief—came pouring out.

As passengers stepped off the train, Ben Grill searched the crowd for his sister, Goldie, a teacher who lived in Brooklyn. They spotted each other and rushed into an embrace. Goldie threw her arms around him as he pressed her face to his and kissed her on the cheek.

Ida Flatow and Ann Cinder, also teachers from Brooklyn, were so overwhelmed with relief at the sight of their families that they collapsed and had to be helped to a nearby hotel to recover.

Eight-year-old Herbert Shprentz of Brooklyn, who rode out the storm with his mother, Freda, told his father, Isidore, that the wreck of the *Dixie* had been "swell." Frank Belcher, the opera-singer-turned-Broadway tobacconist, was happily reunited with Skippy, his Boston terrier. Belcher's wife, Anna, also went through the storm without injury.

As Sunday morning, September 8, dawned in Miami, workers at Woodlawn Cemetery were making final preparations to lay the hurricane victims to rest. The flags that Colonel Ijams had hustled to round up were draped over the coffins, and a veteran stood guard beside each of the flags.

Services for the burial were brief and simple. Representatives from the armed forces and veterans groups made up most of the crowd.

The memorial service, however, was quite a different affair.

At 6:15 p.m. ranks of soldiers, sailors, Coast Guardsmen, and veterans began forming near the entrances to Bayfront Park. Twenty minutes later they marched somberly into the park and stood at attention around a band shell near the center of the park. A few minutes before 7 p.m. three U.S. Navy fighter planes droned overhead and released their payloads—hundreds of roses.

Massed bands from the military groups played "America." As the last notes of the music faded, R. V. Waters stepped to the podium and looked out at the faces of about 20,000 people. Waters tried to make some sense of the veterans' tragic deaths.

"Fellow veterans and citizens," he began. "We are gathered here in solemn assemblage this evening to do honor to a group of American veterans who but a few days ago gave up their lives in the line of duty. We do not believe—we do not say—that this is our last tribute to these departed comrades, for we know that in the heart of every patriotic citizen of these United States there will ever dwell a proper sense of appreciation and of gratitude for the sacrifice and heroic deeds of those veterans and their comrades who a few years ago offered their all upon the altar of civilization.

"Nor do we believe that these men have died in vain. It is rare indeed that such sacrifice is made but some great truth is established—and some noble principle maintained—or some remedy discovered; some agency developed to insure the future welfare of others. Time will surely prove that these veterans did not give up their lives in vain."

A Catholic priest, a Protestant minister, and a rabbi offered prayers, soloists sang "There Is No Death" and "The Vacant Chair," and Colonel Ijams delivered a brief message from President Roosevelt.

"I wish I might be present to express my profound grief and deep sense of loss because of the tragic death of these defenders of the nation," Ijams read. "Will you be good enough to convey my condolences to the families of these gallant men."

It was an impressive ceremony with lots of military flourishes for the earthy, ragtag veterans who were so disdainful of formality and authority. But an anonymous editorial writer for Washington's *Evening Star* gave them a eulogy suffused with a much clearer understanding of the sad irony surrounding their deaths.

"On the hurricane-swept Florida keys has been enacted the final episode of the tragedy of The Bonus Marchers," the editorial said. "The men died as they lived, helpless orphans of the storms. The lightning-lit madness of war tore them loose from the relative simplicity and security of the slow-moving age into which they had been born. When the cannon ball storm had passed over the desolated fields of the earth they were blown into a fast, strange post-war world by the inflating breezes of hero worship. These subsided and they found the calm uncomfortable. After a brief lull they were torn loose from whatever security they had been able to find by the blasts of the great depression."

The *Evening Star* predicted that investigations probably would determine who was responsible for the veterans' deaths, but noted that the real cause of the tragedy "lies beyond the reach of any investigator. They were the victims of a hurricane sweeping the earth whose path no meteorologist can forecast nor understand. It was the tragedy of these men—and perhaps the tragedy of all of us—to be born into an age of hurricanelike transition such as history has not known. Life demanded of them a rapid series of readjustments which they were not equipped by nature to make. Consequently they made them clumsily and with infinite pain."

The "Great War" had been responsible for the vets' inadequacy in dealing with modern life, wrote the anonymous editor. It left some with physical disabilities, but many who'd come back physically intact had been hampered by "spiritual wounds and disabilities" caused by wartime service that were even more difficult for them to overcome.

Some who'd served in World War I had learned skills and self-reliance they hadn't had before going overseas, and "some came back far less adequate than before for any self-directed coping with the multiplying complexities of living," the *Evening Star* said. "Among the latter were many of these poor victims of the hurricane."

As the veterans received a formal send-off in Miami, President Roosevelt was reading Aubrey Williams's report on the circumstances surrounding their deaths.

Williams had arrived in Florida Friday morning. He'd made a flight down to the Keys to see the hurricane's aftermath, interviewed a dozen witnesses, and read transcripts of the testimony of six other witnesses who had been interviewed for an investigation being conducted by Florida State's Attorney George Worley. A fair amount of his time also had been taken up writing the report for FDR. Barely 48 hours after Williams had set foot in Florida, his report was in the hands of President Roosevelt.

"It is impossible for us to reach the conclusion that there has been negligence or mistaken judgment on the part of those charged with the responsibility for the safety of the men engaged on the Keys projects," he wrote.

Williams's report contained a phrase that had been circulating among FERA officials before Williams even left for Florida. "To our mind the catastrophe must be characterized 'as an act of God' and was by its very nature beyond the power of man or instruments at his disposal to foresee sufficiently far enough in advance to permit the taking of adequate precautions capable of preventing the death and desolation which occurred."

Williams listed Colonel Ijams as a contributor to the report, but Ijams had been far too busy organizing the funeral to contribute anything. Still, Williams put the Colonel's name on the report, implying he had helped write it.

Williams's hasty report to FDR exonerating officials of the Federal Emergency Relief Administration and Florida ERA undoubtedly eased the minds of some of his inner circle who were concerned that the veterans' deaths could cause serious political problems for the President. That same night, another event was unfolding that would also improve Roosevelt's chances for reelection.

While the President was looking over the hurricane report, Louisiana Senator Huey Long—who had become a legitimate threat to FDR's hopes for a second term—was in Baton Rouge supervising a session of the state legislature, which he controlled with an iron fist. As the legislators went through a pantomime of democracy under the dictatorial Kingfish's watchful eye, Carl Weiss, a young physician whose father's career as a judge had been ruined by Long, slipped behind a column in the capitol's rotunda.

Around 8 p.m., Long, surrounded by his everpresent heavily armed bodyguards, left the assembly. Suddenly Weiss stepped from behind the column and fired a single bullet into Long's stomach.

Weiss died in a hail of gunfire from Long's protectors, but the senator would linger for two days before dying.

The attack on Long was splashed across the front pages of the nation's newspapers, stealing some of the attention from the news of Williams's "act of God" findings in his report to President Roosevelt.

Still, the hurricane report received plenty of notice.

The Greater Miami Ministerial Association was among the first to howl in protest at Williams's conclusions. As soon as the news appeared in the morning newspapers of Monday, September 9, the indignant clergymen drafted a letter to President Roosevelt telling him that Williams had pointed the finger at the wrong culprit. The clergymen accused Williams of trying to steer responsibility away from Florida ERA administrators by blaming an entity that couldn't be questioned about the part it played in the tragedy.

While the ministers in Miami raised a holy ruckus about Williams's conclusions, Charles Clark, acting director of the U.S. Weather Bureau, was defending his agency's hurricane advisories in a private meeting with his bosses, Secretary of Agriculture Henry Wallace and Undersecretary of Agriculture Rexford Tugwell.

Wallace and Tugwell didn't think the scathing criticism being leveled at the weather bureau was justified, Clark wrote in a memo after the meeting. They believed the weather bureau "had given sufficient and ample warning to influence those proceeding with caution to evacuate the camps, and it was not just or fair that we should take the blame for the destruction of these camps," Clark wrote.

They did have some criticism for the advisories, however. "They, as laymen, did feel that the warnings and advisories were worded in a too stereotyped and technical way to be entirely and clearly understood by the public," Clark noted. Clark, Wallace, and Tugwell had no intention of publicizing this opinion, however.

As the weather bureau administrators critiqued their agency's performance in the hurricane, General Frank Hines, director of the Veterans Administration, was pondering Aubrey Williams's report on the tragedy.

It was becoming clear to Hines that the catastrophe in the Keys and the "act of God" conclusion were creating a serious public image problem for the VA. Clarence Barringer, a veteran in Newark, Ohio, who was furious that the vets in the Keys had been left in harm's way, poured his anger into a letter and mailed it to the "Veterans Extermination Bureau, Washington, D.C." It was delivered to Hines's desk.

Letters and telegrams expressing outrage and heartbreak had been pouring in to the VA from across the United States for days. Most of the people who sent them didn't seem to realize that the VA had had nothing to do with the decision to put the veterans in the Keys. That perception had to be changed.

Hines decided it was time to get some answers about what had really happened on the Keys. He knew the man to provide those answers, but unfortunately, that man wasn't in Washington at the moment. On September 11, Hines told his staff to find VA investigator David Kennamer right away.

chapter nine

Regret to Inform You

It wasn't hard to figure out why the public was heaping so much blame for the tragedy in the Florida Keys on the Veterans Administration. The VA had the difficult and unpleasant task of notifying the families of the men who'd died in the hurricane, and it was only human nature to blame the messenger for the bad news. Every day, telegrams beginning with the phrase "Regret to inform you" were being dispatched from Washington to all parts of the Unites States..

One of those telegrams was delivered to Theresa Kreitzburg in care of the Eckhart Mines in Allegheny County, Maryland. "Regret to inform you that Elmer Kreitzburg is reported among those dead in the Florida hurricane," it read.

A telegram also was sent to Betty Neel in Brandon, Texas. It read: "Regret to inform you that John T. Neel is reported among those dead in the Florida hurricane stop Body was cremated at Snake Creek, Florida stop."

The telegrams went to the big cities—Chicago and Cleveland, Milwaukee and Memphis, Pittsburgh and Philadelphia; they went to Denver, Los Angeles, New York, and Baltimore. But Western Union delivery boys also found their way to front doors in Prague, Nebraska and Tucson, Arizona. They delivered telegrams to Irvington and Elizabeth in New Jersey and to Greensburg and Altoona and Wilkes-Barre in Pennsylvania. The sad tidings went out to Everett, Newtonville, and Roxbury in Massachusetts and to Russell and Covington in Kentucky. The telegrams were delivered to St. Francisville, Louisiana; to Asheville, Concord, and Gastonia in North

Carolina; to Danville and Richmond in Virginia; and to Pensacola and Winter Haven in Florida. They went to Clarksville, West Virginia, and Marietta, Georgia, and Frostburg, Maryland, and to Peebles, Ohio. And they went to Knoxville and Nashville in Tennessee and to dozens of other towns and isolated farms in dozens of states. Regret to inform you...regret to inform you...regret to inform you.

A delivery boy went to 440 Senator Street in Brooklyn with a telegram regretting to inform John Conway—father of Jimmy Conway, the ex-boxer who'd once been a contender for the heavyweight crown—that his son had been killed in a hurricane in Florida. Whoever answered the knock said he'd never heard of John Conway. Hundreds of people were left to wonder. They knew their husbands, fathers, sons, and brothers had been in one of those New Deal work camps someplace in Florida. There had been something in the newspaper about a bad storm down there. They hadn't heard a word in weeks. What had happened?

Many would never know. The burial detail at Woodlawn Cemetery had tried to identify the bodies shipped to them for interment, but in some cases there just wasn't anything to indicate who the man was. Fingerprints were useless because there was no skin left on the fingers.

The workers made notes of whatever details they could. They wrote that one man had a tattoo of an American flag and the words "Sylvia 1906" on his left forearm. Another was missing the second and third fingers of his left hand. Still another had a tattoo on his left forearm of a red shield with "Co. L—28th Inf" in blue letters. They noted that one man was wearing a belt buckle with the initial "F."

It wasn't much, but it was the best they could do.

And then there were the families of veterans who had simply disappeared. There was no body to identify or even any remains to puzzle over. They were just simply gone.

Joseph Karpus of Brooklyn contacted the VA asking what had become of Andrew Beganske. The VA sent a telegram to Karpus that read: "Government and our records show body not recovered as yet stop Continuing search"

Grief and anger inevitably followed the visits from the Western Union delivery boys, and in Phillipsburg, New Jersey, Andrew Koleser was furious.

Koleser, a member of the American Legion post in Phillipsburg, was trying to help a grief-stricken mother whose son, J. Rodney Thompson, had been killed in the hurricane. Thompson's mother wanted to bury her son in his hometown. Federal officials told her that his body would be sent to her, so she'd hired an undertaker in Phillipsburg and made arrangements for her son's funeral. Now some bureaucrat was telling her Thompson had already been buried in Miami.

Koleser went to the Western Union office and told the clerk he wanted to send a telegram to President Franklin Roosevelt in Hyde Park, New York. In the terse, abbreviated language used in telegrams, Koleser explained the situation and asked FDR if there wasn't something he could do to help.

"Aged widowed mother heartbroken stop....Won't you help us have this veteran sent home," Koleser said in the message.

Lots of other people were just as angry and bewildered as Koleser about what had happened in Florida. They weren't buying Aubrey Williams's "act of God" conclusion, and they were pouring their anger and cynicism into letters to President Roosevelt, General Frank Hines, and anybody else they could think of.

"May our Great Savior forgive the ones who are guilty, who caused these poor sick and crippled men to be placed in a death trap," Joseph Hilbun of Eudora, Kansas, said in a letter to President Roosevelt.

A. M. Coffin of Cisco, Texas, told FDR the tragedy reflected poorly on him because he was ultimately responsible for hiring the men who'd been so indifferent to the veterans' welfare. The men in charge of the work camps should have had the "ordinary common sense" to remove the vets at least 24 hours before the hurricane struck, he wrote.

Edward Felker, a veteran in Erie, Pennsylvania, told Roosevelt that a gruesome news photo showing veterans' bodies lashed to a crude sled tied to an automobile's rear bumper had affected him deeply and prompted him to write FDR. Felker said he'd campaigned for Roosevelt in 1932 but said he blamed officials in Florida for the vets' deaths and feared many other veterans would as well.

A few days later, the photo that had shocked Felker was published in *Time* magazine with a story about the hurricane.

Roosevelt supporter Charles Pemburn, a veteran in Akron, Ohio, warned FDR's secretary Marvin McIntyre that Democrats hadn't been responsible for the storm but were responsible for putting the veterans on the Keys. Should people be convinced that FDR was responsible for the vets' deaths, public opinion would shift dramatically against him, and veterans would be working diligently to make sure that perception was maintained, he said. "[A] veteran will fight and work hard against a candidate—yes, much harder against than for," Pemburn wrote.

Others were astonished that those in charge had waited to decide whether to move the men. Frank Hamilton, pastor of the First Methodist Episcopal Church in Daytona Beach, Florida, said the Keys were "a place of great danger" during the hurricane season. "The delay of that train in getting away from Miami and in getting down to the Keys is by this time a nationwide fiasco," he wrote.

Anthony Morse of Jacksonville, Florida, predicted political repercussions if FDR didn't determine who'd left the veterans in harm's way. "There seems to be a disposition to whitewash everybody connected with the matter, but believe it or not, for your own political good you better not let it go that way," Morse said.

"I have had great respect for your motives, Mr. President, even though I have not always agreed with your methods," wrote L. Garland Biggers of West Palm Beach, Florida. "Your action in this matter will determine whether or not I shall continue to respect your motives."

Letters from veterans' groups across the United States underscored many veterans' intense dislike of FDR and revealed smoldering anger that could cost the President dearly in the upcoming campaign.

Albert Grosskopf and Thomas M. Daugherty of the National American Veterans in San Francisco told the President they were speaking for all members of their group when they said the deaths in the Keys were proof of the Roosevelt Administration's "undying enmity toward the veteran."

Veterans of Foreign Wars national commander James E. Van Zandt called Aubrey Williams's hasty report "a whitewash as wide as the breadth of the combined white crosses that cover America's heroic dead buried in France." He urged the President to disregard Williams's conclusion and order a new investigation. Just to be safe, the VFW decided to conduct its own investigation into the veterans' deaths.

"If these officials had heeded the storm warnings or been in the least familiar with seasonal climatic conditions, the tragedy could have been averted, all witnesses agree," Van Zandt said.

Ernest Hemingway had been deeply affected by what he saw when he and friends went to the Upper Keys to help with the rescue effort two days after the hurricane. Soon after he returned to Key West, Hemingway—who had no use for Franklin Roosevelt and the New Deal—vented his emotions in an essay that was published by *New Masses* magazine.

In his essay, Hemingway noted that the wealthy are fond of fishing in the Keys during the mild winters, but they avoid the area during the summer. "There is a known danger to property" during those months, he wrote. "But veterans, especially the bonus-marching variety of veterans, are not property. They are only human beings, unsuccessful human beings, and all they have to lose is their lives."

Hemingway didn't actually accuse the Roosevelt Administration of being responsible for the veterans' deaths, but the accusation was clearly implied. "Whom did they annoy, and to whom was their possible presence a political danger," he wrote. "Who sent them down to the Florida Keys and left them there in hurricane months? Who is responsible for their deaths?"

The *Chicago Daily Tribune* also was taking aim at Williams's "act of God" verdict. In an editorial published September 12, the *Tribune* conceded that the hurricane may have been an act of God, but putting the veterans on the Keys during the hurricane season was "a piece of criminal folly committed by some one in Washington.

"The camps on the Florida Keys were established to avert another bonus march on Washington, with all the political embarrassments involved in such a demonstration of discontent," the editorial said. "Naturally, a site was selected as far from Washington as it conveniently could be while still providing free labor for a southern constituency which wanted public improvements at somebody else's expense."

Senators and representatives were getting into the act, and the White House was deflecting some of the demands to an overloaded General Hines. On September 10, Florida Senator Duncan Fletcher sent a telegram to President Roosevelt telling him that his constituents demanded a thorough investigation. A copy of the message was forwarded to the VA director, and now the general had a memo awaiting his attention from Rudolph Forster, the executive clerk at the White House. Although the request was politely phrased in the form of a delicate understatement, Hines knew he had to respond immediately. "Will you not be good enough to let us have draft of appropriate reply to Senator Fletcher for the President's signature?" Forster wrote.

Hines met with WPA director Harry Hopkins to discuss the situation. They decided to launch a joint investigation in Florida, using investigators from the Veterans Administration and the Works Progress Adminstration, which had absorbed the Federal Emergency Relief Administration. The VA and WPA then would prepare a joint report for President Roosevelt.

Hines explained the plan to Stephen Early, who said he'd pass it on to Marvin McIntyre at the President's temporary offices in Poughkeepsie, New York.

If Early had any thoughts about the joint investigation or any-thing else about the hurricane in the Keys, he still wasn't bothering to jot them down in his White House diary.

At the U.S. Weather Bureau, acting director Charles Clark was wrapping up a "Special and Confidential" report on his agency's per-formance during the hurricane to Secretary of Agriculture Henry Wallace. In a September 12 letter to Wallace, Clark said he was keep-ing the report under wraps because the veterans' deaths had become a highly charged political issue and he didn't want anything he said to be interpreted as criticizing other government agencies and thus adding to the controversy.

Clark gave a detailed accounting of the weather bureau's actions from August 27—when meteorologists first realized that a disturbance of some sort had formed somewhere northeast of Puerto Rico—until the remnants of the hurricane went back to sea near Norfolk, Virginia, on September 6.

In Clark's estimation, the weather bureau had done a good job of tracking the hurricane and warning people in its path. To under-score his contention, he included letters from Pan American Airways, Barnett National Bank, the Superintendent of Lighthouses, the Collier County (Florida) Board of Commissioners, and others commending the weather bureau on the timeliness and accuracy of the advisories.

Without knowing it, Clark refuted Lawrence Westbrook's silly notion that the veterans were safer on the sparsely populated Keys because there was less danger of them being killed by flying debris than in a city. Clark pointed out that most of the deaths on the Key were caused by the massive storm surge that inundated the narrow, low-lying islands. There simply was no place for the veterans to escape this deadly flood. If they'd been on the mainland, the veterans almost certainly would have escaped the storm surge, and the loss of life would have been minimal, Clark said.

As far as Clark was concerned, the catastrophe in the work camps was due to the inexperience of the men in charge.

"The warnings issued by the weather bureau were sufficiently accurate and timely to urge a person reasonably familiar with the dangers of seas due to gales washing over low-lying keys to leave the keys and go to a place of safety on the mainland," Clark said. "Many persons in the southern part of Florida did act on the same advices of the weather bureau and took steps to protect lives and property."

Across town, Hines still hadn't heard from his ace investigator, David Kennamer. Where was he?

At last the VA director got a radiogram from a VA official in upstate New York. They'd found Kennamer in the small town of Canandaigua. He was leaving immediately and would be in Washington the following morning.

The general had Kennamer's orders waiting for him. Hines wanted him to determine whether the men in charge of the camps had received hurricane advisories and, if they had, what they'd done in response. Kennamer was instructed to work with John J. Abt, a lawyer who was handling the investigation for the WPA, which had taken over the Federal Emergency Relief Administration.

Hines told Kennamer to interview every survivor he could find.

David Wendall Kennamer had taken a winding route to his position as an investigator for the Veterans Administration. He had grown up in northeastern Alabama, and his relatives who were still living there in 1935 would soon benefit greatly from the electricity provided by the Tennessee Valley Authority, which had been created by the New Deal. But Kennamer and his family were not especially fond of President Franklin Roosevelt. They had been die-hard Republicans since before the Civil War, and President Calvin Coolidge—also a Republican—had a great deal of respect for the legal skills of the Kennamer family, appointing his brother Charles to a federal judge's position in Alabama and his cousin Elmore to an identical post in Oklahoma.

David Kennamer had been a shy young man who hadn't been especially interested in legal matters when he was growing up in Alabama. After earning a degree in veterinary medicine, Kennamer entered the U.S. Marine Corps and saw combat in France during World War I. He joined the Veterans Administration in 1924. By the summer of 1935 Kennamer was 47 years old and one of the VA's most capable investigators.

Kennamer arrived in Miami Thursday morning, September 12. He checked in to the McAllister Hotel and met briefly with Capt. Harry Farmer, who'd come down to Florida with Col. George Ijams and stayed on after the colonel went back to Washington.

Kennamer and Farmer then met with John Abt and asked the lawyer about the joint investigation they were supposed to conduct. Abt said he knew nothing about it and didn't think it was a good idea to continue looking into the matter. Nor did he want Kennamer interviewing Florida ERA employees. Abt reluctantly gave Kennamer copies of transcripts of some of the testimony he'd taken with Aubrey Williams.

Kennamer was deeply concerned about Abt's belief that there was no need to keep digging into the tragedy on the Keys.

He had quickly looked over some of the transcripts Abt had given him and was already questioning Williams's "act of God" conclusion. Maybe the weather bureau advisories hadn't been 100 percent accurate, but they had warned that a bad storm was out there in the vicinity of the Keys. "I cannot agree with Mr. Abt that no one was guilty of negligence," he wrote in a September 12 letter to Sam Jared, director of the VA's investigative division.

Kennamer also mentioned some of his concerns to Abt after he'd looked at the statements of Fred Ghent, Ray Sheldon, and meteorologist Gerald Kennedy of Key West, who'd advised Sheldon to return to the work camps at 5 a.m. Sunday morning, September 1. Abt said the meteorologist hadn't advised Sheldon to go back to the camps because there was impending danger, but because of the uncertainty about whether the ferry service would continue uninterrupted.

Kennamer saw it differently, especially since Kennedy said in a second interview that he told Sheldon the Keys might be in danger.

The VA investigator was suspicious of Abt's influence on the no-fault report that Aubrey Williams had submitted to President Roosevelt. And he had deep misgivings about whether he should even be working with the FERA attorney on this so-called joint investigation—so deep that he wanted Harry Hopkins to designate someone else to handle FERA's part of the inquiry.

General Hines sent a letter to Hopkins on Saturday, September 14, telling him that Abt hadn't been given any instructions about continuing a joint investigation with the VA. Hines didn't mention Kennamer's concerns about working with the FERA attorney.

Hopkins was surprised. That same day, Aubrey Williams had a telephone chat with the reluctant Abt in Florida.

Williams scolded Abt and told the lawyer he didn't want him giving anyone the impression that the WPA wasn't being cooperative. Abt warned Williams that Kennamer thought the administrators of the work camps had been at fault for the veterans' deaths. But Williams told Abt not to worry about that because they could deal with that problem in Washington.

Abt was persistent. "It would be a terrible mistake to start going through those witnesses again," he said.

"We can't help that," Williams said. President Roosevelt had placed General Hines in charge of the investigation, and FERA had to give the appearance that it was cooperating fully. Williams told Abt he didn't want Kennamer returning to Washington with doubts about FERA's motives. "I want you to develop a very cordial relationship," Williams said.

Abt stuck to his guns. "I think it would be a mistake to go through the whole thing again," he protested.

"But we can't say anything about that," Williams said. He reminded Abt that they'd have a chance to shape the final report before it went to the President, and they could take care of any problems then. "Say whatever he wants, we want too, and when we write the report...."

Williams ordered Abt to make it clear to Kennamer that the WPA and FERA would do anything the VA wanted. Then, Williams said to Abt, when Kennamer's report arrived in Washington they would untangle any problems before it reached the President.

While Williams and Abt discussed their plans for dealing with Kennamer's investigation, Sam Jared was making a few inquiries of his own in Washington, and he'd come across something he wanted to know more about—immediately. He sent a telegram to Kennamer telling him to find out if Ray Sheldon had received the weather bureau's advisory of 3:30 a.m. September 2 warning of high tides and gale-force winds on the Keys.

"Wire prompt report of all circumstances pertaining to this matter," Jared ordered.

Kennamer asked Abt where he could find Sheldon. The lawyer said he had no idea, and said he thought Sheldon had left the area to take another job.

On Saturday, September 14, Kennamer and Farmer went to Jackson Memorial Hospital in Miami, where John Russell was still recovering from the injuries he received during the hurricane two weeks earlier. The postmaster was known up and down the Keys as a man of wisdom and honesty. The investigators wanted to know how he had prepared his family for the hurricane.

"We were afraid because it was in our area and because it is the custom of these storms to make a turn," Russell said. "We were afraid it would turn and we had not wanted to wait until the last moment."

Kennamer asked Russell if Ray Sheldon or anybody else from the Florida ERA asked him whether the hurricane would be dangerous to the Keys. "No, they did not," Russell answered. "They didn't ask me anything about it at all."

Kennamer asked when he thought the vets should have been

evacuated from the Keys. "They should have been moved out on Sunday," Russell said. "The indications were there would be a storm. When there is a storm in the straits we always get a heavy wind from it."

Kennamer asked him if he thought a "prudent man" would have evacuated the veterans on Sunday, September 1.

"Yes," Russell said. "If I had been in charge of the camps, I would have moved out every man from the camps. You see, their situation was different from ours. Those in Camp 1 were in a very low piece of land, right open to the sea. Any sea at all would sweep it. There was nothing to shelter them in their little huts at all. No anchorage. They were just set up on piers, and I told them some time ago when they first built them that they wouldn't have the huts when the storm was over."

Kennamer asked Russell if he thought there had been "carelessness or negligence" on the part of administrators who hadn't evacuated the veterans in time.

"I do," he answered. "I think they should have been moved on Sunday, and they had plenty of time on Monday morning with continuous warnings. Even midday Monday they could have taken them."

Russell said the officials—"those in charge of the camps"—were responsible for the deaths of the veterans.

Farmer and Kennamer still had work to do after they finished interviewing John Russell. They had to track down Ray Sheldon to ask him about the weather bureau advisory of 3:30 a.m. September 2.

The investigators went to the Florida ERA offices in Miami to ask where they could find Sheldon. A worker there said Sheldon told them he was leaving Miami because he didn't want to be questioned about the hurricane. He might be in West Palm Beach, someone offered.

In West Palm Beach, Kennamer and Farmer learned that a Mr. Gordon might know where Sheldon was. Farmer got Gordon on the phone. Gordon was suspicious. He didn't know where Sheldon was. Why did they want to talk to him?

Farmer told Gordon they needed to talk to Sheldon about the tragedy in the Keys. Gordon said to call him in 10 minutes.

The investigators waited exactly 10 minutes, and then Farmer dialed Gordon's number. Sheldon was at the Flagler Apartments on Trinity Place, a block or so from Lake Worth and near the bridge that goes over to Palm Beach.

Sheldon was edgy, and said didn't want to talk to Kennamer and Farmer unless Abt, the WPA lawyer, was present. Sheldon said he had already chewed out one snoop who had tried to talk to him about the hurricane.

A few days earlier, Edward O'Ryan, a WPA writer, had been sent to talk to Sheldon for a report on the hurricane he was doing for Florida ERA director Conrad Van Hyning. O'Ryan knocked on Sheldon's door, but there was no answer. The writer started to leave, but he could hear someone moving around inside the apartment. He wrote an explanation of who he was and what he wanted on a piece of paper and slid it under the door. Minutes passed. Nothing happened. Finally an angry Ray Sheldon snatched open the door. He was furious, he said, because O'Ryan was making it appear as though he was trying to hide.

Kennamer tried to ease Sheldon's concerns. He didn't want Sheldon to make any statements without Abt, he just wanted him to clear up one small detail. Sheldon asked what it was. Kennamer asked Sheldon if he'd received the 3:30 a.m. weather bureau advisory of September 2. Not exactly, Sheldon answered. He'd had one of his clerks sleeping next to the office phone in case the weather bureau called, he said, and when he went in to the office around 8:30 a.m. the clerk reported there had been "no change" in the advisories.

That didn't fit the version given by clerk Robert Ayer, Jr. Ayer told Kennamer that he had repeated the advisory exactly as it was read to him over the phone.

Sheldon told the VA investigators that there had been so much "passing the buck" and so many investigators poking into what happened on the Keys that he was going to be careful what he said. And another thing—he wasn't happy at all at with the way Kennamer and Farmer had tracked him down like he was hiding out or something.

The investigators told Sheldon that Abt said he didn't know where he was, and the employees at the Florida ERA office had said the same thing.

Not true, Sheldon said. Lots of people knew his telephone number and home address, and lots of people—including Aubrey Williams, Conrad Van Hyning, and Abt himself—had told him he needed to get away for a while, get some rest. They all knew where he was staying.

Immediately after meeting with Sheldon, Kennamer sent a letter to Sam Jared. He reported what Sheldon had said about the 3:30 a.m. warning, and added that he thought many of the statements taken by Abt and Williams were "incomplete and unsatisfactory" and he'd need to question the respondents again.

Kennamer then left for Camp Foster, an Army camp in Jacksonville, where he was going to interview veterans who'd survived the storm and been sent to a VA hospital there. He was going to conduct the interviews with the suddenly cooperative Abt.

At the moment, however, the veterans were in no mood to talk.

Many of the survivors who'd come out of the Keys after the hurricane were still in shock. Those who weren't in shock were seething with anger. They'd been put on a special train in Miami and arrived at Camp Foster on September 9. Soon after their arrival, an Army captain told them they'd be enrolled immediately in the Civilian Conservation Corps and shipped out to CCC camps.

But the weary vets would have none of that, and they made their feelings clear about the matter. They weren't joining the CCC, and they weren't leaving Camp Foster anytime soon. The men were "in a very bad frame of mind and in open rebellion," camp administrators reported.

Two VA officials—J. G. Wright and Gladstone Pitt—went to meet the surly veterans in their barracks. Henry Redkey, a Florida ERA official, and Col. Thomas Lowe went with the VA officials.

They walked into a hornet's nest. "The men were in a very ugly mood," Wright said.

The four men tried to explain their plans for helping the survivors, but angry veterans interrupted and shouted insults. They'd been promised reimbursement for the personal items they'd lost in the storm. Where was their money? They'd been promised new clothing to replace the storm-torn rags they were still wearing. Where was that?

No one had any intention of helping them, they angrily accused. The only reason they'd been sent to Camp Foster was to keep them from talking to investigators and newspaper reporters and contradicting the whitewash that had been applied to the Keys catastrophe. They absolutely would not agree to anything until Ben Davis—the former superintendent of Camp 3—arrived from Miami. They would trust him, and nobody else.

The VA delegation gave up and trudged back to their headquarters to talk things over. Henry Redkey, the Florida ERA official, said he'd talk to clothiers about providing some clothes and see if he could hire a dentist and an optometrist to replace false teeth and eyeglasses the men had lost in the hurricane.

On Tuesday, September 10, J. G. Wright walked around Camp Foster chatting with the vets. If nothing else, the outbursts the previous night had provided an outlet for much of the simmering anger and frustration. Many of the vets seemed willing to cooperate. A few said they were interestied in joining the Civilian Conservation Corps— just as quickly as the promises of Mr. Redkey had been carried out.

Still, many men at Camp Foster would never accept the official verdict that no one was to blame for their awful experience. Oscar D. Griffin, a veteran from Union City, Tennessee, who survived the hurricane, told Wright that old-timers on the Keys had warned camp administrators to get the men off the islands. Griffin said Ray Sheldon and Fred Ghent were responsible for the tragedy and neither of them would be truthful about what had really happened.

Monto French of Chicago, who'd been at Camp 3 when the hurricane struck, was heartbroken that his brother John had been killed in the storm. It wouldn't take any investigators to figure out why his brother had died, French told Wright. The reason, he said, was simple—"pure damned carelessness."

At the other end of Florida's long coast another survivor tried to make some sense of his own experience in the storm.

James Duane, Jr., and the Long Key survivors had walked south from Long Key after the hurricane, crossing railroad bridges until they reached Marathon. There they were picked up by a repair train and arrived in Key West on the evening of Thursday, September 5. Duane's family was astonished, and then overjoyed. They had assumed he was dead.

Duane told the *Key West Citizen* that he thought the wind had reached 175 to 200 miles per hour at times, and the ocean had been terrifying. He told the *Citizen* he thought he'd be ready to go back to work after a few hot meals and a little rest, but he didn't care to experience another storm like the hurricane of September 2.

Duane took it easy for a week, then sat down at a typewriter at his residence at 703 Eaton Street and wrote a report about the hurricane to the U.S. Weather Bureau. He penned a more personal report to Ernest Carson at the Miami office of the weather bureau. Despite his harrowing experience, the conscientious Duane asked Carson to critique his report on the hurricane that had nearly taken his life.

"I am writing you to find out if you found anything wrong or anything I failed to do in making these few observations during this last storm," Duane wrote. He apologized for not phoning or telegraphing his 6 p.m. report to Miami on the day of the hurricane, but explained that the lines had been torn down.

Duane described the eeriness of the hurricane's eye as it passed over Long Key.

"During lull there was always a very light breeze—somewhat shifting," he wrote. "Sky clear, stars shining brightly, water was a terrible sight to see on the ocean side. Never will I forget the water raising—no, not a wave but looked just like the vacuum drew it right up, then let go. Raining very, very fast, then it began to pound."

Still, he remained a detached observer in the midst of this deadly chaos. "Very interesting, these storms, and have learned that this last kind are ones to avoid in the future." And after his rest and hot meals, Duane's interest in hurricanes was returning. He told Carson he wished some type of weather station could be established on Long Key. "I'd like to have the job down here, as I'm very, very interested."

Duane had one final question for Carson. "What would your figures be on the velocity of wind with pressure at 26.98 inches?"

While James Duane pondered his personal questions about the hurricane—such as how he'd lived through it—David Kennamer and his staff, who had set up headquarters at Miami's McAllister Hotel, were working 16-hour days to collect and analyze information about the actions of Florida ERA officials before and after the hurricane.

The investigators were digging into every possible source of information. Capt. Harry Farmer dug up evidence contradicting the rumors that Sheldon had prevented the veterans from leaving the camps before the evacuation train arrived. When Farmer asked Paul Pugh, a veteran who had been at Camp 3, whether the vets had been stopped from leaving, Pugh said he'd "never heard of such a thing."

Pugh denied that he'd repeatedly insisted that Sheldon order the train long before Monday afternoon. Pugh said he'd talked with Sheldon about the storm and possible plans to move the men out several times between Sunday afternoon and Monday afternoon, but had never demanded that the camps administrator order the train immediately.

Nor did he doubt Sheldon's abilities as an administrator.

"I had confidence in the man," Pugh said. "The man had a responsible job and I felt like he was capable of handling it."

But much of what Ray Sheldon said bothered Kennamer, starting with his conversation with weather bureau meteorologist Gerald Kennedy early Sunday morning, September 1.

In testimony taken on September 7 by Florida State's Attorney George Worley in Miami, Sheldon had said Kennedy suggested he return to the Keys because seas might be too rough for the ferry to run Monday. Kennedy had a different version of the conversation, however. He said he told Sheldon that conditions on the Keys were likely to become dangerous, and he might want to get back to the work camps as quickly as possible.

There were other inconsistencies. Sheldon denied telling anyone that two trains were waiting in Miami to be dispatched at a moment's notice. But two people—Florida ERA administrator M. E. Gilfond and *Miami Daily News* reporter William Johns—testified under oath to Aubrey Williams and John Abt, respectively, that Sheldon had told them exactly that.

When Kennamer questioned Sheldon about these inconsistencies, the administrator said someone must have misunderstood him.

Kennamer also noticed Sheldon's habit of ignoring advice. "Mr. Sheldon...said he had been through hurricanes, and from the testimony it seems that no one could tell him anything about a hurricane," the investigator observed.

Sheldon was blaming everyone but himself for the tragedy and considered himself a victim of everyone else's mistakes. Sheldon told Kennamer that if the train had arrived when the FEC had promised, he could have moved every man in the camps to safety. The fact that the train crew braved the hurricane, were delayed by the crane cable on Windley Key, and worked heroically in deadly conditions to free the train didn't penetrate Sheldon's thinking.

"He cannot conceive or imagine why it would take one hour and 20 minutes to remove a guyline cable," Kennamer noted.

Kennamer understood Fred Ghent's difficult position but was puzzled by his failure to evacuate the veterans from the Keys before the hurricane struck.

"No one was more sympathetic with the veterans or more interested in their welfare and problems," Kennamer said of Ghent. "His failure to act is not satisfactorily explained by the evidence."

Kennamer also was puzzled about why Ghent, Sheldon, and Conrad Van Hyning—who all had abilities as administrators—did not do more to protect the veterans from the hurricane. The answer, he decided, was because there had been friction and pettiness among Ghent, Sheldon, Sam Cutler, and Van Hyning.

"Mr. Cutler had been at the camps months and had a very high regard for Mr. Ghent," Kennamer said. "Mr. Sheldon had only been at the camps a month. Cutler has more ability than Sheldon and didn't have a very high personal regard for him or his ability. Possibly Sheldon didn't become alarmed [about the hurricane] when he returned to the camps to prove that Cutler's judgment wasn't so good."

The tension that lingered after Van Hyning told Ghent in August that he was going to be dismissed soon may have prompted the two administrators to avoid talking to each other at a critical time during the three days before the hurricane arrived, Kennamer said.

Kennamer didn't at all like it that other investigators had allowed Sheldon to be present when they were questioning survivors. Sheldon had even been allowed to ask leading questions of several witnesses and draw answers from them that supported his actions.

During Ed Butters's testimony to John Abt in Miami on September 9, Sheldon blurted out, "I would like to have you tell these fellows if, according to your opinion, there was anything more under the circumstances that could have been done to safeguard these men?"

"No, I do not" the obliging Butters responded. "I have said that all the time. No, sir."

Sheldon asked similar questions to Sam Cutler and other witnesses during their testimony the same day: Was there anything more that could have been done to protect the men?

"Sam, there has been quite a little talk been heard, and various ones have said this and that, and a lot of it we haven't paid any attention to," Sheldon said to his assistant. "I have asked each and every one in here if they thought that, with the information we received at headquarters, whether we did everything that was humanly possible for a person to do. What is your opinion?"

Cutler, unexpectedly on the spot, didn't mention that the weather reports and other information he'd received Sunday had prompted him and others to urge Sheldon to move the veterans off the island late Sunday afternoon, September 1.

"As I say, I never went through a hurricane," Cutler responded. "I knew nothing about it, and I never did know anything about that, but as far as what I have read, you did everything that you could, with the reports that you received."

"Thank you," Sheldon said.

When Camp 3 superintendent Ben Davis was questioned, he also supported Sheldon's leadership.

"Why, I think we did everything we could possibly do with the information we had," Davis said.

If a witness was reluctant to grant his endorsement of Sheldon's actions or didn't remember an event exactly as Sheldon wanted, he kept prompting and pushing until he got a response he wanted.

During the testimony of Junius Wigginton, clothing supply officer for the veterans work camps, Sheldon asked him if he'd overheard one of his telephone conversations Monday.

"Did you hear me call anyone and repeat a conversation into the phone that I was getting," Sheldon asked Wigginton.

"If I remember right, you called Mr. Ghent," Wigginton said. "Yes, you told him something that somebody had told you, if I remember right."

This wasn't what Sheldon wanted to hear. "No, this was a little earlier than that," he prompted. "You remember we were playing cards there, and it was about time to go to lunch, and I went to the telephone, and called a Miami number, and asked them regarding the storm, and I repeated their story back to them on the phone. Do you remember what that was I said?"

"If I remember right, they said that the storm was still...," Wiggington tried. "I...if I remember the report right, the storm was central near Santa Clara province, Cuba, about 160 or 200 miles—now I won't say which it was—miles east of Havana, moving slowly, and in a westerly direction, and that their opinion was that there was no immediate danger to the Florida Keys. Now, as near as I can remember, I heard Mr. Sheldon repeat that message. Now, I don't know whether he was talking to Mr. Ghent, but at the time that he repeated it, I thought he was. I don't know."

Sheldon pushed ahead. "Well, could it have been the weather bureau I was talking to?"

"It could have," Wigginton said.

"Well, that's who it was," Sheldon said. "That's all."

Sheldon's presence—and his questioning—during the testimony of other witnesses was "unusual and undoubtedly subjected them to intimidation," Kennamer said.

John Abt's refusal to hand over the transcript of Ghent's testimony of September 7 to Aubrey Williams puzzled and annoyed the investigator. And he sparred with the WPA lawyer over how the weather bureau advisory of 3:30 a.m. September 2 should have been interpreted. The advisory predicted gale-force winds and high tides on the Keys, and Kennamer thought this warning clearly indicated that the veterans camps were endangered by the hurricane.

Abt disputed that interpretation of the warning.

While Kennamer sorted through testimony and documents, workers continued sifting through the wreckage on the Keys. They also continued finding bodies.

On September 18, rescue workers found 11 corpses that had been washed up onto a mud flat 25 miles north of Tavernier. The workers speculated that the victims' bodies had been carried along by the Gulf Stream and gradually pushed back to the shore by the tides.

That same day, workers discovered Ben Davis's 1934 Dodge in which George Pepper and Rosalind Grooms Palmer had left Camp 3 with the intention of picking up a group of veterans' wives at the Hotel Matecumbe. Pepper and Palmer never showed up.

The car was submerged in Florida Bay, between Upper Matecumbe Key and Lower Matecumbe Key, about 100 feet from the shore.

A diver went down to take a look. There were no bodies in the Dodge. The car's doors were locked, and its oilcloth roof had been pushed out from the inside.

The diver found one other clue about the car's occupants—a pair of white high-heeled pumps.

The following day, rescuers found the owner of those shoes. A passing boater discovered Rosalind Grooms Palmer's body on Buttonwood Key, one of the dozens of tiny islands that dot Florida Bay.

There's no way of knowing exactly what happened to Pepper and Palmer. The young couple left Camp 3 sometime around 5 p.m. on Monday, September 2—at the same time that the winds increased so much it astonished even Ed Sheeran, who had been in six other hurricanes and had never seen winds escalate so dramatically in such a short time. Others also described the terrifying escalation of the storm's winds between 5 p.m. and 6 p.m. One of the storm's fierce gusts shoved O. D. King's car into the ditch as he drove from the Hotel Matecumbe to his home.

It's possible a vicious blast from the hurricane swept Davis' Dodge and its young occupants off the causeway and into Florida Bay, although the railroad embankment on the same causeway could have provided them some protection from the wind. It's possible that Pepper's well-known fondness for fast driving could have played a role. The combination of terrible weather conditions and high speed could have caused him to lose control of the car on the narrow causeway, sending it plunging into the bay, and the high winds and giant waves made it impossible for Rosalind and him to swim back to safety.

Pepper and Palmer fought their way out of the sinking car. Both were young, and Palmer was a strong swimmer—so strong that she was still alive when she was swept onto Buttonwood Key. But she was badly injured and soon died.

George Pepper's body was found a few weeks later near Cape Sable. He'd been carried across Florida Bay by the hurricane.

Slowly, the survivors of the decimated Russell family learned what had happened to dozens of their kinsmen who'd disappeared during the horrible evening of September 2.

The body of Emma Russell, Bernard Russell's mother, was found near the beach of Florida Bay, not far from her family's hurricane shelter. She was identified by the plain gold wedding band she wore, engraved with the initials "ELR" and "Feb. 1910."

Rev. S. E. Carlson lost his struggle to escape the rising waters of the storm surge. The surge carried Carlson's home several hundred feet, and his body was found not far from the nearby Hotel Matecumbe. His wife's body was found beneath a big pile of seaweed.

On September 10 the crew of a Coast Guard cutter from Biloxi, Mississippi, found the body of a young woman and an infant boy near the beach at Cape Sable. The dead woman was wearing a school ring engraved "MGS 1932."

Playing a hunch, Coast Guard Lt. Comdr. L. H. Baker wrote a letter describing the ring and the woman to Charles Albury, principal of Matecumbe School in Islamorada. Albury told Baker that the body was that of Ruth Booth.

Booth was Bernard Russell's first cousin. She'd clung to her son as the hurricane blew her across 40 miles of open water. Miraculously, she was still alive when the storm hurled her onto the beach. She crawled a few hundred feet from the pounding surf, lay down, and curled her body around her son. That's how the Coast Guardsmen found the mother and child. They buried them both where they lay.

Key West residents mourned the death of a teacher at the Harris Elementary School. Mary Ingraham was visiting her brother Robert Ingraham and his family on Upper Matecumbe Key when the hurricane struck. They were all killed in the storm. The flag at Harris Elementary flew at half-mast for a month in remembrance of Ingraham and Ruby Roberts, a member of the school's PTA who also died in the hurricane.

The body of Sarah Hodge—who'd gone with her sister Myrtle to spend Labor Day with their friend Rita Berteau—was found September 17 on Pelican Key in Florida Bay. Her sister's body was found a few weeks later on Bony Key—32 miles from Islamorada. Rescue workers identified her by the comb and powder puff she'd stuffed into her pocket before leaving Homestead.

The bodies were so badly decomposed that rescue workers didn't even bother trying to bury them. The black smoke from cremation fires became a common sight on the Keys.

On French Reef, salvagers had gotten the *Dixie* ready to refloat. On September 19 two tugs from the Merritt-Chapman & Scott Salvage Company pulled the passenger liner off the reef. The ship was towed into harbor for some temporary repairs, and then towed to New York.

On September 30 the Merritt-Chapman & Scott tug *Relief*, with the battered *Dixie* in tow, chugged into New York Harbor. The ships glided past the Statue of Liberty, and the *Dixie* was docked at Pier 51 at the foot of West 12th Street in lower Manhattan.

As soon as his ship was secured at the dock, Capt. Einar Sundstrom left the bridge to greet his wife, Marie, and his two daughters. A photo of a happy Einar Sundstrom being welcomed home by his family was published in newspapers across the country.

But the captain had little time for celebrating. On October 1 Sundstrom walked into the offices of the Department of Commerce's Bureau of Marine Inspection and Navigation at 45 Broadway to testify before a board of inquiry. The six-member panel wanted Sundstrom to explain how the *Dixie* had ended up on French Reef.

Sundstrom told the board he knew there was a storm in the Straits of Florida, but he'd sailed from New Orleans on September 1 because he thought he could outmaneuver the disturbance.

When the *Dixie* ran into the hurricane, the huge seas and winds made the ship almost unmanageable and he'd reduced the ship's speed to five knots, Sundstrom said.

"The hurricane was doing so much damage to the windows and we were shipping so much water that I just couldn't give her more speed," Sundstrom said.

The captain told the board the Labor Day hurricane was the fiercest storm he'd encountered in his three decades as a sailor.

"I have never experienced such weather in all my life," he said.

Dennis Folds, the *Dixie*'s second officer, told the board that the gigantic waves almost lifted the ship out of the water at times.

After hearing the officers' story, the board decided the grounding was due to "extreme and unusual weather conditions" and the ship's officers and crew had not been negligent in any way.

The marine salvagers had pulled the *Dixie* out of Florida waters just in time to avoid another hurricane. As the *Relief* was towing the *Dixie* up the East Coast, a tropical storm formed in the Caribbean Sea. The storm crossed Cuba and grew into a minimal hurricane as it churned across the Straits of Florida September 28.

The hurricane continued to strengthen as it approached the Keys. This time, Florida ERA supervisors were taking no chances. They loaded hundreds of rescue workers onto trucks and took them to Miami. But the hurricane turned to the northeast and slid past the Keys with its eye offshore. Winds in Miami peaked at about 40 miles per hour.

As the season's third hurricane spun northeast across the open waters of the Atlantic, the American Legion assembled for its annual convention in St. Louis. The legionnaires quickly decided they'd conduct their own investigation of the veterans' deaths in the Keys. Quimby Melton, editor of the *Griffin Daily News* in Griffin, Georgia, was appointed chairman of the three-member investigation committee. The

Legion also appointed Vice Commander W. E. Whitlock of High Springs, Florida, and Catesby Jones of Selma, Alabama, to the panel.

Melton said his committee would first go to Key West to interview witnesses, then to Miami for more interviews. This would be at least the third investigation into the tragedy in the Keys.

Melton would have to board a steamship in Tampa to get to Key West. The hurricane had destroyed about 40 miles of track between Tavernier and Marathon. The Florida East Coast Railway was still operating under bankruptcy, and FEC officials hadn't announced when— or if—they'd repair the tracks. But rumors were rampant that the FEC was going to abandon its famed Key West Extension. Henry Flagler never would have let that happen, the old Conchs muttered, but bureaucrats were running the FEC now, and they would be too concerned with the cost to spend the money to repair the railroad.

On the morning of Saturday, October 12, the passenger ship carrying the American Legion's investigating committee sailed into Key West's harbor. Melton, Whitlock, and Jones went straight to the auditorium of Key West High School, where Melton called his investigating committee to order.

"We have come into Florida with perfectly open minds," he told participants. "We are not here to whitewash anybody. If there is blame to be fixed, we want to find on whose shoulders it properly rests."

Arthur Brown of Hastings-on-Hudson, New York, who had been the timekeeper at Camp 3, was the first to testify before the Legion committee.

"There was sufficient time to get all veterans out from Camp 3, and the trucks could have picked up men at Camp 5, seven miles to the north, and prevented great loss of life there," Brown said.

The committee also heard testimony in public from U.S. Weather Bureau meteorologist Gerald Kennedy, Maj. William Albury of the National Guard, M. E. Gilfond, and Conrad Van Hyning.

The committee then flew to Miami Sunday morning and interviewed Lawrence Bow and Ed Sheeran in sessions that were closed to the public. From there, the investigators went to Tallahassee to meet with Governor David Sholtz.

Melton told Sholtz that the Legion panel was trying to be open-minded. "We're not looking for a goat, and neither do we have a bucket of whitewash with us," he said. "We've been trying to find out whether the lives of these men were sacrificed through care-lessness—and if so, through whose carelessness—or whether it was an 'act of God.'"

Sholtz gave the committee copies of the hurricane report by State's Attorney George Worley and said he, too, wanted to know whether carelessness had caused the veterans to be killed. But the governor told the Legion board that the storm had been unusual in many ways.

"You must take into consideration in this matter that a modern steamer equipped with the best in radio facilities was in the path of this storm and was tossed upon a reef," Sholtz said. "You must also consider that a modern freighter was picked up by a wave and driv-en aground. Also, you must consider that there was a tidal wave along with the storm, and that civilian residents of the Keys as well as the veterans were the victims."

The American Legion committee disbanded after its visit to Tallahassee, and Melton went home to Georgia to write his report. He'd tried to set up an interview with or at least get a statement from Ray Sheldon but hadn't been able to contact him.

As Melton studied the testimony and organized his thoughts to write his report, FEC workers arrived in Islamorada to start salvage work on the ill-fated evacuation train. They'd built temporary tracks to Upper Matecumbe Key and planned to use a crane to set the derailed passenger cars back on the tracks. Then they'd use another locomotive to pull number 447 and the 11 cars back to the Miami yards. It would be the last train ever to depart from Islamorada.

By late October David Kennamer and his staff were wrapping up the investigation into the deaths of the veterans. Kennamer was writing a massive, detailed report to VA director Gen. Frank Hines that incorporated testimony from more than 400 people and information from hundreds of pages of supporting documents.

It was a thorough and painstaking examination of the tragedy in the Florida Keys. On October 30 the report landed on Hines's desk. In Kennamer's mind, there was no doubt about why the veterans had died during the Labor Day hurricane. Ray Sheldon, Fred Ghent, and, to a lesser degree, Conrad Van Hyning had not done what they should have to protect the men who were their responsibility.

The men in charge of the Keys work camps knew hurricanes posed a threat to the veterans' safety and knew they had to devise a practical, effective way to protect them from this threat. Despite Ghent's and Sheldon's claims to the contrary, they never followed through with their plans for one of the most logical methods for getting the men out of harm's way—loading the men on a train and hauling them out of the islands.

"No definite agreement had been made with the railroad to furnish a train and the railroad had not been advised as to who would have authority to order a train in the event of an emergency," Kennamer wrote in his report. "Mr. Loflin's unanswered letter to Mr. Ghent appears to be about the last positive action taken relative to plans to evacuate the veterans in the event of a hurricane."

Ghent, Sheldon, and Conrad Van Hyning should have made sure that definite arrangements had been made weeks in advance to have a train ready if it was needed, Kennamer said.

Kennamer conceded that the advisories from the weather bureau "were not entirely accurate," but added that they clearly told "of danger lurking in the Atlantic east of the camps and was sufficient to alarm Mr. Cutler and others at the veterans camps." He also decided the advisories "were not as inaccurate as some have alleged."

"They told of danger and were sufficient to alarm several people employed at the camps and were sufficient to have caused any prudent man to have been ready to get the men out when the danger became imminent," Kennamer wrote. "With these facts well established, the weather bureau must be acquitted of any culpability."

Kennamer decided that Sheldon was less than convincing in much of his testimony about receiving warnings of the danger the hurricane posed to the Keys. In several interviews Sheldon said that he hadn't been told the situation was dangerous, but this was not true.

Sheldon also fudged the truth in another way. "His statement that he left Mr. Cutler in charge of the camps and told him to call him if anything came up before leaving for Key West cannot be accepted as entirely true," Kennamer wrote. "He left without saying anything to Mr. Cutler and only told his stenographer where he could be found."

Sheldon had committed a serious error by delaying the evacuation, Kennamer said. "The poor judgment used by Mr. Sheldon was his failure to be ready to move when it became apparent this would be necessary," Kennamer wrote. "The evidence is...conclusive that no time should have been lost getting ready to move after the 10 a.m. advisory Sunday, September 1, and that part of the readiness to move should have included a definite agreement with the railroad to furnish a train."

Kennamer included a long list of actions Sheldon should have taken that would have prevented the tragedy. Among other things, he faulted the camps administrator for allowing beer sales to resume in the canteens; not contacting Ghent after he learned of the weather advisory of 3:30 a.m. September 2 predicting gales and high tides on the Keys; not assuming authority to order the train himself after the advisory of 10 a.m. September 2; and not visiting the camps the afternoon of September 2, to make sure everything was ready to move out.

Kennamer blamed Fred Ghent for not completing arrangements to have an evacuation train ready weeks before the worst part of the hurricane season arrived. Ghent also should have stayed in close contact with the camps during the Labor Day weekend after he'd learned that a hurricane had formed, and not disappeared for two hours on Monday, September 2 when Sheldon was trying to reach him.

Conrad Van Hyning should have made certain that Ghent had arranged for an evacuation train with the FEC and kept in touch with Ghent after he knew a hurricane had formed near the Keys.

Kennamer praised the crew that took the evacuation train into the teeth of the hurricane on the night of September 2. He concluded that the FEC was not in any way responsible for the deaths.

He acknowledged that other investigations had concluded that no one was to blame for the tragedy. But he thought his investigation was far more thorough than the others because he'd assembled much more information.

Kennamer also acknowledged "reasonable men may honestly differ about this matter regardless of the facts." But several inarguable facts led to his conclusion that Florida ERA officials had seriously blundered—Ghent and Sheldon didn't order a train after the crucial 3:30 a.m. advisory, Ghent and Sheldon didn't communicate with each other from 4:50 p.m. Sunday until 1:37 p.m. Monday, Ghent disappeared for almost two hours when he was needed, and Ghent and Van Hyning did not communicate with each other at all. Because of these omissions, Kennamer said he could not conclude "that they did all the things they should have done or all the things demanded of them by nature of the representative positions."

The conclusion, in David Kennamer's mind, was clear and simple—more than 250 veterans were dead because Ray Sheldon, Fred Ghent, and Conrad Van Hyning hadn't done their jobs. But in the minds of some influential insiders in Washington, D.C., the well-reasoned and well-supported conclusions that Kennamer drew from his painstaking investigation would be undermined by his long Republican pedigree.

chapter ten

For the Record

On the morning of April 2, 1936, Ray Sheldon was talking about hurricanes with some very important people in Washington.

Sheldon, who had left the Keys and not worked since the September hurricane, sat before the House Committee on World War Veterans' Legislation, which was chaired by Representative John Rankin, a Democrat from Mississippi and a loyal ally of President Franklin Roosevelt. The committee was conducting an investigation into the deaths of the veterans in the Florida Keys as part of its review of a bill that would compensate the families of the men who had been killed. The members of Rankin's committee—14 Democrats, 6 Republicans, and one member of the Progressive Party—were questioning Sheldon about his experience in the storm.

As far as Sheldon was concerned, no one in the Keys—or the state of Florida, for that matter—knew more about hurricanes than he did. He told the committee that he had lived in Florida since 1923 and that he had been through about half a dozen hurricanes before the Labor Day storm. He had been driving from his home in West Palm Beach to Miami when the infamous hurricane of September 17, 1926, nearly leveled Miami Beach and sent seawater surging through downtown Miami. Two years later he stayed in his home when the terrible hurricane of September 18, 1928, smashed ashore at West Palm Beach and roared inland to kill 1,800 people around Lake Okeechobee. So he was a seasoned and knowledgeable observer of hurricanes whose judgment about the storms was as sound and reliable as anyone else's.

John Rankin had no intention of letting anyone seriously

challenge the image that Sheldon was trying so hard to project to the committee. In fact, Rankin intended to set up as many opportunities as he could to allow Sheldon to polish that image.

People had been clamoring for months for a congressional investigation to answer once and for all the questions surrounding the deaths of the veterans in the hurricane of September 2, 1935. Republicans wanted the hearings because they hoped that powerful political ammunition might be uncovered that could be used against President Roosevelt in the election that was only a few months away. The American Legion, Veterans of Foreign Wars, and other veterans groups that had been causing trouble for FDR for years had been insisting that Congress conduct the hearings since the day after the hurricane tore through the flimsy work camps on the Keys and killed more than 250 of their buddies.

So John Rankin was going to give the Republicans and the veterans their investigation. On January 3, 1936—the first day of the new session of Congress—Rankin introduced a bill in the House of Representatives to compensate the victims' families. A few days later, A. D. Hiller, an assistant director of the Veterans Administration, estimated that it would cost the government about $30,000 per year—or $217 per month to each family—to compensate the dependents of 138 veterans killed in the hurricane. The figure would, of course, go higher as more deaths were certified and more dependents became eligible, Hiller said.

Rankin knew that the bill would be referred to his committee for review and a recommendation on whether to pass it, and that would give him a reason to hold the hearings. He would make a big show of getting to the bottom of the questions surrounding the veterans' deaths, and he would parade a couple dozen witnesses before his committee and let them tell their stories. But as chairman of the committee, he would decide who testified. And he would make sure that no troublesome witnesses were called. Rankin would also make sure that the testimony that went into the permanent record of these

hearings led to one conclusion: that no one, least of all the administrators hired by the Roosevelt Administration to supervise the work
camps in the Keys—had been at fault for the deaths of those veterans.

As a lawyer, Rankin knew how to selectively present facts to steer
a jury to the conclusion he desired. In an ideal situation, a lawyer
would allow only those facts supporting his argument to be submitted as evidence to a jury, and he would block anything that might
diminish or detract from his argument. It didn't matter if the information he blocked was true. If it hurt his argument, he kept it out.

As chairman of the committee holding these hearings, Rankin had
set up that ideal situation. He was not presenting a case to a jury, but
he was presenting it to the American public and to posterity. His committee would collect facts about the disaster that would go into a permanent record of findings. Rankin would decide what facts were
relevant and went into that permanent record, and what facts
were excluded. Period. No one could challenge his decisions or appeal
to a higher authority.

Rankin needed the record to show that Ray Sheldon was knowledgeable about hurricanes and would not have done anything foolish
that would have caused the deaths of the veterans. So if Sheldon wanted to present himself as knowing a great deal about hurricanes, Rankin
would do everything he could to help.

That included fending off questions from Representative Edith
Nourse Rogers of Massachusetts, who was one of the Republicans on
the House Committee on World War Veterans' Legislation. Rogers had
been sniping at Rankin and Roosevelt Administration officials for
weeks, insisting from the floor of the House of Representatives that
the administration was trying to cover up the blundering that had
killed the veterans and complaining that Gen. Frank Hines, director
of the Veterans Administration, was aiding in this cover-up by with-
holding information she was entitled to as a member of Congress.

After listening to Sheldon explain to the committee how to inter-
pret a falling barometer, Rogers asked the camps administrator if he

could have loaded the veterans aboard construction trucks and taken them out of the Keys before the hurricane hit. Yes, he answered, they could have done that. Wouldn't that have been quicker than waiting for a train to arrive? she pressed. But Sheldon would not bite.

"We had no reason to have the train," he replied. "We had no storm, from outward appearances, that was going to hit the Keys, at that time."

"But they do—storms sometimes change their courses?" Rogers asked, trying another approach.

"That is what the records show," Sheldon said.

"They often do that?" Rogers asked.

"Yes," Sheldon answered.

"And in your experience, they have changed their course often?"

"Of storms, there is no telling where they will go," Sheldon said.

"So," Rogers continued, closing in on her point, "you have to be ready to move at once?"

Rogers had backed Sheldon into a corner. Rankin jumped in before Sheldon could answer. Since the start of the hearings eight days earlier, Rankin and fellow Democrat Wright Patman, a committee member from Texas, had been hammering away at the fact that the work camps administrators had not been the only people in the Keys who hadn't evacuated the islands because of the hurricane. The Conchs—who undoubtedly knew more than anyone else about the threat hurricanes posed to the Keys—hadn't left either. As far as Rankin and Patman were concerned, that meant that no one should blame Ray Sheldon or anybody else for not acting sooner to evacuate the veterans.

"Mr. Sheldon, right there," Rankin said, "what was the attitude of the people who lived on the Keys? Were they excited over the storm?"

"Some of them closed and got the boards together to nail up their houses, and some of them did not nail them, but that was done, because if there was a storm, it was a whole lot easier to nail them up during pleasant weather than to wait until the last minute and get out in the rain and struggle with the boards," he replied.

Rankin told Sheldon to continue, but instead of answering

Rogers's barbed question Sheldon started talking again about his experiences with other hurricanes in Florida.

Patman asked Sheldon whether the Russell family left the Keys because of the hurricane. Sheldon answered that they hadn't, and incorrectly told Patman that 73 of the 76 members of the Russell family had died in the hurricane.

"Did they have automobiles?" Patman asked.

"They all had cars," Sheldon said.

"They evidently had the same idea that you had about the storm?"

"Yes, sir."

Sheldon's preposterous statement would go unchallenged. In fact, John Russell hadn't had anything resembling the same idea about the hurricane as Sheldon. During his interview with David Kennamer on September 14, 1935, Russell went into great detail about his conviction that the veterans in the work camps were in great danger and should have been evacuated from the Keys long before the hurricane struck.

Russell wasn't asked to testify at the hearings, however, so the committee members never heard his thoughts about who was responsible for the tragedy of September 2, 1935. And, more important to Rankin and Patman, Sheldon's absurd assertion that John Russell had shared his opinion that the Keys weren't in danger and the veterans didn't need to be evacuated would remain untouched in the record.

Rankin would repeatedly use the fact that John Russell hadn't taken his family out of the Keys as an argument that there was no reason for Sheldon, Ghent, and Van Hyning to have been unduly alarmed. As the hearings progressed, he and Patman developed a standard line of questioning that they used to lead witnesses to the conclusions they sought. One of those witnesses Rankin walked through his routine was Joseph Fecteau, a veteran from Massachusetts who'd been the timekeeper at Camp 5. Rogers had insisted that Rankin call Fecteau, assuming that the hurricane survivor's statement would raise legitimate doubts about the judgment of camp administrators.

"Now, you were down there," Rankin said to Fecteau, "and I am just trying to put myself in your place, because I have no interest what-soever in this hurricane, except as a member of Congress and an American citizen and an ex-serviceman, and my usual interest in human-ity. Those people were down there—you knew Mr. Russell, did you not?"

"Yes, sir," Fecteau answered.

Rankin began the familiar call-and-response questioning that he'd used with other witnesses, establishing that Fecteau knew John Russell, that he knew the Russells had lived on Upper Matecumbe Key for many years, and that Russell hadn't moved his family off the island before the hurricane. He also established that the Methodist minister, the Reverend S. E. Carlson, hadn't left before the storm, and that he and his wife had been killed.

Rankin went into a windy summary leading up to his clincher.

"I want to put myself in the condition of those people down there," he said. "They had been there all their lives. I have long since learned that when you are in Rome, do as Romans do as nearly as is possi-ble. If I go into a strange territory and a cloud comes up, I look around to see how the neighbors feel about it, because I would feel uneasy running into a storm and have everybody laugh at me. But these peo-ple lived there, and they had, according to the testimony here, the usual reports on this storm, and the indications were that if it struck Florida at all it would strike Key West. They had no idea, and you say you had no idea, nobody else had an idea, that there was going to be a flood, because any man with any intelligence at all, whether he was a native or a veteran, would have gotten out of there the day before, every single human being who lived on the Keys, if they had an idea that a flood was coming, they would have gotten out, would they not?"

"I guess they would," Fecteau said. "I know that I would."

Rankin had once again protected the record from Rogers.

It would have been very difficult to find two people in the 1936 House of Representatives more dramatically different from each other than Edith Nourse Rogers and John Elliott Rankin.

Rogers, a Republican representing Massachusetts's Fifth District, was the daughter of a wealthy textile mill manager from Lowell. She had been educated by a private tutor until she was 14, attended a private girls' school in Lowell, and completed her education at a private finishing school for young women in France.

She returned to Lowell and married John Jacob Rogers, a Harvard-educated lawyer, in 1907 and moved with him to Washington, D.C., when he was elected as a Republican to the House of Representatives in 1912.

Her husband enlisted when the United States entered World War I, and Rogers joined the American Red Cross. She toured the battlefields in France, saw the war's awful death and destruction, and developed a deep and enduring concern for the welfare of veterans.

When John Rogers died suddenly in 1925, she entered a special election to fill her husband's House seat and won by an overwhelming margin. After the election, she said she hoped everyone would "forget that I'm a woman as soon as possible." But her finishing-school polish, tasteful wardrobe, aristocratic bearing, and the orchid or gardenia that was often pinned to her shoulder set her apart from her colleagues and guaranteed that her gender would not be overlooked.

Still, she established a reputation for two traits that weren't often associated with women in 1936—toughness and aggressiveness. She wouldn't back down from a fight, and she pursued her political goals with a gentle but unrelenting determination.

She was exactly the kind of woman likely to annoy Rankin—an articulate, sophisticated, uppity Yankee female from Massachusetts who was a Republican to boot.

In Rankin's world, women were the delicate creatures of Old South mythology. They were to be revered, protected, and kept at home.

Rankin, a Democrat, represented Mississippi's First District. He'd grown up in rural Itawamba County in northeastern Mississippi near Brice's Crossroads, the site of a Civil War battle in which Gen. Nathan

Bedford Forrest's badly outnumbered Confederates decisively defeated an invading Union force in June 1864.

Rankin graduated from the University of Mississippi's law school in 1910 and in the following year moved to nearby Tupelo in neighboring Lee County, where he was the county's prosecuting attorney. He served in the Army during World War I and was elected to his first term in the House of Representatives in 1920, polling 10,400 votes to a mere 480 for his opponent.

Rankin was bold, outspoken, and absolutely certain of the correctness of his convictions. He was well known for his long, uninterrupted, impromptu speeches on the floor of the House. During one of his especially lengthy monologues, House clerks worked furiously to keep up with the ceaseless flow of the Rankin oration. One clerk turned to another clerk and asked him if he'd managed to copy everything the loquacious Mississippian had said.

"Yes," the clerk replied, "I got it copied down during a burst of silence by Mr. Rankin."

Rankin also had a dramatically different background from Franklin Delano Roosevelt, who'd grown up with the comforts and advantages of wealth in a part of the country where the opportunity to prosper was taken for granted. But Rankin was a shrewd politician who recognized that Roosevelt could be a useful ally for accomplishing his own objectives, and so he established a political relationship with FDR even before the new President had taken the oath of office. Soon after the election of November 1932, which swept Roosevelt into the White House, Rankin wrote to the President-elect seeking help in his bid to become Speaker of the House of Representatives.

Roosevelt didn't have to do much to fulfill Rankin's request. Rankin asked FDR to stay neutral in the contest for Speaker rather than endorse anyone for the post. Roosevelt responded with a letter saying he'd comply, but Rankin's attempt at taking control of the House of Representatives failed anyway. Still, as chairman of the House

Committee on World War Veterans' Legislation, the representative from Mississippi was a powerful figure in Congress.

The congressional district Rankin represented lay in the heart of an impoverished region that hadn't changed much since General Forrest pulled off his improbable victory. Many housewives still cooked meals on wood-burning stoves and lit kerosene lanterns at dusk. Industries that could have brought prosperity to the region ignored it because there was not enough cheap electricity to power their factories.

The region's greatest potential for energy—its rivers—went untapped. That would change, however, thanks to the efforts of an unlikely benefactor—a Republican senator from the Midwest.

Senator George Norris of Nebraska was an ardent supporter of making cheap electricity available for farming and industrial development, and his passion for this effort went well beyond his party loyalty. He campaigned for Roosevelt in 1932 because he thought FDR would do more to help bring this about than President Hoover.

FDR took up Norris's cause almost immediately after he was sworn in as President, and the first chance to advance it was the creation of the Tennessee Valley Authority, a plan that would bring new opportunity to seven southern states. The TVA also would serve a political function identical to the economic revitalization of Key West—it would become another example of how the programs of the New Deal would pull the nation out of the Depression. If the TVA worked in the South, its principles could be applied nationwide.

There was a political hook as well to the plans for the TVA— the prospect of bringing financial investments and jobs to the South would inevitably pull southern Democrats into the New Deal's camp, and Roosevelt—no slouch as a politician himself—knew he had to have the Southerners aboard if he had any hope of pushing his ambitious programs through Congress. If some of his Deep South supporters such as Rankin had antebellum attitudes about race relations, that was regrettable, but it was a trade-off FDR felt he had to make.

As a representative from one of the poor rural states that would benefit greatly from the TVA, John Rankin was very interested in the project. He pushed the legislation establishing the authority through the House of Representatives, and in May 1933 President Roosevelt signed the bill establishing the Tennessee Valley Authority.

Eighteen months later, FDR made a campaign-style swing through five states that would be served by the TVA. The President visited sites where dams being built with federal money would provide cheap electricity that would, in effect, bring the area into the 20th century. The *Washington Post* reporter accompanying FDR on the tour described the TVA as a "staggering blow to private interests," but thousands of people in Kentucky, Tennessee, Mississippi, Alabama, and Georgia felt otherwise, turning out to hear Roosevelt praise the authority and promise them that it would improve their lives.

More than 40,000 people gathered in Harrodsburg, Kentucky, to hear the President speak, and 80,000 welcomed him at Corinth, Mississippi. John Rankin was at Roosevelt's side, introducing the President during some of his stops in Mississippi. During a stop in Tupelo—the first city to announce that it would buy electricity from the TVA—the President looked out at a crowd of more than 25,000 and told them he was "glad to come into the district of my friend, John Rankin."

Roosevelt noted that during his swing through the South people had come to welcome him "not by the thousands. They have come literally by the acres." And the President undoubtedly understood that many of them had turned out thanks to John Rankin.

When the 74th Congress convened for its second session in January 1936, the establishment of the Tennessee Valley Authority had become an accomplishment that the New Deal coalition could point to with pride as President Roosevelt prepared to begin his campaign for a second term. Rankin—who'd also gone to bat for FDR's tax plan by making a speech supporting it over national radio—had been named to Roosevelt's reelection campaign committee.

The President's backers were more worried about how another issue could cause FDR more problems than being on the losing end of the bonus vote. Although Roosevelt still had a powerful influence in the Democrat-controlled Congress, he undoubtedly knew he'd have a hard time preventing the early payment of the World War veterans bonus. On January 9 the House of Representatives passed a bill approving early payment, and the Senate followed the next day. Roosevelt vetoed the bill, but both chambers of Congress easily overrode his veto, and the veterans had their hard-fought bonus.

There was another New Deal project that many Roosevelt supporters feared contained the potential for disaster at the polls in November. Although the effort to revive Key West's economy with tourism seemed to be showing results, questions were still being raised about why government officials in Florida—who were part of the vast new bureaucracy created by the New Deal—hadn't moved quickly enough to get those veterans building a highway in the Keys out of the way before that hurricane struck in September 1935.

On the same day that Rankin introduced the bill to compensate the dependents of the veterans who'd been killed in the hurricane, the House approved a resolution offered by Representative J. Hardin Peterson, a Democrat from Florida, calling for an investigation of the tragedy.

The following day Representative Edith Nourse Rogers sent a letter to Gen. Frank Hines, asking the director of the Veterans Administration for information about the "Florida Keys tragedy." It was the first step of her effort to bring to light more information about the hurricane of September 2, 1935. And although her well-established concern for the welfare of veterans undoubtedly was a motive for her interest in the catastrophe, there were political ramifications to her request as well.

Republicans were desperate to avoid a repeat of the 1934 mid-term elections, when voters had nearly thrown them out of Washington by handing almost 70 percent of the seats in Congress to Democrats. It was the worst thrashing the Republicans had suffered since the party was formed in the mid-19th century, and the GOP was searching for an issue—any issue—that it could hold up as an example of New Deal inefficiency or bumbling to halt the Democrats' political rout.

A hurricane that had killed more than 250 veterans because their New Deal–appointed bosses hadn't troubled themselves to get the men out of harm's way could be just the ticket. The nation had been incensed when two veterans had been killed during their 1932 march on Washington, and voters had taken it out a few months later on a Republican President. How would they react to the deaths of a couple hundred veterans under a Democratic Chief Executive?

It was logical that Rogers should play a pivotal role in any Republican effort to stop the surge of New Deal reform. She was the senior Republican member of the House Committee on World War Veterans' Legislation. But more important, her seat was safely in the hands of the GOP.

In the five elections in which she'd defended her seat, her Democratic opponents had never posed a serious challenge. Her percentage did slip from 66 percent of the vote in 1930 to 59 percent in 1932, but in 1934—when Republicans were being buried by the New Deal landslide—she increased her take of the balloting to 62 percent. If she could add to her vote total during the most disastrous election in the history of the Republican Party, there was little reason to worry about repercussions if she took on a popular Democratic President.

But if Rogers's seat in the House wasn't likely to be threatened, Rankin's was carved of stone. Rankin won his first term in the House in 1920 with a staggering 96 percent of the votes cast in the election. And he actually upped that percentage when he ran for reelection in 1922, receiving 99.7 percent of the vote.

Rankin ran unopposed from 1924 through 1930. Two opponents dared to challenge him in the 1932 election, and he steamrolled them with 97 percent of the vote. He ran unopposed again in 1934.

In late February Rogers received a response to her request for information about the hurricane that she'd sent to General Hines almost two months earlier. He refused to provide what she'd requested, and suggested she ask Representative Rankin for the information she wanted.

Rogers was infuriated and immediately fired back a letter to Hines on February 24 telling him she was "astounded" by his response.

"Other departments always take the position that Members of Congress are entitled to the fullest and most complete information about any matter pertaining to the work of the departments," Rogers told Hines. "Yours is the only department in Washington that has not cooperated with me."

That same day on the floor of the House of Representatives, Rogers took an indirect jab at the administrators in charge of the veterans work camps when Representative Mark Wilcox, a Democrat from Florida, told the assembly that he wanted to provide more money to the U.S. Weather Bureau for tracking hurricanes. He noted that the tragedy in the veterans work camps had been caused in part by the fact that the U.S. Weather Bureau's tracking of the hurricane had been hindered by inadequate equipment.

But Rogers said there were more reasons why veterans had died.

"Does not the gentleman think that someone was very remiss in not removing the veterans earlier?" Rogers asked Wilcox. "I have the report released in September of the WPA," she said, referring to Aubrey Williams's report, "and it seems to me clear, after reading this report, that there was some mismanagement resulting in great tragedy."

Wilcox refused to be lured into a debate. "There is quite a conflict of opinion as to who, if anyone, was to blame," he said.

On February 25 VA director Hines sent another letter to Rogers about her request for information from his department. He told the representative that the VA was preparing a report for Rankin and would send it to him "within the next few days."

"I am sure it will be made available to members of the Committee," Hines said.

Hines also hinted that Rogers could ask WPA director Harry Hopkins—who'd received copies of Kennamer's documents and report—to give her the information she sought.

"What that organization releases is, of course, a matter entirely in their hands," Hines wrote. "Nevertheless, I do not feel that with propriety I can release the report of the Veterans' Administration in this regard until it has served its original purpose and is available for release."

Hines didn't say what the "original purpose" of the report was, nor did he say when it might be made available to the public.

Rogers was still angry a day later when Wilcox presented the appropriations amendment he'd discussed two days earlier. She saw an opportunity to get in a few more jabs at the Roosevelt Administration and House Democrats.

Rogers said she supported the increased funding for hurricane warning improvements, but instead of explaining why she thought the appropriation should be approved, she attacked the Roosevelt Administration's motives for sending the veterans to the Keys, hinting that the men had been sent to the islands to prevent them from becoming a problem for the President. She charged Democrats with wrapping a veil of secrecy around the catastrophe.

"Why they were sent there no one seems to know," she said. "Were they sent in order that they might be as far away from Washington as possible?"

Rogers said Hines had refused to provide information she had requested. "Why is this veil of secrecy thrown around the veterans' tragedy on the Florida Keys?" she asked. "Why is it that the information from the Veterans' Administration is available only through the chairman of the World War Veterans' Committee? Things have come to a pretty pass if members of Congress are obliged to seek information only through committee. It does not seem open and aboveboard to me."

Six weeks had passed since the House had approved Representative Peterson's motion to investigate the tragedy, and nothing had been done, Rogers said. It was time to end the secrecy surrounding the veterans' deaths.

Rogers's cutting criticism undoubtedly left Rankin seething. But in late March he was ready to give the Republicans and other critics of the Roosevelt Administration what they wanted.

On March 25, 1936, Rankin got permission from the House of Representatives to subpoena witnesses and put them under oath during hearings he planned to conduct on the bill to compensate the families of hurricane victims. Later that day Rankin talked to a reporter for the *New York Times* about his plans for his committee's hearings. "There has been much criticism of the administration policy in this matter, and I intend to build up a record on just what happened," he said.

On the surface, Rankin's promise to build up a record of the events surrounding the veterans' deaths seemed to be a promise to use the power of Congress to gather as much information as possible about what had happened in the Keys and from that determine whether anyone was to blame for the tragedy. But Rankin had more important priorities than leading his committee through an open and unfettered inquiry into the sad events of September 2, 1935. That actually was the last thing he wanted.

Rankin had established a solid working relationship with President Roosevelt that had been useful for both men. He could take a large share of the credit for the creation of the TVA and the dramatic improvements it would mean to his poor, underdeveloped home district, and he had had the opportunity to bask in the reflected glory of a very popular President. In Rankin, FDR had gained a powerful ally who could help keep the New Deal on solid footing in the South.

There was every reason to believe that this mutually beneficial relationship would bear more political fruit during a second Roosevelt Administration, and as a member of the President's reelection campaign committee, Rankin had a responsibility to make sure FDR won that second term. And that meant stamping out any brushfire scandals before the Republicans could stoke them into an inferno that might incinerate Roosevelt's chances of reelection—no matter how fire-proof the President seemed nine months before Election Day.

Rankin had had more than a month to study the information provided to him by the VA—plenty of time to decide what could support the "no fault" finding and who could provide it, and what information could undermine the finding and who to avoid bringing before the committee. David Kennamer's VA report thus became a set of guidelines for Rankin to help him decide in advance what information he would allow into the record and what information to keep out.

At 10 a.m. on Thursday, March 26, 1936, Rankin gaveled his committee to order. Besides Rankin, the panel's Democrats were Charles Buckley of New York, William Carpenter of Kansas, William Connery, Jr., of Massachusetts, Joe Eagle of Texas, Joseph Gray of Pennsylvania, Glenn Griswold of Indiana, John Hoeppel of California, John Houston of Kansas, Joshua Lee of Oklahoma, Herron Pearson of Tennessee, Wright Patman of Texas, Jared Sanders, Jr., of Louisiana, and Joe Starnes of Alabama.

In addition to Edith Nourse Rogers, the Republicans on the committee were Albert Joseph Engel of Michigan, Charles Halleck of Indiana, Charles Plumley of Vermont, Chauncey Reed of Illinois, and Charles Risk of Rhode Island.

Harry Sauthoff, a member of the Progressive Party from Wisconsin, was the committee's 21st member.

Rankin got straight to business, calling as the first witness Representative J. Hardin Peterson of Florida, who had just returned to his home in Lakeland after the marathon first session of Congress ended when the storm struck the Keys. Peterson was the first to angrily call for an investigation to determine why the veterans hadn't been evacuated.

"They had plenty of notice, and I want to fix the responsibility," Peterson said in a telegram to Harry Hopkins on September 4, 1935.

But when he took the stand before John Rankin's committee, it was clear that Peterson's anger had diminished.

As part of his testimony, Peterson read into the record an excerpt from the minutes of the American Legion's executive committee meetings of September 22 and September 26, 1935. The segment included part of a statement by Howard McFarlane, a Tampa lawyer who conducted a quick preliminary investigation into the veterans' deaths for the Legion soon after the hurricane.

McFarlane said he'd found "no culpable or criminal negligence chargeable to any person or groups of persons.

"On the contrary," the Florida lawyer had said, "it is my opinion that so far as the human element and the men involved are concerned, they functioned as well as might reasonably be expected. After a disaster such as this, which shocked the nation, there is always a cry that the blame should be placed, the meaning being that it should be placed upon the shoulders of some one or more men—that a scapegoat should be had. Such is the case now. Such a feeling ordinarily does not involve the doing of justice. In making this investigation, I have attempted to put aside any such feeling, and to place myself as nearly as I could in the shoes of the men who had the decision to make. It appears to me that the loss of life is not fundamentally due to what occurred on the first and second of September, but goes considerably deeper than that."

McFarlane added that the "main cause of the disaster was the nature of the weather bureau reports," and said Sheldon's and Ghent's lack of experience with weather conditions in the Keys had been a contributing factor.

Peterson added that after American Legion officials heard McFarlane's comments, they appointed the committee composed of Quimby Melton, Catesby A. R. Jones, and W. E. Whitlock to do a more thorough investigation. "For the purpose of brevity and in view of the fact that representatives of the American Legion will also be here, I will not go into great detail with reference to the report of the special investigating committee on the Florida hurricane disaster," he said.

Peterson's move seemed reasonable and considerate. Why take up the time of Rankin's committee to discuss information that would be provided again by other witnesses?

But Peterson also knew that the Melton-Jones-Whitlock report of November 2, 1935—the one he'd so considerately refrained from discussing—contained a blistering condemnation of Aubrey Williams's "act of God" conclusion.

In their report, Melton, Jones, and Whitlock acknowledged that, without the authority to summon witnesses and put them under oath, their investigation had been hampered. "But we did gather enough information to satisfy ourselves, at least, that the disaster at Matecumbe was not 'An Act of God' and that the lives of the veterans could have and should have been saved," they wrote. Their report went on to blame the tragedy on the "inefficiency, indifference and ignorance" of the people in charge of the work camps and said the veterans' deaths in the Keys amounted to "murder at Matecumbe."

It was a far different take on the disaster than the one presented in McFarlane's statement. The Melton-Jones-Whitlock report was the justification upon which the American Legion's top officials had based their call for a congressional investigation.

By selectively mentioning one Legion report that exonerated FERA and Florida ERA officials from any blame and acknowledging but not discussing a second Legion report that harshly condemned them, Peterson had subtly supported and protected Rankin's all-important record. Also, by not going into details about the Melton-Jones-Whitlock report, Peterson had avoided putting Rankin—a fellow Democrat—in the awkward position of having to make a ruling about what evidence could be admitted to his record and what would be excluded.

It was a slick performance by the Florida congressman. But he was also fed questions from some Democrats on the committee that allowed him to start laying the foundation for the record of selected facts that Rankin wanted to build. Patman asked Peterson if there was any reason why anyone connected with the work camps in the Keys should have anticipated that this hurricane would be so powerful. Peterson said there wasn't.

Rankin or Patman would ask this question or variations of it to witnesses throughout the hearings. If they didn't get the response they sought, they kept asking until they'd led the witness into saying exactly what they wanted.

The two congressmen would establish a pattern of often interrupting Edith Nourse Rogers when she tried to ask a question or make a statement that challenged the "act of God" conclusion. Patman was the first to jump in when she tried to ask Peterson whether Florida residents were reluctant to leave their homes when they receive a hurricane warning.

"Is it not true that the inhabitants of the area that has been flooded, or has had a hurricane, or disaster of some sort, are always very unwilling to leave their homes?" Rogers said to Peterson. "I know, recently, in Lowell, where we are recovering from a flood, that although the water was in the first floor of people's houses, they had to be hauled out by policemen."

"Yes," Peterson said. "That has been my observation."

Rogers had a letter from Everett McComb, a veteran from Milwaukee who'd been at Camp 1, in which he described his experience in the hurricane. She wanted to make McComb's letter part of the record of the hearings.

"These veterans were not inhabitants of Florida and were very anxious to leave," Rogers said. "Mr. Peterson, did you receive a letter from..."

But Patman jumped in before Rogers could finish, saying he did not understand everything she'd just said. Rogers repeated that the veterans were anxious to leave the Keys before the hurricane struck.

"Is the lady testifying?" Patman asked.

"Here is a letter right here from Mr. McComb, and I ask unanimous consent, if Mr. Peterson is willing, to have this inserted in the record at this point," Rogers said.

But Rankin wouldn't hear of it. He insisted that if Rogers wanted McComb's comments to go into the record, she would have to have him come to Washington and testify. Rogers said she thought McComb would be willing to do that.

"That may be true, but we are not going to fill the record with unsworn testimony, because people who put their statements in this record are going to have to take the responsibility for them," Rankin said, ignoring the fact that he'd already allowed Peterson to read into the record the statement of Howard McFarlane despite the attorney's absence—and obvious inability to swear under oath that he was telling the truth.

Rogers tried to resume her questioning of Peterson, but Patman interrupted repeatedly until an exasperated Rogers started to take another swipe at Rankin.

"I do not believe it is the chairman's fault that we have not had hearings about this matter, and...," Rogers began.

Rankin was incensed. "The truth of the business is, I did not know the lady was so anxious to have the hearings," he shot back.

Rankin also would accumulate testimony to the effect that the Keys were not a dangerous place to put the veterans and that the living conditions in the work camps were quite comfortable for them.

He would establish in his record that Florida ERA administrators had correctly interpreted the hurricane advisories issued by the U.S. Weather Bureau and had taken reasonable and prudent precautions based on their interpretations.

He would allow some witnesses with little knowledge of relevant facts to make statements that couldn't possibly be verified. Many of these statements would be presented as facts, but they would simply be wrong or misleading. Some of these incorrect or misleading statements were undoubtedly inadvertent. Others were just as undoubtedly deliberate. Regardless of the witnesses' motivation, the inaccuracies all became part of Rankin's permanent record.

Finally, Rankin intended to make Edith Nourse Rogers pay for the accusations she'd made on the House floor that the Roosevelt Administration had sent the veterans to the Keys to get them out of sight and that Rankin was being secretive about the Keys tragedy. Rankin and Wright Patman would disrupt or challenge Rogers's questioning at every opportunity.

Rogers was not the only committee member who attempted to ask penetrating questions that might prompt witnesses to make statements casting doubt on the "act of God" conclusion. Harry Sauthoff, the Progressive Party congressman from Wisconsin, frequently asked questions that cut through the no-fault contention, as did Republican Albert Joseph Engel.

Engel, however, gave clear indications that he was going to side with the majority Democrats on the committee—perhaps because he felt there wasn't enough solid evidence to conclude that anyone had been at fault. Or perhaps because he was a first-term Republican who'd wrested Michigan's Ninth District seat from its Democrat incumbent in a close, hard-fought election. Engel's margin of victory was so narrow that the winner hadn't been determined until the day after the balloting. He knew he risked alienating the swing voters in his district who'd put him in office if he went against a popular Democratic President.

Sauthoff's and Engel's attempts to question the no-fault theory often drew defensive responses from Rankin and Patman, but Rogers's efforts to challenge the "act of God" conclusion were often met with open hostility, especially from Rankin.

When Rogers raised questions about the living conditions in the camps, Rankin interrupted with a reference to Douglas MacArthur's 1932 rout of the Bonus Marchers. The vets would have preferred living in the Keys, he accused sharply, to "being driven out of Washington at the point of a bayonet and having their tents burned down."

He continued his tirade. "I do know that a former administration drove these same men out of Washington at the point of a bayonet, when they were looking for work," Rankin said. "If you want facts in the records, those are facts."

Rankin didn't explain what these facts had to do with the veterans dying in the hurricane.

Rankin and Patman used three witnesses—Representative Mark Wilcox, a Democrat from Florida; Julius Stone, the former director of the Florida Emergency Relief Administration; and Aubrey Williams—who'd written the now famous "act of God" report—to establish for the record that the Florida Keys were a safe and comfortable place to send the veterans.

"If you had been one of those soldiers and they left you the selection of the place, you would have gone right there [to the Keys]?" Patman asked Wilcox.

"I expect I would, knowing as much as I do about the climate and the surroundings," Wilcox said.

"You would have considered it one of the most likely places?" Patman continued.

"There is nothing wrong with the location," Wilcox said. "There is nothing wrong with the project."

"And you did not consider it a dangerous place to send them?" Patman asked.

"No," Wilcox said. "I did not consider it a dangerous place to send them."

Patman also asked Wilcox about the actions of Capt. Einar Sundstrom, master of the S.S. *Dixie*, with the objective of establishing that Sundstrom—like Ghent and Sheldon—had been misled about the storm's position and had been driven aground as a result. "If a ship that was well equipped with the proper instruments could not tell which way the hurricane was coming, how would you expect anybody else to do it?" Patman asked Wilcox.

"I am not sure he could not have gotten out, if he had wanted to," Wilcox said. "He probably did not try to get out."

"You do not think he would purposely go into it, do you?" Patman asked.

"I do not know whether he did or not," Wilcox said.

"We will presume he did not," Patman said.

Julius Stone described the work camps by using his unusual talent for weaving fact and fantasy into appealing tales of deception.

Sending the men to remote islands many miles from a city and depriving them of any amusement except drinking was not subjecting them to hardships—it was exactly what the men needed, Stone said.

"The minute you put a group of detached men anywhere near a city, they have got two strikes on them before they start," Stone told the committee. "They are blamed for every crime that is committed in the city, and they do not have a chance at leading anything like a nor-mal life because the environment will not permit it...So we felt that, if the men were to have any chance to do something besides putting some brick and mortar into place, it was necessary to give them a social environment in which they could escape their nerves, calm their nerves, and so on."

Stone didn't mention the excessive drinking among the veterans, nor did he mention the serious sanitation problems that prompted the vets to go on strike in February 1935.

"What do you consider the standard of health conditions in the camp, and in the Keys?" Rankin asked Stone.

"Well, I would say they were excellent, and so did the Florida State Health Department, under whose auspices all of our operations were," Stone answered without flinching. Somehow, the comments from federal inspectors about the filthy living conditions that existed in the camps soon after they were established were left out, as was the fact that two veterans had died from a form of meningitis that is spread by crowded conditions.

Stone also glossed over the reasons why B. M. Duncan and Lawrence Bow were removed from supervising the veterans camps. Instead of telling the committee of the engineers' indifference to the veterans' living conditions, he attributed the change in administration simply to the growth of the camps.

Stone achieved his masterpiece of glibness, however, when he told the committee that the only discomfort the vets experienced in the camps was having to watch millionaires at play as they worked under the hot sun.

"The only feature of these camps that I can think of that was at all unsettling was the fact that whenever these fellows unbent their backs from sawing rocks, they looked out and saw a millionaire's yacht," Stone said. "The millionaires came down to fish in these waters and the weather was wonderful. So we saw no reason why we should not put these fellows in the same weather as where these millionaires went."

Aubrey Williams told the committee that Florida officials were "enthusiastic about having that road built and thought the Keys would be an excellent place for the veterans.

"They felt that this was an excellent type of project for men that were in need of rebuilding and conditioning, out of the way from the ills and troubles that had beset them," Williams said. "And, as a matter of fact, I know of no place I have ever been that I would rather go to and take my chances of rebuilding myself than there."

Williams added that many people had told him how well the camps had been administered "and that anyone who attempted to make a goat of anybody in this thing was either vicious or ignorant, and that it was the height of absurdity to attempt to place—to attempt to make any agent of the government responsible for the freaks of nature, as this sort of thing obviously is."

Williams defended the no-fault conclusion he presented in his report without using the "act of God" phrasing that had upset so many people across the country.

"I was unable to do otherwise than come to the conclusion it was through no one's fault," he said. "It just happened, that is all. It was tragic and deplorable, but something that was beyond the power of anybody to have averted."

Edith Nourse Rogers told Williams his hastily completed report was "not a very complete description of what actually took place."

When she asked Williams for more information, Rankin hurried to Williams's defense, again attacking Republicans for the rout of the Bonus Marchers in 1932.

"Your administration had jurisdiction of these men in 1932," Rankin said. "And these same men, instead of being given jobs in Florida, as I have said, were driven out of Washington at the point of a bayonet. And to come at this late hour and criticize this setup down there and say they did not have enough assistants, when you had no information to that effect developed by the testimony here, under oath, I think is a belated cry."

Rankin allowed Williams's full report, which had been completed in 48 hours, to be made a part of the record.

Gen. Frank Hines, whose top investigator had spent three weeks compiling a detailed report, could have seriously undermined the credibility of Williams's report during his testimony by discussing David Kennamer's investigation for the VA. But the VA director had scarcely been sworn in when he made it clear he wouldn't lift a finger to contradict the no-fault conclusion.

"Mr. Chairman, I would say that the procedure followed by the committee is undoubtedly producing the facts, and I congratulate you on the procedure," Hines said. "I would like, first, to say to the committee that I am sure you appreciate that, in my position, as head of the Veterans Administration, there is little that I can directly testify to regarding this matter; that I must rely upon reports that have come to me, and the official records of the Veterans Administration."

No one asked Hines about David Kennamer's investigation and Hines didn't mention the detailed report his skillful but staunchly Republican investigator had assembled. Nor did Hines mention that he'd defended Kennamer's findings in a March 31, 1936, memo to Undersecretary of the Interior Charles West.

Col. George Ijams did mention Kennamer's report when he testified, but did not discuss any of the VA investigator's conclusions.

Rogers asked Ijams if he thought everything possible had been

done to get vets out of way of the hurricane, and if he'd talked to survivors about this question when he was in Florida immediately after
the storm. Ijams said he "did not go into that end of it." He didn't mention that on January 10, 1936, he'd written a memo to Hines in which
he explained why he completely agreed with Kennamer's findings.

Fred Ghent, who had landed a new federal job in Washington,
tried to explain how he had intended to protect the veterans from hurricanes. He told the committee that he had talked to Ray Sheldon in
Key West around 5:30 a.m. on Sunday, September 1. Immediately after
this conversation, Ghent said, he told a Florida East Coast Railway
dispatcher that he would probably want a special train sent to the
Keys on short notice the following day. Ghent said that since he had
given the railroad 32 hours' notice that he would want a train, the
FEC should have been able to assemble it and get it from Miami to
Camp 3 at Lower Matecumbe Key—a distance of about 80 miles—
within three hours after he gave them a definite order. That meant
that because he had ordered the train at 2 p.m. Monday, it should
have reached Camp 3 around 5 p.m., he said.

Ghent told the committee that his expectations weren't unreasonable. He was very familiar with how the FEC operated, he said. The train
should have been able to travel at 60 miles per hour, he said. But Ghent
either didn't know or didn't tell the committee that the FEC trains never
approached such a high speed in the Keys.

Although Rankin had assured committee members that there was
plenty of money to pay travel expenses for witnesses to come to
Washington to testify, he refused a request from FEC officials to reim-
burse them for travel from Florida to the capital, and so they didn't testify. Had they come before Rankin's committee, it's likely that they would
have told the members that no firm agreement had ever been reached
with Ghent in the summer of 1935 to provide an evacuation train, that
because Ghent hadn't given them a definite order for the train on Sunday
September 1, 1935, they hadn't assembled it then, and that they didn't
allow their trains to travel anywhere near 60 miles per hour in the Keys.

On May 1—after the hearings before Rankin's House Committee on World War Veterans' Legislation had been in session for more than a month—Edith Nourse Rogers discovered she'd been working at an even greater disadvantage than she'd thought. On that day, she learned that copies of transcripts of the testimony taken by VA investigator David Kennamer had been filed in an office just down the hall from where the hearings were being held. Somehow, no one had bothered to tell her that these transcripts were available for her to examine so long as she didn't take them out of the office.

By early May 1936, Rankin was ready to wrap up his committee's hearings and bring the bill to compensate the hurricane victims' families to a vote on the floor of the House of Representatives. But there were a couple of details he still needed to take care of to protect his record from being tarnished by any testimony or statements that might contradict the "act of God" verdict.

On Saturday, May 9, representatives of the Veterans of Foreign Wars and the American Legion came before the House Committee on World War Veterans' Legislation. Rankin knew that both agencies had conducted their own investigations of the hurricane disaster, both had condemned Aubrey Williams's report, and both could and probably would offer testimony that would undermine the no-fault conclusion.

But he disposed of both of them quickly and harmlessly, beginning with Col. John Thomas Taylor of the American Legion.

Taylor told Rankin that he'd brought copies of the American Legion's full report—the report compiled by Quimby Melton, Catesby A.R. Jones, and W.E. Whitlock that concluded that the veterans' deaths had been "murder at Matecumbe"—to give to the committee so that it could become part of the record of the hearings.

Rankin immediately decided that the committee could not accept the Legion's report because "we could not accept conclusions drawn from another investigation such as we have conducted here."

It was a bizarre ruling considering that he'd already allowed two other outside "investigations" to be made part of the record—the statement from Tampa lawyer Howard McFarlane and the hasty investigation of Aubrey Williams. Both of those investigations, of course, had supported the no-fault verdict that Rankin had so tenaciously defended throughout the hearings.

Patman suggested that Taylor leave his documents for the committee to review. "Of course, we are not saying that we will put them in the record," Rankin cautioned.

Edith Nourse Rogers tried to get Rankin to call witnesses from the American Legion who had gone into the Keys after the hurricane, but Rankin refused and Patman hinted at possible repercussions if Rogers pushed to call more witnesses.

"I hope the lady will not insist upon prolonging this investigation," Patman said. "If she is opposed to the compensation bill..."

"The gentleman knows that is not true," Rogers retorted.

"That would be a good way of postponing action on the bill," Patman said. "Why not read the testimony here?" he suggested, referring to the documents Taylor had just turned over. "Perhaps that would pacify the lady?"

Rogers made a motion to call an American Legion witness, and Rankin refused to even put the motion to a vote. Nor did he make the Legion's "murder at Matecumbe" report part of the record.

Rankin dismissed Taylor and turned to Millard Rice, who represented the Veterans of Foreign Wars.

"Mr. Chairman, the VFW did have a special committee that made an investigation relative to this matter," Rice began.

"I know you are not going to say anything, unless you know it of your own knowledge," Patman interrupted patronizingly. "You are under oath, and any suggestion or statement made by someone else is not admissible."

"I was about to say the chairman of the commission is not available," Rice continued. "He is now in Japan. I am not able, under oath, of course, to report what he stated in regard to that investigation, nor, I assume, am I permitted to submit any of the affidavits gathered by the chairman of that committee. They are available if this committee wants them. But they are quite similar to the affidavits gathered by the WPA, although some of these were gathered very shortly after and may differ in some respects."

Rankin didn't ask Rice for his documents. He thanked Rice for offering to testify and declared that the committee was going into an off-the-record executive session.

With that, Rankin's hearings on the Labor Day hurricane of 1935 were over. A few weeks later Rankin submitted a report recommending that the House of Representatives approve the bill to compensate the dependents of the veterans who'd died in the hurricane. Rankin's report included a few sentences saying that camp administrators were not to blame for the veterans' deaths.

Rogers submitted her own report explaining her take on the hearings conducted by Rankin. Not surprisingly, she lambasted Rankin's "no fault" conclusion.

"There is no doubt in our minds that while it would be impossible to place blame for the terrible loss of life, yet the evidence shows a surprising lack of judgment on the part of those responsible for the welfare of the men under their charge," Rogers wrote. "Many blunders were made. This hurricane has been called an act of God. God may be held responsible for this storm, but He cannot be blamed for leaving these men in the path of the storm, nor can He be blamed for depriving them of their only available method of leaving."

Besides Rogers, Rhode Island Republican Charles Risk and Harry Sauthoff, the Progressive Party member from Wisconsin, signed the report.

On June 1, 1936, Rankin's bill to compensate the dependents of the hurricane victims came up for a vote in the House. Rogers said she was in favor of the compensation bill, but she again attacked the no-fault conclusion and the Roosevelt administration.

"I feel that there was gross negligence," Rogers said. "I blame no one person, but a number, and I hold this government directly responsible for the death and injury of those veterans. There has been no more horrible tragedy than the Florida hurricane, which killed so many of our veterans entirely unnecessarily, their wives and their children."

Rankin protested and pointed to his carefully constructed record as proof that no one had been at fault.

"I ask every member of the House to read this record," Rankin said. "I ask you to read these sworn statements. I ask you to consult the members of this committee who are unbiased and who heard all of this testimony. You will see that we reached the only conclusion that we could have reached."

"There have been some silly efforts made by some members of the committee to play politics with this matter," Rankin added, "but I am glad to say that the more responsible minority members of the committee have been sincere in their efforts to get the facts and to assist in arriving at a proper conclusion."

Rankin thanked Albert Joseph Engel, the Republican from Michigan, "for his able and diligent services."

Rogers came back for another attack.

"I am delighted to have the membership of the House read the hearings," Rogers said. "Whitewash is written all over them. If you will read these hearings, you will see the efforts made to ban testimony when certain questions were asked by the ranking minority member, myself, and by others."

Rogers also accused Rankin of refusing to call witnesses who could have cast doubt on the no-fault conclusion.

"I sat through those hearings and allowed my rights to go by because I feared if I did not the hearings would be closed and the testimony end," Rogers said. "They had the votes on the majority side to stop the hearings, and I wanted the facts to appear in the record."

Sauthoff supported Rogers's contentions.

"I have come to the conclusion that the government was negligent in the method in which it provided protection for the people on the Florida Keys," he said. "It must be remembered that the government put them there. The government had a responsibility and a duty. Having put them there, it was the government's duty to take care of them."

Risk criticized Rankin's shameless manipulation of rules of evidence against anyone who might offer testimony or evidence he didn't want to hear.

"I saw the technical rules of evidence which apply in a court of law applied time and time again against the gentlewoman from Massachusetts and other members of the committee," Risk said.

But the other Republicans on the House Committee on World War Veterans' Legislation were silent, offering no reasons why they had passively quietly sided with the Democratic majority. Perhaps they had decided it just wasn't worth the effort and they didn't want to become entangled in a squabble they couldn't possibly win.

The bill to compensate the veterans' dependents was passed, and the House moved on to its next item of business—a bill authorizing the U.S. Marine Corps Band to play at a reunion of Confederate veterans in Louisiana and centennial celebrations in Arkansas and Texas.

On June 4, 1936—after Rankin's hearings had ended and Congress had approved the bill to compensate hurricane victims' families—VA director Frank Hines sent a copy of Kennamer's report to Edith Nourse Rogers. But if Rogers and other Republicans found any of the political ammunition they were seeking, they didn't use it against President Roosevelt in the 1936 election. By the time John Rankin hit the campaign trail to stump for FDR's reelection, the Labor Day hurricane of 1935 was officially on its way to obscurity.

Congress also approved Mark Wilcox's request for more funding to protect Florida residents from hurricanes, and in July 1936 the WPA sent a recently hired engineer from its Jacksonville office to Key West to determine what public buildings there might be converted to hurricane shelters.

The engineer who inspected the structures had learned a great deal about the power of hurricanes and what the storms could do to poorly constructed buildings. His name was Ray Sheldon.

chapter eleven

Forgotten Storm

On September 7, 1936—Labor Day Monday—Bascom Grooms, Sr., and his family were returning to Key West after a two-week trip to Georgia. One year had passed since his daughter Rosalind had been killed in the hurricane, and he and his wife were still grieving over their loss.

They'd learned the awful details of what had happened to her the previous Labor Day—the car carrying her and her fiancée George Pepper, plunging into Florida Bay; their escape from the submerged vehicle, fighting to stay alive as the hurricane carried her across Florida Bay, her lonely, tortuous death on a tiny, isolated island. Those grim facts were in their thoughts as they drove down the islands to catch the ferry at Lower Matecumbe Key.

Reminders of the hurricane were strewn along the roadside. In Tavernier a storm-battered house still stood by the road where the hurricane had left it. Several wrecked cars also remained where they'd landed a year earlier. They were now rusting hulks being gradually overtaken by the returning vegetation. But there was talk of plans to erect a more appropriate reminder of the storm, a monument or memorial of some sort.

They drove through Islamorada, where the American Red Cross was building small houses for hurricane survivors whose homes had been destroyed by the storm. It would take a hurricane of unimaginable power to destroy these houses—their foot-thick walls were made of steel-reinforced concrete.

They passed the spot where the Hotel Matecumbe had stood. Soon after the hurricane, Fern Butters had salvaged the tablecloth stained by Thomas Edison and returned Rosalind's suitcase and the clothing she'd packed for her Labor Day holiday to the Grooms family, but the hotel—and Ed Butters's $80,000 uninsured investment—were gone. They'd left the Keys to look for work.

Grooms reached the southern end of Upper Matecumbe Key and started across Indian Key Fill. As they approached the spot where the car carrying their daughter had left the highway during the hurricane they saw an eerie, unsettling sight—another battered, rusting automobile was sitting by the road. Only this one hadn't been there two weeks ago, and it looked exactly like the car Rosalind Grooms Palmer and George Pepper had been in when the storm had hurled them into Florida Bay a year earlier.

Surely it wasn't real. It had to be a mirage, a fleeting hallucination brought about by their grieving and the fact that it was the anniversary of their daughter's death.

But it wasn't a ghostly apparition. It was indeed the 1934 Dodge the young couple had been in, the car that plunged off the island into Florida Bay.

The automobile had been submerged offshore in Florida Bay since the storm. It had been declared a menace to navigation, and the Coast Guard wanted it removed. But whoever hoisted it out of the bay had just dropped it beside the road and left it there.

Bascom Grooms, Sr., pulled his car off the road and stopped. He and his son got out and walked over to the Dodge. Bascom Jr., prompted by motives only a 14-year-old boy can understand, broke off the chrome plate that covered the front of the Dodge's radiator and took it back to his father's car.

He kept the macabre souvenir for many years.

Bertram Pinder moved his family back to Islamorada in April 1936. Their home had been destroyed in the hurricane, but no one was living in the Methodist parsonage, so they made a temporary home there. The family cleared the storm debris out of the house, and Bertram repaired the damage as best he could. He replaced the windows that had been blown out by the hurricane, but the hole in the ceiling remained as a reminder of Reverend S. E. Carlson's desperate but futile attempt to save himself and his wife from drowning in the storm surge.

They were glad to get back to Islamorada, but their lives would be different after the Labor Day hurricane of 1935. The flooding had carried away much of the thin layer of topsoil on Upper Matecumbe Key, so there would be no more lime groves or tomato gardens. They'd have to find new ways to provide food and earn a living.

Every so often during the years after the Labor Day hurricane of 1935, Alma, Dolores, and Laurette Pinder found odd personal reminders of the tragedy. Dolores found her grandfather's rusted pocket watch. Alma found dishes that had somehow been buried in sand beneath an overturned washtub that kept some of them from breaking, and Laurette found the plate that had held their mother's wedding cake.

Slowly, they recovered from the shock and terror of their awful experience. There were no grief counselors to help them deal with that difficult task. Eventually, they came to accept it simply as part of life.

Amid the dozens of pleas federal officials received from distraught relatives seeking information about missing veterans was a penny postcard from Mrs. Amanda Ambrose of Baton Rouge, Louisiana. She was the mother of John Hanson Ambrose, the talented artist at Camp 5 who'd contributed finely drawn cartoons to the *Key Veteran News* and told readers on August 31, 1935, that perhaps they'd get to see a hurricane "next month."

Amanda Ambrose said she'd heard that her son had been seen at a first aid station soon after the hurricane, but she hadn't heard from him. She theorized that he might be suffering from shock or amnesia and asked if anyone could tell her where he might be.

Nothing was ever heard from him after September 2, 1935, however. VA officials created a carefully indexed file of three-by-five cards on which they jotted notes about veterans who were killed in the hurricane or missing afterward. The card for John Ambrose has only a single notation: "Missing unaccounted for 9/28/35."

In 1937 Julius Stone decided to leave government service and return to Harvard University to study law. When he graduated in 1940 he returned to Key West to set up as an investor and real estate broker. His Florida connections—and his trademark artistry as a word slinger—served him well. He bought a beautiful house overlooking the Gulf of Mexico and prospered—for a while.

By 1960 Stone was deeply in debt and scheming to avoid the IRS. He had one more slick trick up his sleeve, however. He sold his house in a quick, furtive transaction and skipped town to Cuba with a pocketful of cash. He left behind a horde of angry creditors—and a permanent legacy in Key West as the man who saved the city from possible abandonment by turning it into a tourist attraction.

In the summer of 1948 a federal grand jury in New York indicted a dozen Communists on charges of plotting to overthrow the government. A tremor of fear pulsated through the country, and there were more accusations that government officials who were secretly members of the Communist Party had been spying for the Soviet Union. Among those accused was John Abt, the former lawyer for the WPA.

Abt admitted that he'd been a Communist since 1933 but denied he was a spy.

Abt's name popped up again in 1963 when a man who was in a lot of trouble was trying desperately to get in touch with him. Unfortunately the man died before he could speak to Abt.

The prospective client's name was Lee Harvey Oswald.

By the spring of 1937 the *Daily Tribune* of Miami Beach had moved into a beautiful new art deco office building and the newspaper's name had been changed to the *Miami Tribune*. But the ambitions of publisher Moe Annenberg hadn't changed. He still had dreams of making the *Tribune* the dominant newspaper in South Florida by either buying or bankrupting the *Miami Herald*.

It appeared that he had a chance of reaching his goal. Under the leadership of editor Paul Jeans, the *Trib's* circulation had steadily increased. Jeans also had recently finished writing *Tropical Disturbance: The Story of the Making of the* Miami Tribune. The book—which was published as a special insert in the *Trib*—was both a history of the newspaper and Jeans's valentine to himself. Jeans covered the *Trib*—and himself—with glory, describing the newspaper's brief existence as "unique in the annals of American journalism."

Jeans devoted an entire chapter of *Tropical Disturbance* to praising the newspaper's reporting of the Labor Day hurricane of 1935. In his estimation, only the *Trib* had had the courage to fully and accurately report the tragedy. He gave the *Tribune* credit for everything from being the only publication to publish the "real" death toll from the hurricane—he still insisted that 1,000 had died even though there were scarcely that many on the islands when the hurricane struck—to prompting state officials' decision to cremate victims' bodies—due, no doubt, to the *Tribune's* fixation with publishing photos of decaying corpses.

Jeans boasted that the *Tribune's* coverage of the Labor Day hurricane "impressed as perhaps nothing else could have upon the community the value and importance of honest, accurate reporting." He claimed that the *Trib's* hurricane coverage had boosted the newspaper's prestige and increased its daily circulation by 10,000.

On April 18, 1937 Jeans was returning from a trip to Tallahassee with the newspaper's lawyer, Victor Miller, who had skillfully and successfully defended the *Tribune* against several libel suits.

Florida has long been one of the nation's leading producers of cattle, and in 1937 the state had no restrictions on where cattle could graze. Cattlemen weren't required to keep their livestock fenced in, and the animals could wander freely, grazing wherever they found grass—even beside busy highways.

About 20 miles south of St. Augustine, a cow ambled onto U.S. 1 right in front of Jeans's southbound car. The editor swerved to avoid the animal, but his automobile crossed the center line and collided head-on with a northbound car driven by Edward Moore of Cincinnati.

Miller was thrown through the windshield and killed instantly. Jeans was crushed against the steering wheel column and died soon afterward in a St. Augustine hospital.

Moore also was killed.

The *Miami Tribune* gave Jeans' a hero's sendoff, filling its front page with photos of Jeans and Miller and packing its stories of Jeans' death with condolences from local dignitaries. The *Trib* then began a crusade to change Florida law to prohibit unrestricted grazing.

Jeans's sudden death ended Moe Annenberg's dream of journalistic conquest in Miami. In December 1937 he sold the *Miami Tribune* to John Knight, who'd also purchased the *Miami Herald*. Knight closed the *Tribune*, and Annenberg bought the *Philadelphia Inquirer*.

On a clear, hot day in mid-November 1937, nine-year-old Faye Marie Parker, who survived the hurricane with her family, stood in front of a canvas-covered obelisk in Islamorada. She held a short length of rope and was flanked by two Boy Scouts. She looked out at a crowd of 4,000 from beneath an old-fashioned sun bonnet that gave her a 19th-century appearance.

The crowd—more than four times the population of the islands outside of Key West and the largest ever to gather for an event in the Keys—had come for the dedication of a WPA-built memorial to the victims of the Labor Day hurricane.

Although patches of green had returned to the islands that had been blasted by the storm two years earlier, those who made the trip into the Keys for the ceremony saw many lingering scars from the hurricane during their journey. The storm-damaged house in Tavernier was still there, and so were the wrecked cars along the roadside.

Parker tugged the rope and the canvas fell away, revealing an 18-foot-tall shaft of coral with an art deco–style bas-relief sculpture showing waves rolling past windblown palm trees. Beneath the sculpture was a plaque with the inscription: "Dedicated to the memory of the civilians and war veterans whose lives were lost in the hurricane of September second, 1935."

Cameras clicked and the crowd applauded.

The memorial included a crypt in front of the coral shaft. An urn containing the remains of Herman Sauter, a veteran from Philadelphia who was killed in the hurricane, were interred during the unveiling ceremonies, and the crypt's lid served as a frame for a ceramic tile map of the Keys.

O. A. Sanquist, district director of the WPA, presented the memorial "to the people of Monroe County. We leave it in their care and possession."

P. J. O'Shaughnessy, chairman of the committee that planned the dedication ceremonies, reminded the crowd of the 1935 hurricane's awful toll in the Keys. "Out of 270 who made their homes in the Keys, we know that 167 are missing," he said. "Out of 682 World War veterans who were camped on the Keys, 253 are missing."

Thomas Kelly, commander of American Legion Post Number 29 in Miami, made no attempt to mask the anger he and other veterans still felt about the deaths of their comrades two years earlier. Government agencies in charge of the work program may have meant well in sending the vets to the islands, but they failed to protect the men in their care, he said.

"We admire their courage, but we question their judgment."

Florida had been lucky in 1936—no hurricanes had struck the state, he said. But he added that state and federal officials should take immediate action to prepare for the next disaster.

"We should not be lulled into a false sense of security," Kelly warned.

The bankrupt Florida East Coast Railway decided not to rebuild its roadbed to Key West, and once again the city was cut off from the rest of the United States. But the dream of linking Key West to the mainland with a highway didn't die. The FEC sold its right-of-way in the Keys to the Florida State Highway Department, and the state built a highway on the railroad's roadbed.

Steel outriggers were added to the old concrete viaducts and piers that had shrugged off the blasts of the Labor Day hurricane, and they were converted to highway bridges.

When engineers realized they couldn't widen the steel suspension railroad bridge at Bahia Honda, they routed the highway across the top of the span and attached the outriggers there. On July 2, 1938, the Overseas Highway—the final segment of U.S. 1 stretching from Maine to Key West—was opened with a ceremony atop the Bahia Honda Bridge, 75 feet above the Atlantic Ocean.

A few months after the Overseas Highway opened, President Roosevelt briefly drew the nation's attention to the unusual road. On February 18, 1939, the President and his entourage drove the length of the highway to Key West, where Roosevelt boarded the U.S.S. *Houston* to watch naval training exercises in the Caribbean Sea. The presidential caravan stopped briefly on Summerland Key—well south of where the hurricane had done its worst damage four years earlier—to eat a picnic lunch. FDR's route to Key West took him within a few yards of the hurricane memorial erected two years earlier in Islamorada. If the president made any comments about the hurricane, the reporters accompanying him either weren't listening or weren't interested.

The opening of the highway and the construction of a freshwater pipeline from Florida City to Key West in 1942 sparked rapid population growth on the islands. Almost 16,000 people moved into the Keys between 1940 and 1950.

A couple of those new residents weren't exactly newcomers. Fern and Ed Butters returned to Upper Matecumbe Key in the mid-1940s and built the Fern Inn on the site of the old Hotel Matecumbe. Fern Butters became famous for her key lime pies, and they ran the small inn until Ed Butters died in 1965.

Ed Sheeran became an engineer for the Overseas Highway and was given an office at Pigeon Key, a small island beneath the Seven Mile Bridge near Marathon. His devotion to his work didn't diminish in the slightest with advancing age, nor did the thought of retirement even enter his mind. He continued his practice of staying in the Keys during the workweek and returning to his home on weekends.

On a Monday in 1946, Sheeran, as usual, arose around 4 a.m. to drive from Coral Gables to Pigeon Key. He got into his new 1946 Ford and headed south.

It was still dark when he reached the Keys—too dark for him to see the unlighted tractor-trailer truck that had broken down in the southbound lane of U.S. 1. Sheeran's car slammed into the rear of the truck.

Sheeran was seriously injured in the wreck and was hospitalized for many weeks. He recovered from his injuries, but his working days were over. He returned to his comfortable, spacious home in Coral Gables, but he wasn't prepared for life without work.

"He was too involved with his job to be bothered with home-type things," according to his grandson Edward H. Sheeran. "After the accident, he sat at home in front of the radio. He didn't do anything except sit there and wait for death, more or less."

Sheeran died on December 28, 1951. He was buried with full military honors—including a 21-gun salute—in Miami's Woodlawn Cemetery.

Miami newspapers reported that Roland Craig was killed in the 1935 hurricane, so his family was astonished when he walked through the door of his home as though nothing had happened two days after the storm.

Craig rebuilt his business on the ruins of his old one. When he learned the FEC was going to abandon its Key West Extension, he persuaded railroad officials to give him the piece of track that ran in front of his little settlement—the track that had kept him and Jack Crow from being blown off the island on the evening of September 2, 1935. Always a shrewd entrepreneur, Craig mounted the track in front of his store and turned it into a tourist attraction. On the rail he painted "This Is the Rail that Saved Poor Old Craig's Life during the 1935 Hurricane."

Craig decided not to take his chances on surviving a second powerful storm in 1960 when Hurricane Donna struck the Keys. He left the islands before the hurricane arrived. When he returned, his business was gone. This time he didn't rebuild. The only reminder of Poor Old Craig's little empire is the Florida almond tree that his wife planted by U.S. 1 after he rebuilt following the 1935 hurricane.

You can stand in front of the almond tree, look to your left, and, if the day isn't too hazy, you can see the Alligator Reef Lighthouse. On a clear day the white spire stands out sharply against the blue sky.

Between 1950 and 1960 another 18,000 new residents moved to the islands, and by the end of the decade Monroe County's population had swelled to 47,921. With the exception of a few hundred Indians of the Seminole and Miccosukee tribes who still live in the Everglades, the population was packed onto the narrow 130-mile stretch of islands.

Visitors became fascinated with the Keys. One visitor in particular attracted a great deal of attention to the islands. President Harry Truman started coming to Key West regularly in the late 1940s and loved it so much he once quipped that he had a notion to move the nation's capital there so he could stay.

By December 1951 Truman had visited Key West ten times in five years. The President was drawn by the city's remoteness and relaxed environment. Here he could run the country by day while dressed in comfortable tropical attire, play poker and drink bourbon with his staff at night, and take brisk early morning walks.

But the city that once had been too broke to pay its bills was becoming linked with celebrities. Authors Elizabeth Bishop and Tennessee Williams bought houses in Key West, and although Ernest Hemingway moved to Cuba after his marriage to Pauline Pfeiffer Hemingway ended in 1939, he still visited Key West occasionally. By the time President Truman became a regular visitor, the isolation that made the Keys and Key West so unusual and so appealing as an escape from the rest of the world was endangered because the rest of the world had discovered the islands.

Frequent visitors such as *New Yorker* writer Richard Rovers were already fretting about the disappearance of Key West's unique ambiance in the early 1950s.

"The old town is too small for the present flow of visitors and the fear now, as more marl is pumped up daily from the sea to be used as fill for enlarging the island, is that the motels and drive-ins will eventually surround and overwhelm it," Rovers said in the December 15, 1951, edition of *The New Yorker*. "It is not resentment of outsiders that makes some people worry about this possibility but the fact that if Key West succumbs to the motels and drive-ins, there will be much less for the tourists to enjoy. Even the illusion of remoteness will be gone."

The Keys provided much of the inspiration for singer-songwriter Jimmy Buffett's rise to the top of popular music in the 1970s and doubtless enticed more people to visit the islands. "Margaritaville" was more than a hit song for Buffett—it became a marketable state of mind.

Between 1978 and 1983, the former FEC bridges that withstood the fierce Labor Day hurricane and were converted for automobile traffic were replaced with modern, wider spans, and U.S. 1 was rerouted slightly in places to line up with the new bridges. But Henry Flagler's old railroad bridges, which have endured for almost a century, are still there, as a monument to what can be accomplished by a wealthy, determined man when he's not hindered by government regulations.

By the late 1990s, Key West had achieved a bizarre pinnacle of distinction as a tourist attraction. The city became the theme for a new amusement park in Orlando—"Key West at SeaWorld." The five-acre park offers a manufactured, sanitized, family-safe fantasy of Key West, an illusion of the town's once remote charm without the inconveniences of homeless panhandlers, Duval Street drunks, traffic jams, and hurricane evacuations. Advertisements for Key West at SeaWorld describe the park as "wacky," "exotic," "funky," "quirky," and "festive."

It's difficult to imagine the hard-up residents of Key West thinking of their destitute, dying city in those terms in 1934.

Three decades after the Labor Day hurricane of 1935, federal officials were still unwilling to release details of the deaths of the veterans to the public.

In January 1968 Mathias von Brauchitsch, a writer and television producer in Pittsburgh, asked Veterans Administration officials for permission to see the report on the tragedy written by David Kennamer in October 1935. In a January 23, 1968, letter to John Radowich of the VA's Information Service, von Brauchitsch said he'd already read the testimony of witnesses interviewed by Kennamer—which was on file at the National Archives—and might write a book about the tragedy.

Von Brauchitsch's request was passed on to Manuel Mota, a VA special investigator, who reviewed the documents at the National Archives. Mota passed along his findings to W. L. Retew, Jr., the VA's assistant director for investigations. Retew dug into the VA's files on the hurricane and Kennamer's report and wrote a memo to his boss, the VA's director of investigation and security service, saying he didn't think it was a good idea to allow von Brauchitsch to see Kennamer's report and supporting documents.

In his memo of February 26, 1968, Retew said he'd found "documents, as well as a lack of documents, which indicate there could be problems in the release of Kennamer's report itself."

Retew noted that Aubrey Williams had submitted a report to President Roosevelt concluding that government administrators were not to blame for the veterans' deaths. After Williams had sent his report to FDR, Retew said, Kennamer conducted a joint investigation with John Abt, the attorney for the Federal Emergency Relief Administration and the WPA. Kennamer and Abt were supposedly going to submit separate reports on the disaster to President Roosevelt.

Retew had found several documents in the VA file clearly indicating that Abt had indeed written a report on the disaster. But neither Abt's report nor the one written by Kennamer ever reached FDR's desk, he wrote.

A copy of Kennamer's report and supporting documents were still in the VA's files, but Abt's report had simply vanished.

Retew added that Kennamer's report was "highly critical" of federal officials.

"Kennamer's comments and conclusions appear quite harsh in relation to the facts developed," Retew said. The investigator "appears to have been 'hard-headed' about his report and any attempts to modify it. FERA disagreed with his conclusions of negligence and publicly took the position that there was no negligence. While the records do not establish the VA's final position with respect to negligence of FERA officials, there is much evidence to indicate that it was considerably milder than as expressed in Kennamer's report. The only known report to the President was the VA-FERA report prior to the Kennamer investigation which concluded there was no negligence."

Though he could find no legal basis for denying Mathias von Brauchitsch access to the files, Retew did just that, noting that allowing the writer access "would present a misleading picture of the VA position in this matter and do a grave injustice to the FERA officials the report criticizes."

In a March 26, 1968, letter to von Brauchitsch, Retew told the Pittsburgh writer his request was being turned down.

Retew justified his decision by citing a provision of the Freedom of Information Act allowing federal agencies to refuse to make public the same internal memos or letters they could legally withhold if they were involved in a lawsuit. Since Kennamer's report was never sent to

President Roosevelt, it was still technically an internal memo and therefore he wasn't legally required to allow von Brauchitsch to see it.

There's no way of knowing why the reports written by Kennamer and Abt never reached President Roosevelt's desk. They may have been deliberately withheld from him by one of his subordinates, who decided on his own that there was no reason for FDR to see these reports—especially after the carefully orchestrated hearings conducted by Representative John Rankin put the final stamp of exoneration on FERA and Florida ERA officials.

Or it may have been accidental. Filing accidents happen, especially when office workers are trying to keep track of the thousands of pages of documents that are produced by the office of the President of the United States. But if it was accidental, no one bothered to check up on whether the chief had been sent the reports as promised, or to track down extra copies to replace the ones that had gone astray so FDR could take a look at them. And it has to be noted that, of the thousands of pages of documents related to the Labor Day hurricane of 1935 that eventually were turned over to the National Archives, the Abt report is the only known major document that went missing somewhere between Abt's desk and the archives.

Regardless of how this little mystery unfolded, President Roosevelt never saw the reports written by Kennamer and Abt, and he never had to reconsider whatever impression of the tragedy he may have formed after reading the hasty, incomplete report that Aubrey Williams threw together during a weekend in Florida. Being ignorant of the facts and conclusions developed by Kennamer—and presumably Abt— also means that FDR never had to make any decisions or take any action that might have gotten the attention of reporters and Republicans and kept the tragedy in the public spotlight longer than it was.

There's also no way of knowing how a scandal might have affected the 1936 election. Roosevelt won another landslide, this time over Alf Landon, receiving 523 electoral votes to the Republican's 8. It was another ringing endorsement of the New Deal, and it's hard to believe that anything—even a scandal over the deaths of more than 250 veterans—would have derailed FDR. Representative John Rankin apparently made sure the Republicans didn't get any help from his committee's "investigation" of the tragedy. A file at the National Archives intended to preserve documents from Rankin's hearings on the hurricane is empty. Archivist Kate Snodgrass said Rankin left very few documents from his committee's activities during the 74th Congress. The Rankin family also denied a request to allow their collection of the Congressman's documents to be used for research for this book.

On a warm afternoon in mid-November 1997 almost 60 years to the day after the dedication of the hurricane memorial in Islamorada, Bernard Russell walked up to the foundation of the old Islamorada post office, picked up a chunk of coral about the size of a cantaloupe, and inspected it. "You know," he said, thinking of the time when he and his neighbors gathered tailings from the road grading to build the post office, "we probably picked this up by the side of the road in 1928." DeLeon Street is paved now, and there's a branch of the Marine Bank next to the old foundation. Bank officials wanted to remove the foundation to expand the parking lot, but preservationists led by Jerry Wilkinson of Tavernier, president of the Historical Preservation Society of the Upper Keys, talked them out of it. Now there's a plaque explaining the significance of the site next to the foundation, but the bank couldn't resist trying to spiff things up somehow. They've landscaped the old foundation, planted trees in it, and filled it with mulch. It's become a historical planter.

The road that once was Upper Matecumbe Key's only highway runs past the old post office site, and Russell's house is about a mile and a half south of the foundation. The road is now designated as Florida State Highway 4-A, and there's a brief stretch where you can still get a good idea of what Islamorada looked like in 1935. The vegetation is so thick it looks like an impenetrable leafy wall, and you get the feeling you're driving through a green corridor.

A few hundred feet up DeLeon Street from the old foundation, the new Islamorada post office sits where the FEC station stood until the hurricane blew it to pieces. Any trace of the old railroad is long gone. Every day hundreds of cars on U.S. 1 whiz past the spot where the train cars came to rest after the powerful storm surge swept them off the tracks.

Bernard Russell married Laurette Pinder in 1939. They've shared a bond beyond their love for each other—both of them somehow survived one of the most cataclysmic events in recorded history.

The same year they were married they moved into one of the steel-and-concrete houses built by the American Red Cross. They still live there, a stone's throw from the hurricane memorial, a couple of blocks from the Atlantic Ocean, and not much farther from Florida Bay.

Russell has compared their sturdy little home to living in a bank vault. There are about two dozen of the concrete houses scattered in Islamorada and Tavernier. The locals call them Red Cross houses.

Russell is an elderly man now, and his hands tremble from the debilitating effects of Parkinson's disease. Almost 70 years after the Labor Day hurricane, he still finds it difficult to talk about his experience. Tears come to his eyes as he tries to describe the moment his sister and nephew were torn away from him when the storm surge came ashore. Yet, he's almost apologetic for his sorrow.

"Those memories of what happened, you don't blot them out overnight," he said. "You lost everything but the shirt on your back. Some of us didn't even have a shirt on our back."

In some ways, he is still trying to understand what happened.

"I can remember being so numb, all of it happened at once," he said. "A flash, and everything was gone, and everything had to be new."

Russell also remembers the terrifying sound the winds made on the night of September 2, 1935. He's been through many hurricanes since then, but he's never heard a noise like the unearthly screech he heard that long-ago Labor Day.

"You didn't have time to dwell on it," he said. "It sounds silly, or crazy. You say, 'Didn't it bother you?' Sure, it bothered you, but that wasn't the answer. The answer was, we had to buckle down and say, 'Look, we got to make it here. And we got nobody to help, but we'll do it on our own.' Like Dad said, he said, 'Son, whatever we do, we just got to buckle down and do it. Not look for any frills or anything like that. 'Cause we don't have it and it's not here. We're going to make it on our own.'"

Picking up the pieces of their lives after the 1935 hurricane meant pursuing small goals and keeping expectations to a minimum, Russell said.

"You know, a lot of things you want to blank out," he said. "It's not right, but you want to blank it out, because you can't live yesterday, and you can't live tomorrow until it gets here. Better live today, one day at a time. And that's the only way you could plan it. You couldn't plan anything; you couldn't say, 'I'm going to do this next week.' You had to play it a day at a time, and live it a day at a time."

Russell and his father returned to Islamorada in November 1935. They lived on a boat for about a year until they got a house built.

Russell has been wondering why he's still alive since the moment the Atlantic Ocean suddenly drained off Upper Matecumbe Key and he climbed down off the pile of wreckage that saved his life during that awful Monday evening so long ago. Except for a stint in the Army during World War II, he's remained in Islamorada. He did well as a cabinetmaker, and he and Laurette raised a daughter who's now married and living in central Florida.

Russell has given a lot to his community. He still attends Matecumbe Methodist Church, which was rebuilt across the street from the hurricane memorial. He was the driving force in establishing Upper Matecumbe Key's first fire department and rescue squad.

He's seen thousands upon thousands of newcomers move into the once remote Keys. He shakes his head in disbelief when he hears them say they'd like to experience a hurricane. He heard the doomed veterans say the same thing in the summer of 1935, and he's warned many of the newcomers about the lethal power of the storms, assuring them that a hurricane is something to be avoided, not experienced.

"People don't stop to realize that once you get so far into one of them, there's nothing you can do," he said. "You're going to ride it out, one way or another. There's no way to get away from it. They say, 'Well, if it gets so bad we'll get in the car and leave.' You just don't do that."

Still, Russell has ridden out every hurricane that's hit the Keys since 1935. He hasn't left because he felt he might be needed.

Russell was in Islamorada on another sinister September day in 1960 when Hurricane Donna—the most powerful storm to strike the Keys since 1935—hit. Donna, which crossed the Keys on September 8, 1960, resembled the 1935 hurricane in several ways. Besides its incredible strength (at the time it was the fourth strongest hurricane to strike the United States) it followed a path through the islands that was nearly identical to that of its predecessor.

The steel-and-concrete houses and a school built by the Red Cross easily withstood Donna's fierce winds. After the worst of the hurricane passed, Russell—who was now Islamorada's fire chief—directed the search-and-rescue effort on Upper Matecumbe Key. His experience in the 1935 hurricane was very much on his mind.

"When I took the guys out, this is exactly what I told them—go yell," Russell said. "Yell and scream when you get to a place where there's damaged buildings. Yell. Scream. Somebody might be pinned down, can't get up. And I had them out doing that when the wind was still howling. I found out that that was the way to do it."

Despite Hurricane Donna's fearsome winds, only four people in the Keys were killed by the storm.

The beach where the Matecumbe Methodist Church and the Matecumbe School once stood is now part of the Cheeca Lodge, a luxury oceanfront resort. But the cemetery remains. The 1935 hurricane blew the marble angel off Etta Pinder's grave, but survivors found the statue. Part of the angel's left wing had been broken off, but

306

otherwise the statue was intact. The statue was returned to its pedestal, and it's still there.

A short distance down State Highway 4-A is the building that housed O.D. King's service station and tavern in 1935. The building was heavily damaged by the hurricane, but there was enough of it left to prompt King to repair it, and he built it strong enough to withstand Hurricane Donna 25 years later.

Today, King's former service station is the Green Turtle Inn, which opened in 1947. Now, where terrified survivors huddled to escape the hurricane in 1935, tourists enjoy seafood specialties and listen to a pianist play dinner music on a grand piano.

Down at the southern tip of Lower Matecumbe Key, where Camp 3 and the ferry landing stood in 1935, there's now a Boy Scout camp and a pricey gated community called Tollgate Shores. Not many of the people living there have any idea of the story behind the eight concrete piers protruding from Florida Bay several hundred yards offshore. The piers are an enduring but nearly forgotten reminder of the tragedy of that long ago Labor Day.

The piers were the beginning of the bridge that was being built by the Florida State Highway Department and the veterans in the work camps.

Ed Sheeran directed the workers who set the cofferdams for the piers into Florida Bay, built the forms, lowered the coral blocks into the forms, and poured the concrete. John Ambrose, the talented draftsman from Louisiana who tempted fate with his sardonic comments on hurricanes, drew a detailed cartoon of the bridge construction work for the July 27, 1935, issue of the *Key Veteran News*. Plans called for dozens of the piers to be built.

But the Labor Day hurricane of 1935 stopped the construction and the piers were abandoned. Curious boaters who come in close to the piers today can see, just beneath the surface of the water, the corrugated steel sides of the cofferdams, twisted and torn by the action of the massive storm surge that inundated the islands.

Now the old piers are a hangout for cormorants. The long-necked birds perch on the concrete and spread their wings to dry during the day, and they roost there at night. Boaters who happen to be downwind of the piers as they cruise slowly past them can tell instantly that the cormorants have been roosting there for a very long time.

The causeway that was being built to link the bridge to Lower Matecumbe Key is overgrown with mangroves and other vegetation. A few of the locals refer to it as Veterans Island, but it doesn't have an official name.

Next Time It'll Be Worse

The mass grave in Miami's Woodlawn Cemetery for victims of the Labor Day hurricane of 1935 is just off Southwest 8th Street. The city's Little Havana neighborhood has evolved around the cemetery, and if you drive to the site with your car windows down you'll probably hear the rhythms of salsa and perhaps catch a whiff of tangy Cuban cuisine or hear a middle-aged baseball coach shouting instructions in Spanish to his young players during a practice session.

An American flag and a massive granite block mark the gravesite. The engraving reads: "Erected by Harvey W. Seeds Post No. 29 The American Legion In Memory Of Our Comrades Who Lost Their Lives On The Florida Keys During The 1935 Hurricane 'Lest We Forget.'

It's a plea from the past to remember what happened on September 2, 1935. And in one sense, it's been honored. Every couple of years, one of the newspapers in South Florida will publish a story about the Labor Day hurricane of 1935 on the anniversary of its landfall in the Keys.

It's always a compelling tale. The reporters explain that the 1935 storm was a Category 5 hurricane on the Saffir-Simpson scale (the classification given to the storms that achieve winds exceeding 155 miles per hour and produce storm surges exceeding 18 feet). Only two other hurricanes have rated a category 5 ranking at the time of their U.S. landfall; Camille, which devastated the Gulf Coast in 1969, and Andrew, which hit South Florida in 1992.

Bernard Russell, who feels a personal responsibility to warn people about the fearsome power of hurricanes, is usually quoted in these anniversary stories. The reporters do an excellent job of conveying the drama, and readers inevitably are enthralled and sometimes write letters to the editors praising the stories.

Yet, there's a clear and pervasive attitude among many residents—so many of whom are newcomers—that this kind of storm won't strike the Keys again. It's almost as though people believe the Labor Day hurricane of 1935 was some sort of prehistoric sea monster that is now extinct and will never threaten them again.

So every summer when the Atlantic Ocean starts heating up, thunderstorms begin rolling off the coast of western Africa, and tropical depressions start popping up on radar screens, Billy Wagner and Irene Toner of the Monroe County Department of Emergency Management—who are responsible for deciding whether to order thousands of people to leave their homes when they think a severe hurricane could strike the Keys—cross their fingers and hope this isn't the year the Big One heads their way.

Still, they know it's only a matter of time before a Category 5 monster lands a deadly, crushing blow to the Florida Keys.

"I hope it's not in my lifetime," Toner said. "In this business—those of us who are responsible for the public's safety—we know it's going to happen. It's not if, it's when."

Chris Landsea, a meteorologist with the National Oceanic and Atmospheric Administration's Hurricane Research Division in Miami, always wonders if the upcoming hurricane season will be the year it does finally happen.

"A repeat of the meteorology that led up to the 1935 hurricane is inevitable—a rapidly developing hurricane, going from a Category 1 to a Category 5 in about 36 hours right as it is headed toward the Keys," Landsea said.

Meteorologists are still studying the Labor Day hurricane of 1935 hoping to discover secrets that might prevent another catastrophe on the Keys. They're particularly interested in learning why some hurricanes undergo the rapid intensification that transforms them from tropical storms to Category 5 killers in less than two days.

"We still have extremely poor skill predicting the future intensity of hurricanes," said Sam Houston, a meteorologist with the National Weather Service's Central Pacific Hurricane Center in Hawaii. "The possibility of a weak tropical disturbance strengthening to an extremely violent hurricane just before landfall without sufficient warning still exists today. The uncertainty of future intensity causes even more problems for those who have to put up warnings."

Researchers also are still trying to determine how strong the Labor Day hurricane was. Soon after the storm, U.S. Weather Bureau meteorologists in Washington conducted careful tests on the barometer belonging to Ivar Olson and determined that it was an excellent instrument that gave very reliable readings. They also determined from their tests that the lowest reading registered by Olson's barometer was 26.35 inches—still the lowest reading ever for a hurricane making landfall in the United States.

Ed Butters said the needle on his barometer dropped to 26.00 inches, but unfortunately Butters hurled his barometer into the storm rather than endure the fear of watching the needle steadily fall. So meteorologists couldn't test his barometer to determine whether his reading of 26.00 inches was valid. Olson's reading of 26.35 inches remains the official benchmark for the Labor Day hurricane of 1935.

Meteorologists are less certain about the maximum sustained wind speeds—that is, the strength of winds blowing for at least one minute—of the storm.

For years, it was generally accepted that the hurricane's maximum sustained winds were well in excess of 200 miles per hour, and it was believed by many that at times its winds might have briefly gusted to 250 miles per hour.

Today, scientists are less willing to accept those earlier estimates. Some estimates place the peak sustained winds at 160 miles per hour while others continue to maintain they reached speeds of 200 miles per hour. Scientists do agree that winds probably gusted to 200 miles per hour—or more.

Wind, storm surge, and barometic pressure combined to make

311

the Labor Day hurricane of 1935 the most powerful storm to strike the United States in recorded history. In 1999, it earned the dubious distinction of "Storm of the Century" in a ranking done by The Weather Channel.

Every time a hurricane does appear to be taking aim at the Keys, Wagner and Toner face a decision identical to the one faced by Ray Sheldon on September 2, 1935—do they stay or do they go? They have the advantage of monitoring hurricanes with high-tech equipment that Sheldon couldn't have imagined. But they don't have the luxury of waiting, as he did, until the hurricane is less than 100 miles offshore before deciding whether to empty the Keys. It takes at least a day and a half to evacuate the islands, so they have to make their decision while the hurricane is still at least 36 hours away. And as horrible as the death toll was during the 1935 hurricane, Wagner and Toner know that thousands of lives could be lost if they make the wrong call.

The days when getting people out of harm's way in the Keys meant loading a few hundred people onto a train are long gone. More than 80,000 people now live on the islands that were populated by fewer than 1,000 in 1935. On any given day there also are likely to be upward of 40,000 tourists on the islands. The only way in and out by automobile is U.S. 1—a single highway that is only two lanes for much of its length. Wagner said that turning U.S. 1 into a one-way, northbound-only road during evacuations can't be done because there's not enough gasoline in the Keys to fill the tanks of all the automobiles, and so a southbound lane has to be kept open so fuel trucks can get in and out.

During hurricane evacuations, there's only one place for Monroe County evacuees to go—north into Dade County, where another two million people live. And if there's a hurricane in the vicinity of the Keys, there's a good chance that many of those people in Dade will be trying to get out of harm's way as well, adding to the traffic jam.

Wagner and Toner are not going to debate very long on whether to order an evacuation. If there's even a slight chance that a powerful hurricane is going to come their way, they're going to order people to get out of the Keys.

"We may decide eight times to evacuate, and it may be unnecessary every time," Toner said. "But we will make the decision to evacuate. That one time that you may slack off could be the biggest mistake of your life."

Telling people to get out of the Keys for their own safety doesn't eliminate the possibility of a major catastrophe from a 1935-type hurricane because, inevitably, there will be those who refuse to leave.

Wagner has a well-rehearsed one-liner he uses to describe his dilemma: "We're dealing with Mother Nature and human nature, and you never know what either of them is going to do."

Even with weather satellites that pinpoint the precise position of a storm and track its movement exactly, there's no way of knowing for certain where it's going to be in 12 or 24 or 36 hours. Forecasters warn that when they predict where a hurricane is likely to make landfall, there's always a margin of error of 100 miles on either side of the point where it's expected to strike.

The Monroe County Department of Emergency Management has conducted surveys asking residents whether they intend to leave the next time an evacuation is ordered.

When they're responding to the surveys, residents usually obey the dictates of common sense and say they'll evacuate. But something strange and inexplicable seems to overcome many of them when the hurricane warning flags go up—they stay put.

The instant availability on the Internet of detailed, up-to-the-minute information and sophisticated graphics during the hurricane season has thrown a new wrinkle into evacuation planning. When a hurricane threatens, many Keys residents are going online, studying satellite photos of the storm and weather forecasts, and making their own decisions about the necessity to leave their homes.

Wagner and Toner think that's flirting with disaster.

"A lot of people are getting a lot of information, and they don't understand the shortcomings of forecasts," Wagner said. "They're basing their decision on what they see at the time and not paying attention to what the average error on a storm track is for 24 hours, which is 90 or 100 miles."

When people do evacuate, there's no way of predicting how they're going to behave when they get on the road.

In order for an evacuation of the Keys to go smoothly, tens of thousands of people would have to behave almost perfectly. They would have to be prepared to leave immediately when the order came for them to evacuate. When they got out onto U.S. 1, they would have to accept the fact that they would be in a long line of slowly moving traffic for several hours. They would have to resist impulses to become impatient and pass other cars recklessly and possibly cause an accident that could block the Keys' only escape route for hours. And they would have to maintain an even temper in a highly stressful setting.

It's a lot to ask. It hasn't happened in earlier evacuations.

In October 1999 Wagner and Toner ordered an evacuation after Hurricane Irene crossed Cuba and took aim at the Keys. Traffic backed up on U.S. 1. An impatient driver tried to pass a long line of cars and collided with a tanker truck. The truck's trailer jackknifed across the highway. The evacuation was halted for two precious hours.

After another evacuation, police officers blocked the road leading from Florida City into the Keys and permitted only residents to return. One motorist said he was a resident but couldn't prove it, so the police wouldn't let him through the roadblock. He responded by pulling a gun and demanding to be allowed to pass. No one was hurt, but the incident was an indication of the extraordinary—and often dangerous—tensions that accompany an evacuation.

The most recent evacuation was ordered in November 2001, when powerful Hurricane Michelle roared out of the Caribbean with 140-mile-per-hour winds and slammed into Cuba's southern coast.

Keys residents largely ignored the evacuation order, Wagner said. Luckily, Hurricane Michelle lost much of its strength as it crossed Cuba, and luckily the storm maintained its northeasterly movement when it went back to sea in the Straits of Florida, and so the Keys were spared.

But things could have turned out quite differently, Wagner said.

There's no guarantee that hurricanes coming off Cuba and into the Straits of Florida will always be steered away from the Keys and toward the open water of the Atlantic Ocean.

The Keys also were lucky when Hurricane Georges struck Key West in September 1998. The hurricane had briefly reached Category 5 status as it roared across the Atlantic and killed 602 people during its rampage through Puerto Rico, the Dominican Republic, Haiti, and Cuba. Then Georges took dead aim at Key West.

People went to the shrine at the Grotto of Our Lady of Lourdes and prayed. Many of them obeyed the evacuation order. By the time Hurricane Georges reached Key West it had weakened dramatically. Its eye moved across Key West with winds of 100 miles per hour during the morning of September 25, soaking the city but leaving it intact.

And then there was Hurricane Andrew.

When Andrew struck southern Dade County with winds of 155 miles per hour or better on August 24, 1992, the third most powerful hurricane to hit the United States since 1900 bore a chilling resemblance to the Labor Day hurricane of 1935. Like its ferocious predecessor, Hurricane Andrew exploded from a minimal hurricane to a monster in barely 36 hours.

Wagner ordered an evacuation of the Keys as Andrew approached Florida, but luckily the storm's eye—and its 16-foot storm surge—went ashore at the southern tip of the Florida peninsula. Florida City and Homestead took the brunt of Andrew's fearsome punch and the hurricane became the most expensive natural disaster in the nation's history, causing about $25 billion in damage in Florida and Louisiana, where it made a second landfall several days later.

Still, Andrew's death toll was minimal compared with what it could have been if its eye had wobbled to the north toward Miami or to the south toward Key West.

"If Andrew had hit the Lower Keys, we would've lost thousands of people," Wagner said.

It's the sudden intensification—also referred to as bombing out—of a minimal hurricane as it nears the Keys that deeply concerns meteorologists and emergency planners. That's the mysterious process that turned the 1935 hurricane and Hurricane Andrew into fearsome monsters as they drew within striking distance of Florida. It's almost impossible to predict when a hurricane is likely to do this. And sooner or later it will happen again.

"Our inability to skillfully forecast the phenomenon of rapid intensification means that when a hurricane like the 1935 hurricane occurs and makes landfall, it will likely be under predicted as to its intensity," Landsea said. "An under forecasted hurricane, combined with a very susceptible and dangerous region like the Keys and either a late or incomplete evacuation, will mean hundreds or thousands dead. Unfortunately, it is not that outlandish a proposition."

When a hurricane does suddenly bomb out just offshore and come barreling toward the Keys, there's the awful possibility that hundreds of residents who ignored earlier orders to evacuate will dash to their cars and flee in near panic, only to be caught in a miles-long traffic jam on U.S. 1 with other terrified motorists. The consequences of a hurricane with winds exceeding 155 miles per hour and a 20-foot storm surge coming ashore at that moment on slender islands that are only a few feet above sea level are almost too horrible to contemplate.

It's nearly happened a couple of times at other areas of the coast.

In October 1995 Hurricane Opal bombed out as it roared across the Gulf of Mexico toward the Florida Panhandle. Its winds reached 150 miles per hour. Even worse, the storm suddenly shifted into high gear, increasing its speed from 8 miles per hour to 18 miles per hour.

Residents who had ignored earlier evacuation advisories poured onto highways, and suddenly there were traffic jams upward of 10 miles long with a powerful hurricane rushing toward them. Some residents leaving Santa Rosa Island near Pensacola were caught in stalled traffic, panicked, and fled on foot, abandoning their cars on the bridge connecting the island with the mainland.

It was a situation that had all the makings of a worst-case scenario. Luckily, Opal weakened and veered eastward away from heavily populated areas just before it made landfall about 30 miles east of Pensacola in the beach town of Destin. In an additional piece of luck, the hurricane came ashore at low tide on a weekday during the off-season when there weren't many tourists in town.

It could have happened again four years later when Hurricane Floyd, with winds exceeding 150 miles per hour, moved ominously toward Florida, then turned north to menace the entire Southeast coast. Evacuations were ordered in Florida, Georgia, South Carolina and North Carolina.

Luckily, Floyd's eye stayed offshore as the storm turned, and the hurricane's winds weakened considerably before its eye went ashore in North Carolina on September 16, 1999. Still, Hurricane Floyd caused enormous flood damage and prompted one of the largest mass evacuations in the nation's history. The evacuations caused gigantic traffic jams as about two million people from Florida to North Carolina tried to leave the coast.

But the luck won't hold forever, and meteorologists think weather cycles have changed and we've entered a period when more hurricanes are likely to be forming every summer. There are also clear indications that Keys residents have fallen into that false sense of security that Thomas Kelly warned about in 1937 when he spoke at the dedication of the hurricane monument at Islamorada.

So when the next hurricane season arrives, it may be that the only thing standing between the Keys and a catastrophe are the faithful who still follow Sister Mary Louis Gabriel's example and go to the shrine at the Grotto of Our Lady of Lourdes to pray for deliverance when a screaming killer is roaming the seas.

acknowledgments

Many generous people helped me tell this story. Jerry Wilkinson, president of the Upper Keys Historical Preservation Society in Tavernier, opened his extensive files on Florida Keys history and his home on Key Largo to me. His collection provided a treasure trove of information, and the hospitality he and his wife Mary Lou offered made it much easier for me to do research. Mary Lou put up with two guys obsessively discussing a long-ago event from early morning until late at night, and those discussions shaped the eventual content of the book. Jerry's passion for this project and Keys history is boundless. He has spent the past decade carefully documenting the Keys' colorful history, and this book could not have been written without him.

Laurette Pinder Russell, Alma Pinder Dalton, Dolores Pinder Brothers and Wilbur Jones told me about their experiences in the hurricane. Bernard Russell, who spent many hours talking with me, added great depth and immediacy to the manuscript. Bascom Grooms Jr. talked candidly with me about losing his sister, Rosalind Grooms Palmer.

Gayle Butters of Archer, Florida generously gave me a copy of Fern Butters' personal account of her experience, and Edward Sheeran of Stuart, Florida helped me flesh out the personality of his grandfather, Ed Sheeran. Louis Wendall Page Sr. of Scottsboro, Alabama provided vital information about VA investigator David Wendall Kennamer.

Archivists Marjorie Ciarlianti, Bill Creech, Trevor Plante, David Wallace, Gene Morris and Rebecca Livingston steered me to the records in the National Archives that provided a huge part of the source material for the book.

Meteorologists Chris Landsea, Sam Houston, Wilson Shaffer and Brian Jarvinen answered my questions about hurricanes, and engineer Herbert Saffir of Coral Gables, Florida—who helped devise the Saffir-Simpson Scale used to categorize hurricanes—offered invaluable insights.

Dr. Dean Hawley, professor of forensic pathology at the Indiana University School of Medicine, helped me visualize the conditions that rescuers faced after the 1935 hurricane. Dr. Michael Higginbotham at Duke University Medical Center also provided helpful information.

Chester "Bo" Morgan, chairman of the department of history at Delta State University in Mississippi, advised me on New Deal-era politics in the South, while David Sansing at the University of Mississippi provided some colorful facts about John Rankin. And John Viele of Big Pine Key, Florida and author of *The Florida Keys: A History of the Pioneers*, helped with facts about the Keys in the 1930s.

Tom Knowles at Florida State University graciously shared some of his research on the Labor Day hurricane of 1935.

Librarians helped me greatly. I want to thank Michael Cotter at East Carolina University, John McMinn and Esperanza DeVarona at the University of Miami , and the staffs at the University of Wyoming library, the Franklin D. Roosevelt Presidential Library in Hyde Park, New York; the Mariner's Museum in Newport News, Virginia; the MacArthur Memorial Library and Archives in Norfolk; and the Pigeon Key National Historic District in Marathon, Florida.

Tom Hambright, historian at the Monroe County Public Library in Key West, provided insights of Keys history, as well as newspaper clips and other documents. Jim Clupper at the Islamorada branch of the library had American Red Cross records and other documents from the storm.

Lt. Cmndr. Glen Freeman, Lt. Paul Lange, and Wrnt. Ofcr. Dave Umberger of the U.S. Coast Guard told me about storms at sea, and John McAfee of the law firm of McCotter, McAfee and Ashton in New Bern, North Carolina helped me understand the political aspects of this story.

Colonel D.J. Kieley of the National Museum of Naval Aviation Foundation in Pensacola, Florida provided helpful contacts and details about 1930s-era aircraft.

Robin Smith of Candler, North Carolina used her savvy from years in publishing to guide me through the sometimes perplexing process of finding a publisher, and Nancy, Stanley and David Colbert of Wilmington, North Carolina gave me the benefit of their experience in the business. My agent, Craig Nelson of New York City, worked diligently on my behalf even in the terrible days immediately following September 11, 2001.

Sarah Duran, who is now a reporter for the *Tacoma News-Tribune* in Washington, took on research missions to the University of Miami library. Mary Dellert Griffin of York, Pennsylvania and Tom Gunning of Omaha, Nebraska edited early chapters. Ed Grisamore, an author and columnist for the *Macon Telegraph* provided helpful news clips, and Alan Snel, publisher of Hudsonian Magazine.com of New Paltz, New York let me use his home as an office while I did research at Hyde Park.

Historian Paul George of Miami convinced me that my topic was worth writing a book about and helped with early planning. The late Wright Langley, founder of Langley Press in Key West, offered encouragement and advice, and I deeply regret that he didn't live to see the finished product. I also owe thanks to Larry Wiggins, who allowed me to make copies of Homestead newspapers from the mid-1930s.

The Pamlico Writers Group of Washington, North Carolina helped shape early versions of the manuscript, and David Jenkins of Cape Carteret, North Carolina provided information sources for Al Dubin.

Lisa Thomas, my editor at National Geographic, made this a much better book.

Finally, I'd like to thank Phil Meyer at the University of North Carolina at Chapel Hill, who taught me to always keep digging for facts. And of course, my parents, Ola and Claude Dry of Misenheimer, North Carolina.

Plymouth, North Carolina
May 14, 2002

postscript

I'm not the first person to realize that sometimes, in order to get something you really want, you have to stop chasing it and let it come to you. When I was researching this book, I made many attempts to find a member of Ray Sheldon's family, but everything came up empty. When the book was published, I stopped looking. Then, purely by accident, I met Rae Sheldon Cummings—Ray Sheldon's only surviving child— during a trip to Florida. She gave me some fascinating documents that allowed me to add a little more to the story of this long-ago tragedy.

Ray Sheldon didn't talk much about the Labor Day hurricane after the investigators, lawyers, and politicians finally left him alone. But he did not put the memories of that terrible holiday entirely out of his mind. For the rest of his life he kept a small collection of reminders of the storm. His keepsakes included a packet of postcards showing the gruesome aftermath of the hurricane and two memos from the U.S. Department of Commerce about the wrecks of the passenger liner *Dixie* and the freighter *Leise Maersk*. But the centerpiece of his souvenirs was an unsigned carbon copy of WPA attorney John Abt's 56-page report absolving him of any blame for the veterans' deaths. The original report was intended for President Roosevelt, but the document never made it to FDR and somehow went missing from the National Archives files that contain hundreds of other documents about the catastrophe.

Sheldon's only surviving child, 67-year-old Rae Sheldon Cummings of Vero Beach, Florida, has had the documents since her mother died in 1976. She has no idea how her father managed to obtain a copy of a sensitive, classified report that was intended for the President of the United States. Her father didn't discuss his experience in the hurricane with her.

Abt completed his report on the disaster for WPA chief Harry Hopkins in late 1935. In Abt's view, Sheldon and his boss, Fred Ghent, handled the hurricane emergency exactly as they should have. They made no mistakes, nor were they guilty of even minor lapses of judgment. The camps' directors were, in Abt's opinion, victims of the unprecedented and unpredictable fury of nature and the human shortcomings of those around them.

If Ed Sheeran was concerned about the hurricane, he didn't bother telling Sheldon until the evacuation train had already been ordered, Abt wrote. He acknowledged that Sam Cutler was concerned about the storm from the moment he learned of it, but everyone knew

Cutler was too nervous to be taken seriously. The Weather Bureau advisories were inaccurate and understated the danger the hurricane posed to the Keys, so no reasonable person would have been alarmed, he wrote. And Abt defended Sheldon's and Ghent's delay in ordering the evacuation train by saying, in effect, that as long as they couldn't see obvious indications of danger, they weren't compelled to act.

Abt acknowledged that some witnesses gave testimony that blamed Sheldon and Ghent for the veterans' deaths. But he brushed these aside simply by concluding that the witnesses' recollections of events had been addled and distorted by their awful ordeal and therefore their testimony wasn't reliable.

"The contradictions which appear in the evidence are readily explainable in the light of the fact that, almost without exception, the witnesses had been subjected to the most severe mental and physical strain, either in the hurricane itself or in the arduous task of rescuing the survivors and disposing of the dead," Abt wrote, concluding that "we cannot condemn the judgment which they made."

In January 1936, Hopkins sent a copy of Abt's report to General Frank Hines, director of the Veterans Administration. Hines gave the report to his assistant, Colonel George Ijams, who responded with a detailed memo that pointed out many fallacies in Abt's contentions—especially that no one was to blame for the tragedy on the Keys. Ijams reinforced his own support for VA investigator David Kennamer's conclusions that the vets died because Sheldon, Ghent and Conrad Van Hyning had ignored obvious danger signals.

In February 1936, Frank Hines sent a letter to Harry Hopkins that included Ijams' comments on Abt's conclusions. Hines said it was "practically impossible to agree entirely on all the points at issue" and suggested he and Hopkins send copies of both Kennamer's and Abt's reports to President Roosevelt so FDR "may have the views of all points at issue."

Decades later, however, VA investigators would discover that President Roosevelt hadn't received either report.

Ray Sheldon got on with his life after Rep. John Rankin's hearings exonerated him from any blame for the veterans' deaths. His daughter, Rae, was born in 1936. He worked as an engineer for the WPA for a few years, and then started his own construction company in West Palm

Beach. He moved his family into a modest house, built a small office behind his home, and became a loving, middle-aged, first-time father.

"He really doted on me, I think because of his age," said Rae Sheldon Cummings, who now lives with her husband in a comfortable, well-manicured subdivision in Vero Beach, Florida. "First child and all that. He couldn't do enough for me. He was a very loving father."

Cummings recalled only one oblique reference that her father made to the 1935 hurricane. It came during a brief vacation in the Keys sometime in the 1940s. "We took a trip down to the Keys, and stayed in Key West," Cummings said. "And I think at some point he was talking to my mother and they said things, but you know, I was so young I wasn't that interested. Now, of course, I wish I'd stayed right there and listened."

Cummings said her parents might have stopped at the hurricane monument in Islamorada, and this may have been where Sheldon made a few comments about the storm. She has one other memory of that long-ago trip to the Keys. "I remember being really struck at how close the water was on both sides of the road," she said, adding that her father used to say, you could stand in the center of the road and spit in either direction and hit water."

Ray and Gayle Sheldon had a son in 1938. Sheldon did well in his contracting business. One of his first big jobs was building a blimp hangar for the U.S. Navy during World War II. He also did a lot of work in West Palm Beach. At least five of his buildings on West Palm Beach's Dixie Highway are still in use, including a theatre and a hardware store.

Eventually, Sheldon was able to buy a big, expensive Packard and build a dream house for his family on Monceaux Road in West Palm Beach. He made sure his home would stand up to almost anything nature could throw at it and built his home about four feet off the ground with steel reinforcements for added strength.

Sheldon loved the handsome, two-story house, and became especially fond of a slender fir tree he planted at one of the house's front corners. He sometimes relaxed by settling into a lawn chair in his back yard to smoke a Lucky Strike cigarette and sip a tall glass of iced coffee. But Sheldon's happiness was brief. Not long after he moved his family to Monceaux Road, his health started failing.

In 1952, Sheldon was admitted to Good Samaritan Hospital in West Palm Beach, where he died of heart failure at the age of 64.

select bibliography

The sources listed below represent a selction of material constulted during the preparation of this book.

BOOKS AND PAMPHLETS

Barnes, Jay. *Florida's Hurricane History.* Chapel Hill, NC: The University of North Carolina Press. 1998.

Best, Gary Dean. *FDR and the Bonus Marchers, 1933-1935.* Westport, Connecticut: Praeger, 1992.

Bowditch, Nathaniel. *American Practical Navigator*, vol. I. Washington, D.C.: Defense Mapping Agency Hydrographic/Topographic Center, 1984.

Burnett, Gene M. *Florida's Past: People and Events that Shaped the State.* Sarasota, Florida.: Pineapple Press, 1986.

Chambers, Clarke A., ed. *The New Deal at Home and Abroad, 1929-1945.* Vol. 8 of *Sources in American History*, edited by George H. Knoles. New York: The Free Press, 1965.

Daniels, Roger. *The Bonus March: An Episode of the Great Depression.* Westport, Connecticut: Greenwood Publishing Co., 1971.

Dean, Love. *Lighthouses of the Florida Keys.* Key West, Florida.: Historic Florida Keys Foundation, Inc., 1992.

Douglas, Marjorie Stoneman. *Hurricane.* New York: Rhinehart, 1958.

Dunn, Gordon E. and Banner I. Miller. *Atlantic Hurricanes.* Baton Rouge, Louisiana: Louisiana State University Press, 1960.

Emery, Edwin. *The Press and America: An Interpretive History of Journalism.* Englewood Cliffs, New Jersey: Prentice-Hall, 1962

Gallagher, Dan. *Pigeon Key and the Seven-Mile Bridge 1908-1912.* Marathon, FL: Pigeon Key Foundation, Inc., 1995.

Kaufelt, Lynn Mitsuko. *Key West Writers and their Houses.* Sarasota, Florida: Pineapple Press and Fort Lauderdale,

Florida: Omnigraphics, Inc., 1986.

Kobal, John. *Gotta Sing Gotta Dance: A History of Musicals.* New York: Exeter Books : distributed by Bookthrift, 1983

Larson, Erik. *Isaac's Storm: A Man, a Time, and the Deadliest Hurricane in History.* New York: Crown Publishers, 1999.

Lisio, Donald J. *The President and Protest: Hoover, Conspiracy, and the Bonus Riot.* Columbia, Missouri: University of Missouri Press, 1974

Manchester, William. *The Glory and the Dream: A Narrative History of America — 1932-1972*, Vol. 1 & 2. Boston: Little, Brown and Company, 1973-4.

McIver, Stuart B. *Dreamers, Schemers and Scalawags.* Sarasota, Florida: Pineapple Press, 1994.

McIver, Stuart B. *Hemingway's Key West.* Sarasota, Florida: Pineapple Press, 1993.

McLendon, James. *Papa: Hemingway in Key West.* 3rd ed. Key West, Florida: Langley Press, 1993

Murphy, George, ed. *The Key West Reader: The Best of Key West's Writers 1830-1990.* Key West, Florida: Tortugas Ltd., 1989.

O'Sullivan, Maurice and Jack C. Lane. *The Florida Reader: Visions of Paradise from 1530 to the Present.* Sarasota, Fla.: Pineapple Press, 1991.

Opel, Frank and Tony Meisel, ed. *Tales of Old Florida.* Seacaucus, New Jersey: Castle, a division of Book Sales Inc., 1987.

Parks, Pat. *The Railroad that Died at Sea: The Florida East Coast's Key West Extension.* Key West, Florida: Langley Press, Inc., 1968.

Sloan, Bill. *"I Watched a Wild Hog Eat My Baby!": A Colorful History of Tabloids and their Cultural Impact.* Amherst, N ew York.: Prometheus Books, 2001

Smiley, Nixon. *Knights of the Fourth Estate:*

The Story of the Miami Herald. Miami, Florida: E.A. Seemann Publishing Co., 1974.

Smith, Richard Norton. *The Colonel: The Life and Legend of Robert R. McCormick, 1880-1955.* Boston: Houghton-Mifflin Co., 1997.

Swanberg, W.A. *Citizen Hearst: A Biography of William Randolph Hearst.* New York: Galahad Books, 1996.

Tufty, Barbara. *1001 Questions Answered About Hurricanes, Tornadoes, and Other Natural Air Disasters.* New York: Dodd, Mead & Co., 1970; New York: Dover Publications, Inc. 1987.

Viele, John. *The Florida Keys: A History of the Pioneers.* Sarasota, Florida: Pineapple Press, 1996.

JOURNALS AND PERIODICALS

"Report of Special Investigating Committee, Florida Hurricane Disaster." *Digest of Minutes,* National Executive Committee Meeting, American Legion magazine, November 1936.

Bellamy, Jeanne. "Newspapers of America's Last Frontier." *Tequesta: The Journal of the Historical Association of Southern Florida,* Number 12, 1952.

Boulard, Garry. "State of Emergency: Key West in the Great Depression." *Florida Historical Quarterly,* vol. 67, no. 2, October 1988

Bremer, William W. "Along the 'American Way': The New Deal's Work Relief Programs for the Unemployed." *The Journal of American History* 62, no. 3 (1975): 636-652.

Burt, Al. "Fury in the Keys." *Tropic* magazine, August 20, 1978.

Cox, Merlin G. "David Sholtz: New Deal Governor of Florida." *Florida Historical Quarterly,* vol. 43, no. 2, October 1964.

Davis, Elmer. "New World Symphony." *Harper's Magazine,* May 1935.

Gentry, Richard E. "Early Families of Upper Matecumbe." *Tequesta: The Journal of the Historical Association of Southern Florida,* vol. 34, 1974.

Hemingway, Earnest. "The Sights of Whitehead Street: A Key West Letter." *Esquire,* April 1935.

Hemingway, Earnest. "Who Murdered The Vets?" *New Masses,* September 17, 1935.

Jeans, Paul. "Tropical Disturbance: The Story of the Making of the Miami Tribune." *Miami Tribune,* April 4, 1937.

McDonald, W.F. "Lowest Barometer Reading in the Florida Keys Storm of September 2, 1935." *Monthly Weather Review,* October 1935.

McDonald, W.F. "The Hurricane of August 31 to September 6, 1935." *Monthly Weather Review,* September 1935.

Mitchell, Charles L. "The West Indian Hurricane of September 14-22, 1926." *Monthly Weather Review,* October 1926

Painton, Fred C. "Rendezvous with Death." *The American Legion Magazine,* November 1935.

Rovers, Richard. "End of the Line." *The New Yorker,* December 15, 1951.

Weightman, R. Hanborn. "West Indian Hurricanes of August 1928." *Monthly Weather Review,* October 1928

Saunders, William H. "The Wreck of Houseboat No. 4 October 1906." *Tequesta: The Journal of the Historical Association of Southern Florida,* Vol. 19, 1959.

WEBSITES

www.rice.edu/fondren/woodson/exhibits/wac/rogers.html; Edith Nourse Rogers biography by Dorothy M. Brown.

www.indo.com/distance/; a website maintained by Darrell Kindred that provides a link to a navigation computer.